PEOPLE GET READY

Improvisation, Community, and Social Practice

A new series edited by Daniel Fischlin

Books in this new series advocate musical improvisation as a crucial model
for political, cultural, and ethical dialogue and action—for imagining and
creating alternative ways of knowing and being in the world. The books are
collaborations among performers, scholars, and activists from a wide range
of disciplines. They study the creative risk-taking imbued with the sense
of movement and momentum that makes improvisation an exciting,
unpredictable, ubiquitous, and necessary endeavor.

PEOPLE GET READY

the future of jazz is now!

AJAY HEBLE AND ROB WALLACE,
EDITORS

Duke University Press   Durham and London

2013

Printed in the United States of America
on acid-free paper ∞
Designed by C. H. Westmoreland
Typeset in Charis with Block display by
Tseng Information Systems, Inc.
Library of Congress Cataloging-in-
Publication Data
People get ready : the future of jazz is
now! / Ajay Heble and Rob Wallace, eds.
pages cm—(Improvisation, community,
and social practice)
Includes bibliographical references and index.
ISBN 978-0-8223-5408-6 (cloth : alk. paper)
ISBN 978-0-8223-5425-3 (pbk. : alk. paper)
1. Jazz—History and criticism. 2. Improvisation
(Music) I. Heble, Ajay. II. Wallace, Rob, 1976.
III. Series: Improvisation, community, and
social practice.
ML3506.P46 2013
781.65'5—dc23
2013003139

In memoriam

Dr. Madhav Heble
(1925–2012)

and
Bernice Wallace
(1933–2012)

CONTENTS

ACKNOWLEDGMENTS

The inspiration for this book comes in large measure from the Guelph Jazz Festival Colloquium, an annual international conference that for seventeen years running has continued to bring together scholars and creative practitioners for engaging dialogue and critical exchange. It's a place where vital, new, and timely research issues get put on the table, and where we've been privileged to work actively in a rich, collaborative environment fueled by motivating interactions between leading practitioners and scholars in the field. Many of the pieces included in this book were first presented at the colloquium.

We'd also like to acknowledge the extraordinary support of the Improvisation, Community, and Social Practice (ICASP) research project, centered at the University of Guelph. This large-scale multi-institutional collaborative project focuses on the social implications of improvised music and brings together a dynamic international research team of thirty-five researchers from twenty different institutions. Special thanks to ICASP's project manager Kim Thorne, and to our research team members, especially our dear friends and colleagues Frédérique Arroyas, Daniel Fischlin, Ric Knowles, Eric Lewis, and Ellen Waterman. Huge thanks also to the many research assistants who've worked with us, either directly on this book or on related projects, including the colloquium and ICASP's peer-reviewed journal, *Critical Studies in Improvisation / Études critiques en improvisation*: Maureen Cannon, Stephanie Cheung, Karl Coulthard, Paul Danyluk, Greg Fenton, Elizabeth Groeneveld, Cory Lavender, Natalie Onuška, Michelle Peek, Rachel Shoup, Hanna Smith, Melissa Walker, Ben Walsh, and Claire Whitehead.

Christie Menzo deserves special mention here. As a mainstay of the project, Christie worked as our research assistant for several semesters, and she gave the book extraordinary care through the various stages of its production. She compiled the list of works cited, maintained regular contact with our contributors, and kept us on track, especially when deadlines loomed. Rachel Shoup stepped into a similar role upon Christie's departure, and we appreciate her dedication and attention to the final stages of the manuscript.

The ICASP research project is funded through a generous grant from the Major Collaborative Research Initiatives (MCRI) program of the Social Sciences and Humanities Research Council of Canada (SSHRC). We're hugely grateful to SSHRC, and also to the project's various partners and institutions, especially the office of the vice-president, research, at the University of Guelph.

Thanks to the staff at Duke University Press, especially to our editor, Ken Wissoker, for his immediate and enthusiastic support of this project, and to Susan Albury and Mandy Earley. Thanks also to our anonymous readers.

Thanks to all our contributors for permitting us to include your work here. It has been a pleasure working with you throughout the process, and we're tremendously grateful for your support and encouragement. A much earlier version of chapter 4, by Eric Porter, first appeared as "Jeanne Lee's Voice" in *Critical Studies in Improvisation / Études critiques en improvisation* 2, no. 1 (2006). A much earlier version of chapter 11, by Greg Tate, first appeared as "Black Jazz in the Digital Age" in *Critical Studies in Improvisation / Études critiques en improvisation* 3, no. 1 (2007). A much earlier version of chapter 12, by Paul D. Miller (DJ Spooky) and Vijay Iyer, first appeared as "Improvising Digital Culture" in *Critical Studies in Improvisation / Études critiques en improvisation* 5, no. 1 (2009). All of these earlier versions can be found online at www.criticalimprov.com.

Thanks to all the artists who appear in the photos we've included in the book. We'd also like to thank Derek Andrews, Jean Burrows, Kevin Hall, Julie Hastings, Elizabeth Jackson, Pete Johnston, George Lewis, George Lipsitz, Lewis Melville, Ingrid Mündel, Bill Shoemaker, Joe Sorbara, Jesse Stewart, and Alan Wildeman for their support. Thanks to the many musicians working every day to make the future of jazz *now*. Rob would especially like to thank Ajay Heble, whose intellectual spirit, enthusiasm, piano-playing, and humor have made this project a true blessing and honor to be a part of. Ajay is enormously grateful to Rob Wallace for his dedication, his intellectual energy, his friendship, his drumming, and for being such an inspirational collaborator. Ajay would also like to extend a special thanks to Dr. Eric Schnell, a perfect stranger who turned up out of the blue when most needed, and who improvised a quiet miracle.

And, most importantly, we give thanks to our families: to our parents, to our siblings, to Kiran Heble and Maya Heble, and to Kara Attrep and Sheila O'Reilly. This book wouldn't be possible without your guidance, your encouragement, and your love.

This book is dedicated to the memory of Ajay's father, Dr. Madhav Heble (1925–2012), and Rob's mother, Bernice Wallace (1933–2012). Both passed away as we were seeing this book through the final stages of the production process.

Ajay Heble and Rob Wallace

INTRODUCTION

"PEOPLE GET READY"

The Future of Jazz Is Now!

Offered as something of an attempt to correct the historical record, and as an intervention into current debates both about where the music has been and where it might be going, the essays collected in *People Get Ready: The Future of Jazz Is Now!* attest to the vibrancy (and the challenges) associated with much of the music that falls under the rubric of "jazz" today. Our book takes its inspiration and borrows its title, "People Get Ready," from the New York bassist William Parker's tribute to the songs of Curtis Mayfield—a project that draws on deeply intertwined musical traditions which might initially seem disconnected if viewed from the perspective of marketing terms like "soul," "rock 'n' roll," "funk," or "jazz." Parker's improvised takes on Mayfield, along with collaborator Amiri Baraka's conception of "inside songs"—messages within and between the lines of Mayfield's original lyrics—cause us to reflect on the continuing relevance of both musical forms and the social conditions from which they sprang. An anthem for the civil rights movement, Mayfield's song encouraged its listeners to "get on board" in the spirit of hope, possibility, and profound conviction. Amid current uncertainties about markets, audiences, technologies, and public subsidies, in the context of emerging anxieties, trends, and questions in jazz scholarship, and in the face of a status quo that so many contemporary artists and activists refuse to take for granted, it seems apt to ready ourselves for the (artistic, social, critical, cultural, and institutional) changes that might be a-coming, by reflecting on the shape of jazz to come.

William Parker's Mayfield Project, in this context, provides a telling example. It reminds us that jazz has long functioned as a powerful repository of cultural memory, as a site for the expression of history and identity, and as a means for calling communities into being. Think of "The Inside Songs of Curtis Mayfield," then, not so much as a tribute or retrospective, as a standard "history lesson," but rather as a contemporary remix, as a vital example of a "living art form," of how historical documents and sources can be recalled, reworked, and reenvisioned as part of a new network of musical and cultural conversations.[1] Parker puts it this way: "Every song written or improvised has an inside song which lies in the shadows, in between the sounds and silences and behind the words, pulsating, waiting to be reborn as a new song" (liner notes, *I Plan to Stay a Believer*). This music, Parker is telling us, is going somewhere, and it is sustained by the communities cultivating it, even as they themselves change and grow over time.

Between Innovation and Nostalgia

Jazz has a future, but that future is as susceptible to varying interpretations as its past has been. In the past few decades, several influential views of jazz history have come to the fore in popular and academic discourse. Despite useful critiques and debates about the history of jazz that have appeared in recent years—many of them made in various places by some of the contributors to this book—there are still at least two narratives that seem to have significant traction in many discussions of jazz history. One is the notion that jazz has had its day—or, at, least, the jazz that matters, since all the heroes of the past are dead or elderly, and their improvisational voices are no longer as relevant as they were in their prime. The other perspective tells us that jazz is alive and well, but only if we subscribe to carefully prescribed models of jazz performance, history, and education.

The idea that jazz is dead is, in short, part of a distinct mode of experiencing and looking at the world, a mode reinforcing the view that the only history of jazz that matters is *one* that has already happened. Exaggerated pronouncements of the music's demise are thus premised on an investment in the belief that no significant profile-raising and pattern-shifting impacts are possible in the music's present or future tenses.

Yet if we concede that jazz is alive and well, but only in a certain orthodox manner, we overlook a substantial amount of music that is clearly, if not explicitly, jazz-based. How, then, do we meaningfully describe a music under a rubric that has so many potential definitions? John Szwed noted in 2000 that "today many writers wisely avoid definitions altogether, and only by what they exclude and what they prize is it possible to know what they mean by jazz" (*Jazz 101* 22). While readers should be wary of thinking that any excluded voices are deemed unworthy of analysis in this volume, making a convenient checklist of characteristic features to define jazz, as Szwed demonstrates, is also problematic. Any such list inevitably circumscribes the music while ironically "letting in" music that might not normally be granted access to the canon—in other words, "if it swings, it must be jazz" is not necessarily a useful yardstick for describing the range of music that even a conservative account of jazz would contain, even as it gives priority to stale or doctrinaire music that fits the prescribed patterns. The exception in this case does not prove the rule, because there are too many exceptions to convincingly support one rule.

Like this last point, our book's title should make clear that there is something compelling to us about the musics historically connected with the word *jazz*, and, moreover, that we see value in continuing to use *jazz* as a catch-all term for a variety of different, even disparate, stylistic, geographical, and historical elements. Jazz, as a living art form, is large enough to accommodate them all, and, furthermore, we are committed to advocating for a jazz that is continually open to innovation, even innovation that threatens to change our previous perspective on the music we thought we knew. Certainly, such a change in perspective can be threatening, but we argue (as do our contributors throughout this volume) that it can also be exhilarating, rewarding, even paradigm-shifting. Believing otherwise, we remain virtually drugged, as Burton Peretti's assessment of recent developments in jazz historiography suggests: "Like the heroin that some bebop musicians took to escape the pain of the present, nostalgia has been a narcotic of choice for people terrified by the unfamiliarity of the ever-changing present. Almost regularly in the twentieth century, Americans have expressed disgust with the present and yearned for the imagined 'normalcy' of yesteryear" (188).

Peretti continues: "Perhaps we can only tentatively conclude that innovation and nostalgia are fundamentally inter-related in modern popular music and culture" (188). We contend that relegating jazz to either a glorious past *or* a straight-jacketed present simultaneously dooms its future, ignores the wealth of present innovation in the music being carried out as we write, and forgets (or misreads) the sheer complexity of the music's history. Navigating beyond a fear of innovation and a soothing dose of nostalgia, this book seeks to commit firmly to a continually changing future of jazz informed by a complex past and active present.

The essays collected here run counter to the prevailing orthodoxy in popular discourses about jazz. They illustrate how assumptions about the death of jazz are patently false and how the nostalgia for a more limited definition of relevant music ignores continuing and important contributions; they reveal not only the complexity, resilience, and vitality of the innovative music of the past forty years, but also the implications of how that music connects to earlier moments and how it will literally and figuratively "play out" in the future.

Indeed, as Greg Tate reminds us in his essay in this volume, any conversation about the future of jazz must also ask, "Why does jazz have to be going anywhere, since where it has been already staggers the imagination with its telltale monuments?" From Afro-Futurist strains of jazz (Sun Ra) to Amiri Baraka's notion of black music's potential to usher in a new future based on love, to Liberation Music (Charlie Haden and Carla Bley), to Deep Listening (Pauline Oliveros), there is a long and illustrious history that understands jazz and related improvised musics as a potent arena for inventive, adventurous, and creative responses to predefined (and often unjust) social scripts. In an era of globalization and hybridization, when diverse peoples and communities of interest struggle to forge historically new forms of affiliation across cultural divides, the participatory virtues of respect and collaboration inculcated through jazz and improvised music take on a particular urgency.

This collection thus seeks to build on recent work, such as George Lewis's history of the Association for the Advancement of Creative Musicians (AACM) in *A Power Stronger than Itself*, to develop a more nuanced history of the music stemming from post-1960s jazz: the avant-garde, the New Thing, Free Jazz, "non-idiomatic" improvisation, fusion, etc. But more than just history, we seek to show the ongoing relevance of these musical practices, especially given the fact that many of the key participants are still active. We do not subscribe to a history of jazz that has "evolved" into some perfect form of democratic innovation—whether it be from a neoliberal or anarchic perspective. Jazz does not have to "go anywhere" to prove the relevance of where it has been, but the "where" it has been is still a map missing key continents, oceans, and directions. We offer in this book a particular correction to the compass-rose of jazz history, even as we hope to continue sailing on to new areas off the map.

Our perspective on the oscillation between past, present, and future in debates about jazz is guided here, at least implicitly, by the lifework of Sun Ra. In Robert Mugge's documentary *A Joyful Noise*, Sun Ra states, "Every song that I write tells a story . . . no two songs tell the same story. They say that history repeats itself. But history is only his-story. You haven't heard my story yet . . . my story is endless—it never repeats itself . . . I'm not part of history. I'm more part of the mystery, which is *my* story."[2] Our volume presents the diversity and complexity of improvised music through an analogously diverse and eclectic range of contributors. While none of the following essays focus primarily on Sun Ra, his playful but serious wordplay reminds us that every history is provisional and that every individual has a potentially significant story to tell, a story whose mystery is a source of both confusion and strength. We believe that too often the *history* of the music discussed herein has been glossed as *mysterious* in mostly negative ways. Our "history" features pieces focusing specifically on music produced in the 1960s and 1970s that has been largely unacknowledged and underdocumented in the scholarly literature, while at the same time accounting for the continuing "mystery," in order more fully to document how subsequent musical movements are alive, well, and part of a complex, sometimes contradictory, and complicated history.

The essays included here offer various ways of linking the past, present, and future in a dynamic relationship by revealing the "living histories" of musicians who are still working, still making important musical and social statements, as well as offering some revisions to the standard and canonized jazz historiography of both well-known and "underground" figures. Additionally, a series of original black and white photographs by Thomas King, portraying many of the musicians discussed by the contributors, provides a visual record of the sonic histories and mysteries discussed. Taken as a whole, this book offers a touchstone for those seeking a more complete record of recent jazz history, a history that continues to be ignored or vastly underrepresented in standard accounts, while offering a vision for the future of the music as a vital, relevant, energetic force with important lessons for how society might change and grow.

It is our contention that despite the sometime replication of oppressive social structures, to the detriment of more hopeful and helpful social elements, and despite supposed critical and popular insignificance, the music and cultural conditions stemming from the so-called New Thing (and subsequent related movements) are sites of provocative and often positive social relations and antihegemonic practice. Modeled on the strong ties to community and on the social function of the music and musicians discussed in this volume, we anticipate that *People Get Ready* will be a pivotal pedagogical text for rethinking institutionalized narratives about jazz histories and jazz futures. Scholars such as Ingrid Monson, Ronald Radano, David Ake, John Szwed, Eric Porter, Iain Anderson, and George Lewis have all, of course, addressed as a living history jazz produced after 1965, and their work has played a significant role in revitalizing and reinvigorating our understanding of the music. Our work here is certainly indebted to these writers. We note, however, that much of this scholarship comes primarily from the perspective of a single author and is often focused on a single artist (such as Sun Ra or Anthony Braxton). And while anthologies such as *Jazz among the Discourses, The Other Side of Nowhere, Uptown Conversations,* and *Keeping Time* have connected artists, scholars, and other voices from jazz historiography to various ideological, conceptual, and historical frameworks, our book is unique in its breadth and depth regarding specifically post-1965 jazz, and, perhaps more significantly, a commitment to a fuller representation of the continuing legacies of that music—the future of jazz. Our project therefore strives to map out the negotiation of freedom within those lines of circulation and transit outside, underneath, and inbetween the frequencies—as Ralph Ellison says in *Invisible Man*—of mass-mediated culture. The future of jazz has been a long time coming.

Back to the Present

You can't really talk about one thing without talking about everything. Then you know you're talking a real truth.—Henry Threadgill

This quotation from composer and multi-instrumentalist Henry Threadgill (as spoken to jazz critic Howard Mandel) provides one reason for the disconnect between the vivid and vital life of musics associated with "jazz" performed after 1960 and the apparent lack of critical attention (outside more open-minded writers like Mandel, for example) to that music.[3] Threadgill's statement also gives us an opportunity to acknowledge the limitations of any project trying to address a diverse and contested field of historical inquiry and future practice. Most notably, our book does not make much sustained reference to music and musicians outside North America. This is partly a function of the importance of specific post-1960 musicians to the wider global scene (the AACM, for example) but also an inevitable function of the vicissitudes of trying to include everything in one book. We trust that the lack of attention to musicians and scholarship outside North America will not detract from the wealth of issues raised in the following pieces, and will, indeed, encourage others to fill in some of our gaps.[4] In some ways, jazz has always been more appreciated (if not more understood) outside the nation of its origin, and many jazz musicians from the earliest days of the music decided to escape blatant racism in the United States for more latent racist primitivism—which did not prevent musicians from getting gigs, at least—in Europe and elsewhere. One of the weaker moments in Ken Burns's documentary *Jazz*, in fact, critiques a vitally important musical collective performing after 1960, the Art Ensemble of Chicago (AEC), for only having a small audience made up of college students "in *France*." Even though earlier and more supposedly "authentic" musicians like Sidney Bechet and Kenny Clarke had found solace in the more appreciative jazz climate in France, the Burns documentary criticizes the AEC for being detached from the American roots (and audiences) of jazz.

Moreover, jazz has *always* been global—and "post-national," as Taylor Atkins puts it in the introduction to his revelatory volume on global jazz.[5] Jazz was created by people from a diverse set of class, ethnic, and aesthetic origins, even if we limit that group of creators to the African American community of early twentieth-century New Orleans. And those black New Orleans musicians—whether or not they considered themselves to be mixed-race creoles or "negroes"—were all, by legal decree, considered second-class citizens in the white-supremacist United States. The multiethnic cast of African Americans, Native Americans, Latinos and Latinas, and otherwise Creole people who created jazz (Creole, after all, originally designated anyone born in the Americas, regardless of skin color) were relegated to a caste of artists automatically separated from their nation—creatively diverse and innovative yet separate and unequal.

In fact, this very same diversity of aesthetic, political, and social categories within Afrodiasporic music-making has inadvertently brought the music scorn on the one hand and artistic resilience on the other. It was reprehensible to many white and black commentators during the early days of jazz that a music stemming from the "low" culture of black urban centers could be so popular. The threat of jazz combined racist fear in whites with a concomitant fear in blacks aspiring to higher social status, a fear that ruling whites would judge them based on the good-time, boisterous, sexualized music of the dance hall and brothel. Langston Hughes would have to argue as late as 1926 that a "racial mountain" faced those black artists trying to ascend aesthetic heights, a mountain made by whites and blacks who undervalued the contributions of black popular culture provided by jazz and blues. The racial mountain was surmountable, according to Hughes, by heeding the call of the "eternal tom-tom" in the black artist's soul, a drum that "laughs" and "cries" in its musical chronicling of black life.⁶ Hughes, in other words, emphasizes that black artistic production could either satisfy white and black audiences or not; it did not matter, as long as the artists were true to themselves. Hughes's protoblack nationalism, then, like the later sign of "blackness" in the Black Power movement, was a strategic call for a truly democratic society where blackness operated as a sign of freedom, resistance to social norms, and paradoxical greatness at a time when all things and people labeled as "black" were deemed dangerous and morally repugnant.

Jazz, too, as a word and as a collection of musical styles, shared a similarly paradoxical life with its black creators. *Jazz*, from almost its first usage, was a word associated as much with sexual depravity and debauchery as with optimism, modernity, and American (that is, United States) essentialism and supremacy. From its uneasy alliance with the traditionally downtrodden masses, jazz joined world musical and political life as an ambivalent child of twentieth-century pain and joy. We often forget that *the Jazz Age*, F. Scott Fitzgerald's moniker for the post–World War I, pre-Depression era, was not as positive a label as is sometimes perceived. Jazz, in Fitzgerald's most famous novel, *The Great Gatsby*, provides a soundtrack to the childish, nihilist libertinism of the Lost Generation, even as in real life it was granting new opportunities for African American performers to codify their cultural contributions into an innovative art form that would captivate the world.⁷ The partying would continue as the band played on, but that band was more than just a group hired to entertain revelers.

As Paul Gilroy has argued, cultural developments like jazz fulfilled important social, political, and spiritual roles for a community divested of many formal means of legal and civic expression.⁸ Jazz, blues, and other genres of black music became exotic and attractive to white audiences, even as they confirmed the resilience and power of African American cultural forms in the face of centuries of oppression. When placed in a party context at a black juke joint or community center, jazz and the merry-making that it accompanied were humanity writ and sounded large against dehumanization. Nonblack musicians often recognized this potential for liberation in the music, and while some musicians only initially heard aesthetic implications of the new sounds, jazz not coincidentally attracted people from analogously oppressed groups: jazz's first non-American star, for example, was the Roma musician Django Reinhardt, and the somewhat dubiously dubbed "King of Swing," Benny Goodman, was Jewish.

If this brief account of early jazz history seems at odds with a section titled "Back to the Present," then perhaps it's worth remembering that these same issues of political and aesthetic diversity and contradiction still define much of the jazz world. Some might argue, in fact, that jazz's relative lack of popularity and cultural visibility confirms its lack of importance and political force. Yet we argue, following from Ralph Ellison, that invisibility does not equal disempowerment. Moreover, thinking about jazz in terms of the visual—especially via the signs of race—often distracts us from the sounds of the music, the eternal or provisional tom-toms, saxophones, pianos, and electric guitars that signal new and old histories and mysteries of the possible futures for society still conflicted by racist, classist, and sexist divisions. And, finally, we maintain that the musicians in post-1960s jazz are *not* invisible after all: their sounds and images, like the photos and echoes of their music and words found throughout these pages, confirm the ongoing relevance of their collective missions.

The historical circumstances surrounding jazz and its development from the early to the middle of the twentieth century, and the various ways jazz musicians have adapted to their surroundings, are also important for a fuller understanding of the period when jazz was considered most "politically conscious," most tuned-in to the history it was shaping, that of the 1960s and early 1970s. While earlier jazz had certainly not neglected political or social concerns—indeed, following from Gilroy, we can see how African American cultural forms can be read as an expression of resistance—the advent of the civil rights movement in the late 1950s and early 1960s joined a corresponding movement throughout the jazz world that more explicitly demanded justice and equality for all. And while these musical maneuvers were often cued by the titles of pieces (Sonny Rollins's *Freedom Suite* and John Coltrane's "Alabama," for example), the life of musicians and the sound of their music began to more openly engage with political discourse. As in earlier moments in jazz history, these politicized musicians encountered misunderstanding and resistance from whites and blacks alike, including older generations of jazz musicians who were uncomfortable giving up the gains they had made in a music mostly pushed to the margins after the zenith of the big-band era. There was no single solution, musical or political, to social injustice, but by the 1960s jazz musicians had articulated some common themes that were in some cases organically developed by the musicians themselves or morphed into marketing categories by the music industry: Free Jazz, the New Thing, Fire Music, Great Black Music, Improvised Music, Free Improvisation, and others.

Within each of these categories were gathered a diverse set of musicians and musical styles, but they all shared a perceived, if not in all cases actual, rupture with the past—or with the present—social and musical norms. When combined with overtly political rhetoric, then, this new kind of jazz-based music was often heard and seen as radical, dangerous, or nihilistic by some, and alternatively liberatory, refreshing, and spiritually renewing by others—again, the same sorts of reactions that jazz had garnered from various audiences throughout its history. Yet the fact that this new music brought with it a host of political and social demands that explicitly took it out of the realm of entertainment or aesthetic concerns was something of a critical moment in jazz history, and the concerns inspired subsequent generations of musicians to foreground the possibly transformative powers of their sounds. It is this foregrounding of social change harnessed to musical change that we find especially compelling in much of the music discussed in this book. It seems to us that the artists representing post-1960s jazz have often developed a set of sometimes implicit, sometimes explicit, critical perspectives on the social power of music. As we have suggested above, jazz was often a music forged from the uneven distributions of power, as well as the sometimes paradoxical collision of cultures learning to negotiate aesthetic and social space together. Moving from an initial strategic deployment of "blackness" as a positive category in a primitivist or largely hostile, white-supremacist social context, the musics growing from the rich soil of jazz have created a significantly pluralistic outlook on collaboration—across racial, class, gender, generational, and national boundaries. The essays in our book, when read alongside one another, open up an implicit dialogue around such positions. While some of our contributors are elegiac, for example, about the ability of black music to provide a reference point for black people, others, in their own ways, would seem to favor a pluralist stance that sees the music as encoding certain longings for change while sometimes suggesting that the music has made vital changes along the way in order to survive.[9] The implications of such a pluralism represent not an "anything goes" approach, but rather a commitment to the complicated task of learning how we can best learn to live together.

Politics in Music, Politics and Music

[Music] can serve to articulate new "structures of desire" through the consolidation of "affective alliances" between elements in a heterogeneous field organised around contradictory and conflicting social-sexual appetencies, aspirations, inclinations, dispositions, drives. Attempts are continually being made (from within the music industry) to stabilise this complex and volatile amalgam of forces through the fixing of more or less enabling, more or less proscriptive social-sexual "identities."—Dick Hebdige, *Hiding in the Light*

The question of what exactly is "political" in music and what effect in "real" life that music can have continues to be a contentious topic. But it is our contention that a serious focus on the social and political potential in post-1960s jazz demonstrates very real and important forms of social change that continue to inspire and transform contemporary life. While we would like to follow Henry Threadgill's dictum that one should talk about everything to get at truth, a few important examples of the kinds of transformation we have in mind will help contextualize the issues addressed in this volume, and hopefully provide some correctives to the frequent disavowal or lack of knowledge about post-1960s jazz.

   Discussing the European dimension of free jazz and politics, the ethnomusicologist and musician Mike Heffley reminds us that "musicians often have an immediate grasp of forces, concepts, and relationships that political programs and gestures manifest more dimly, with less enduring depth. The art can last, grow, satisfy for life, after the politics burn out and fade. Or, as Jost Gebers, of the German *Emanzipators* . . . put it, 'The truth of the music was stranger than the fiction of those politics'" (11). But even musicians not directly interested in, or explicitly involved with, political action and rhetoric find themselves at the crossroads of political debate; the continued use of jazz as an analogue for American democracy bears this out in contradictory ways. As Penny Von Eschen has detailed, for example, in her work on State Department-sponsored jazz tours by U.S. jazz artists during the Cold War, jazz musicians have often been oppressed at home even as they are wielded as ideological weapons in defending and expanding U.S.-style democracy.[10] This arguably remains the case today, as the essays in this volume concerning performance spaces and public funding of the music point out. While the public face of jazz in the United States seems more firmly institutionalized and "respectable" than ever, musicians for the most part are struggling to make ends meet.

The Cold War journeys of jazz form one part of the continuing story linking jazz explicitly with politics. With its public recognition as "America's music," jazz has seemingly become another example of the best kind of political, cultural force; no longer viewed as an imperialist agent of the U.S. monoculture intent on dumbing-down local cultural forms, jazz is democracy in melody and rhythm. Yet while many critics, musicians, and listeners seem to be content with the connection between democracy and jazz, when alternative forms of democratic philosophy—usually left-leaning, anarchic, and sometimes feminist perspectives—are linked explicitly to jazz, defenders of the cultural and political power of jazz tend to balk at the suggestion that the music could be so potentially transformative. To cite one recent example, Ted Gioia has dismissed the "Hegelian" (Gioia's term) revolutionary rhetoric of the 1960s "New Thing" as unrealistic. Hegelian (or its successor in the form of Marxian) teleology aside, stripping any political agency from the music seems equally unrealistic. It is worth quoting Gioia at length here, since we believe his argument dismisses the issues and musicians highlighted in this book:

> This is the jazz world we have inherited, a happily-ever-after in which anything goes, everything goes, and pluralism (*not* freedom or atonality) is the single guiding principle. There is no sign that this will change anytime soon. Indeed, it is almost inconceivable that it could change. No one in the jazz world believes in the Hegelian force of history any more, even if they pay it lip service. No one believes that jazz styles move ahead like science, each generation progressing beyond the last, superseding and replacing what went before. Sometimes they talk as if they believed these things, because the language in which jazz criticism is written still smacks of this positivistic attitude. But the reality, which everyone can plainly see, is that jazz styles are

more like Paris fashions, which must change with the season, but not with some linear sense of inevitability, more just for the sheer fun of it.

And *fun* is the catchword that first comes to my mind when I think of jazz today. Call me, if you will, the advocate of *The Fun Principle* in jazz. (My motto: I can't solve socio-political problems, only show you a good time.) But the rhetoric of jazz—as opposed to the reality—is still mired in the old paradigm.

While some musicians themselves share Gioia's contention that the emancipatory potential of (free) jazz is gone (or was never there), we believe that the real story is about how we define "solving socio-political problems."[11] The revolution, to paraphrase Gil Scott-Heron, will not be jazzercised, because if we accept the argument that music doesn't help but is merely fun, then we also accept that the musicians (and audiences) who have explicitly struggled for political and social change have failed. This not only relegates music to a realm of entertainment (already dubious if we follow Gilroy's arguments about African American cultural contributions); it also egregiously misrepresents history and politics. If all political and social changes were judged by a complete, overnight transformation of society, then we would have to deem most forms of political and social change useless. This seems to be the logical conclusion of Gioia's argument. We think such an argument runs the risk of denying the real accomplishments of real people who are still active in the jazz world, even people such as Wynton Marsalis, who has been held up as an example of safe, "neo-traditional jazz." But the transformations that Marsalis, with the help of many other musicians and fellow travelers, has accomplished in the name of jazz are remarkable by any standard. While the focus of our book is on musicians sometimes openly opposed to the "Marsalisization" of jazz, it must be acknowledged that his efforts are paradoxically in line with the same kinds of arguments made by politicized jazz musicians coming out of the 1960s: that jazz was important to American life, that it necessitates serious interest and discipline, and that it requires respect and institutions to further its dissemination. Wynton Marsalis's efforts to realize these goals are fairly well known and amply critiqued; our goal in this book is to exhibit other and equally important examples of this history, and to demonstrate that—counter to critics like Gioia, who would like to downplay or disregard the actual social and political life of the music—jazz has made things happen (to twist a paraphrase of W. H. Auden). We'd now like to turn to a few brief examples of how and what has happened, and how these happenings are further contextualized and improvised on by the contributors to this volume.

Interculturalizing the Field

One of the most potent arenas in which jazz has played (and will continue to play) a role in solving (to rework Gioia's argument) "socio-political problems," may well be related to its staging of cultural and sonic hybridity, to its efforts, in the trombonist and scholar George Lewis's words, to "interculturalize the field" ("Rethinking Diversity"). As Chris Searle argues, "The future of jazz is embedded within its internationalism. Its migratory powers . . . have taken its blue and joyous notes across the world, and they have frequently . . . been welded to a message of peace, justice and political freedom" (18). And as Alexander Gelfand reminds us in his article "Life after the Death of Jazz," "hybridization and cross-pollination have become the way of the world." Recent trends in contemporary jazz and improvised music indeed make clear that the future of jazz is largely being shaped by artists engaged in making intercultural connections in an effort to broaden the music's expressive resources. And, in doing so, they have been engaged in a process of meaning-making that enables negotiation of what the cultural theorist Ien Ang has referred to as "one of the most urgent predicaments of our time": the deceptively simple, yet utterly profound, question, "how are we to live together in this new century?" (193). The negotiation of that predicament through the act of music-making is, we argue, one of the things that gives contemporary jazz its critical force. In an essay on improvisation and composition in a collaboratively authored book on *The Future of Jazz*, John Szwed explains that jazz "is a music that is learned in the doing, in collective play: it began as a social music, and some of the features of early African American performance and social organization are still evident in its execution. As such, it is a way of being as well as a way of doing. It is an emergent form, a social form, and as much an ethic as it is an aesthetic. No wonder, then, that many jazz musicians speak of their music in metaphysical or spiritual terms, or justify the music in terms of personal and collective survival" (69).

From William Parker's tour de force project with the classical Indian vocalist Sangeeta Bandyopadhyay, on *Double Sunrise over Neptune*; to

Jane Bunnett's long-standing collaborations with Cuban musicians; to the
Lebanese oud virtuoso Rabih Abou-Khalil's many groundbreaking recordings with musicians from around the world; to D. D. Jackson's multicultural jazz opera *Québécité*; to the koto player and composer-improviser
Miya Masaoka's trio, with Reggie Workman and Andrew Cyrille, on *Monk's
Japanese Folk Song*; to Evan Parker's *Synergetics Phonomanie III*; to George
Lewis's "Dream Team," contemporary artists are, in effect, offering testimony to the efficacy of improvised music-making as a vital form of social practice, as a way (to borrow from Szwed's terminology) of being
together in the world, as well as a way of doing things together. They show
us how (and to what extent) diverse identities, cultures, and viewpoints
can be brought together through improvisational music-making. In modeling (and offering a sonic articulation of) how difference might be negotiated within the context of a community, the work of these artists is very
much in keeping with George Lewis's claim that improvisation is "a *social*
location inhabited by a considerable number of present-day musicians,
coming from diverse cultural backgrounds and musical practices, who
have chosen to make improvisation a central part of their musical discourse." "Individual improvisers," Lewis writes, "are now able to reference
an intercultural establishment of techniques, styles, aesthetic attitudes,
antecedents, and networks of cultural and social practice" ("Improvised
Music after 1950," 149, emphasis added).

   But, of course, as the range of essays we've included in this book should
make clear, any conversation about the future of jazz must also take stock
of where the music has been. And where it's been, to quote again from
Greg Tate's essay in this volume, staggers the imagination with its telltale monuments. True, there's nothing particularly new, then, about such
forms of intercultural cross-fertilization in jazz, as we have tried to emphasize above in our brief account of the diverse, international (and arguably
global) beginnings of jazz. After all, as many commentators have correctly
noted, jazz has long been a vital vehicle for the expression and articulation of hybridized identities. Jason Stanyek's work on the development
of a Pan-African intercultural community through forms of musical improvisation, for instance, reminds us about the central role played in this
context by the musical collaborations between Dizzy Gillespie and Chano
Pozo. Stanyek writes, "What Gillespie and Pozo did was to set a number of
precedents for future Pan-African collaborations in jazz; an emphasis on
composition with a simultaneous affirmation of improvisation; the inser-

tion of nonjazz repertoires into jazz; the accommodation of instruments not typically found in jazz ensembles; the use of non-English and multilingual texts; the highlighting of African spirituality. But perhaps most important were (1) their ability to juxtapose different histories without sacrificing identity and (2) their reflexive use of notions of cultural difference as a basis for collaboration" (88–89).

Many of the precedents that Stanyek sees as having been established by intercultural collaborations between Gillespie and Pozo continue to shape, to inform, and, indeed, to transform contemporary music-making. What's new, what's more pronounced, may have something to do with the inventive flexibility, the subtleties of nuance, associated with players working both ends of the in-out spectrum, the force (and, indeed, the ease) with which artists such as Hamid Drake, Rob Mazurek, Matana Roberts, Marilyn Crispell, Nils Petter Molvaer, Vijay Iyer, Joe McPhee, Pauline Oliveros, Cuong Vu, Myra Melford, and many others are confounding orthodox assumptions, unsettling categorically sanctioned ways of seeing, thinking, and listening. These inside-out, outside-in players compel us to dispense with customary frameworks of assumption, they determinedly elude any inclusive analysis or interpretation of the effects they produce, they continually keep us on edge, and they subject our assessments to an ongoing process of critical inquiry.

Are Generic Boundaries Still Relevant?

If the conventions associated with fixed genres "contribute to an ahistorical view of the world as always the same" and if the "pleasures of predictability encourage an investment in the status quo" (Lipsitz, *American Studies in a Moment of Danger* 185)—indeed, if the fixity of genres has often functioned as a locus of racialized and other forms of power—then the musics we find ourselves drawn to, the musics that move us, inspire us, provoke us, surprise us, and compel us to keep listening so often serve as prods to reconsider our very notion, our very understanding, of genre. We have already noted the problematic history of jazz and its various definitions; therefore, the reader will notice that our (and many of our contributors') provisional use of *jazz* often dovetails with the equally ambiguous, but we think equally powerful, term *improvisation* to describe the musical practices we discuss herein. With Nathaniel Mackey, we celebrate improvisation's "discontent with categories and the boundaries they enforce, with the impediment to social and aesthetic mobility such enforcement effects" ("Paracritical Hinge" 368). To cite just one example from recent history and mystery—in reference to the Chicago Underground projects (duo, trio, etc.) featuring Rob Mazurek (cornet and electronics) and Chad Taylor (drums, vibraphone, percussion), the *New York Times* has declared, "No one interested in the future of jazz can afford to ignore them" (Shantz). We wholeheartedly agree. We agree, too, with Peter Margasak's assessment: "The way they [the Chicago Underground projects] dissolve any stylistic hegemony is inspiring" (56). The group's one-of-a-kind mix of elements from jazz (including influences from the AACM), post-rock, electronics, found sounds, and studio bricolage has resulted in an impressively wide, diverse, and young following (indeed, the last time they played at the Guelph Jazz Festival, the venue was packed for a late night show with teens and twenty-somethings aplenty). Their recordings and performances offer an effortless demonstration of music's mobility, of how various musical styles can seep into one another in utterly compelling ways, creating something we might genuinely call sui generis, even as Mazurek and Taylor's improvisations sometimes echo the now very deep roots of those two previous "underground" trumpet-percussion collaborators, Dizzy Gillespie and Chano Pozo (listen, for example, to Mazurek's trumpet blending with Taylor's Afro-Cuban *bembe* patterns played on the drum set on "January 15th," from the album *12° of Freedom*).

Mobility of practice is also reflected in the opportunities that current technologies allow for connecting people, via the Internet, for example, in real-time improvised musical settings across different geographical locations. While explorations of the possibilities and implications of such technologies may still be in their infancy, musicians such as Pauline Oliveros, Mark Dresser, Myra Melford, and others are already participating in (and leading) telematic performances across a range of international and institutional sites. A telematic performance of improvised music led by Oliveros at the Guelph Jazz Festival in 2010 connected her and others performing live and in real-time in Guelph, Canada, with artists in the United States and in Colombia.

Efforts to expand the sonic vocabularies and expressive resources associated with the music (whether through intercultural collaborations, through the incorporation of what Stanyek calls "nonjazz" elements and repertoires, through the wiping out of time-honored distinctions between inner and outer regions of musical expression, through the use and negotiation of technologies, or through "extended" techniques such as multiphonics, circular breathing, playing the inside of the piano, etc.) may be indicative of jazz's ongoing insistence on finding new kinds of solutions to familiar problems and challenges. Think again of Ien Ang's question about the most urgent predicament of our time, of how we can best live together in the new century. Think, too, about how institutionalized versions of jazz history crowd out alternative accounts and interpretations. And recall that jazz, as George Lipsitz has compellingly argued in *Dangerous Crossroads* (178), has always been about relentless innovation, rather than static tradition (this despite the claims promulgated by those most visible, those most institutionalized, of jazz historians, Ken Burns and Wynton Marsalis). And if, as Stephen Shukaitis has argued, "the emergence of a radical future . . . is almost always necessarily defined by its very otherness from the world as is" (112), then it's no wonder that jazz, with its destinations out and other planes of there, its ascensions, giant steps, and changes of the century, has, in so many of its most provocative historical instances, been forward looking and future directed, the music's out-ness (its experimentations, improvisations, provocations, dissonances) a sonic expression of social practices, hopes, and possibilities not constrained by dominant (and often racist) frameworks of assumption.

Markets, Institutions, Publics

In an article entitled "Can Jazz Be Saved?" in the August 2009 issue of the *Wall Street Journal*, Terry Teachout tells us that "it is precisely because jazz is now widely viewed as a high-culture art form that its makers must start to grapple with the same problems of presentation, marketing, and audience development as do symphony orchestras, drama companies and art museums—a task that will be made all the more daunting by the fact that jazz is made for the most part by individuals, not established institutions with deep pockets." As the discussion on venues, markets, and subsidies we've included in our volume should make clear, these are, indeed, lively issues. However, we're reluctant to buy wholesale into an understanding of jazz that's predicated on such a separation between high art and popular culture. We're reluctant to let "deep pockets" do all the talking, this despite the fact that we are, of course, all too aware of the complex ways circuits of commodity production and forces of commercialization (read: Burns, Marsalis, Lincoln Center) shape, inform, and legitimize certain assumptions about the music (what counts as jazz, what gets disqualified as noise, as self-indulgent, etc.). We're reluctant to assume that jazz is a music that, in any kind of way, is in need of "saving." Better, we suggest, to reflect on how assertions about the essentialization of cultural activity, such as those promulgated in the *Wall Street Journal* article, might run the risk of directing our attention away from the complexity and heterogeneity of the networks through which jazz happens. Better to consider the institutional frameworks shaping not only how and what we listen to, but also the very ways we construct and negotiate meanings. Better to think about the future of jazz, then, in the context of a broader set of institutions and practices through which the music is taught, received, mobilized, talked about, marketed, reviewed, circulated, distributed, and celebrated. These are important, perhaps even urgent, matters, for they are connected in complex (and sometimes unsuspected) ways to issues of resources, power, and public interest. Dominant cultural institutions play a powerful role in inculcating prescribed values and behaviors; they can and do define and determine our very frameworks of reference and understanding.

Disruptions to such dominant consensual assumptions, however, take many trenchant forms in contemporary jazz culture, as independent artists and networks of practice continue to find purposeful and innovative strategies to enlarge our base of valued knowledge, and continue to develop their own strategies around issues of "presentation, marketing, and audience development." Individual agency and counterhistories (demonstrated in the work, for example, of independent record labels, musicians' collectives such as the AACM, and small, and often artist-run, festivals, of venues battling, and providing an alternative to, the corporate music business) should, of course, not be underestimated; nor can we ignore the capacity of the living histories we discuss here to shatter, to transform—perhaps even to reinvigorate—our understanding of the past, present, and future tenses of the music.

In regard to such transformative actions, we feel that it is important to add a brief note about the significance of pedagogy in the forms of music discussed in this volume, and our own role as teachers. While jazz music has been institutionalized in many schools throughout the world—from grade-school to the university—the musicians themselves, as Cecil Taylor once said, are their "own academies" (quoted in Wilmer 51). From another perspective, the more traditional definition of the "academic" take on jazz has been perennially viewed as irrelevant to the "authentic" experience of performers (another version of that tired cliché, "those who do, do; those who can't, teach"). But the presence of a significant number of "out" jazz musicians in the academy should give pause to those who feel that the more spiritual, free, or experimental versions of jazz cannot be taught, as well as to those who feel that free jazz has not made significant in-roads into public institutions. Again, with *significant* we do not intend to neglect the very real lack of appreciation and funding that most of these musicians—even those with jobs in the academy—still often face. Nevertheless, it is significant that musicians are currently directly educating young students in an institutional format: musicians like Anthony Braxton, at Wesleyan; Wadada Leo Smith, Charlie Haden, and Vinny Golia, at Cal Arts; Roscoe Mitchell and Fred Frith, at Mills; George Lewis, at Columbia; Andrew Cyrille, at the New School; Anthony Davis and Mark Dresser, at UCSD; Gerry Hemingway, at the Hochschule Luzern; Pauline Oliveros, at Rensselaer Polytechnic Institute; Myra Melford, at Berkeley; and Bobby Bradford, at Pomona. This shortlist of multigenerational (and mostly U.S.-based) musicians is, as of this writing, a small representation of how the music discussed in this volume is being commented on, learned, practiced, transformed, and "gotten ready for." And these current musicians follow in the footsteps of retired teachers (some no longer with us; some merely no longer teaching officially but still actively performing) like Max Roach, Bill Dixon, Archie Shepp, Yusef Lateef, Milford Graves, George Russell, Cecil Taylor, and others. These musicians dedicated their time to mentoring students, some of whom have become professional musicians and teachers in their own right, some of whom have become scholars, educated listeners, fans, and supporters of the music.[12] We suggest that more research on the vital pedagogical role played by "famous" jazz artists of the free jazz movement is essential for understanding the transformative power of this music, outside of the ways jazz and other forms of music are often judged in the marketplace. How many students of each of these musicians have gone on to become musicians? How many attend, support, or promote performances? How do they talk about their encounters with the living legacies of a supposedly "dead" music? All of these questions remain rich terrain for future scholarship.

Just as the musicians in the above list belie the truism about teaching versus doing, we believe that the scholarship and discourse expressed in this volume gives the lie to the often-repeated lines, attributed to Louis Armstrong, that "if you have to ask [about jazz], you'll never understand." Despite our sympathy for Satchmo's pre-Sun Ra tricksterism, we believe that there is much to be asked and much to be said, and that it is more and more important to ask and try to understand as the history and mystery of jazz become more complicated in our increasingly globalized moment. Musicians (often stereotyped as baffling mystics or inarticulate oafs) and scholars (often stereotyped as highfalutin eggheads with little of value for true fans or practitioners) have equally complex, complicated, and valid ways of writing and talking about music. Furthermore, the distinction between teacher, scholar, critic, and musician breaks down in the following pages, in a way that we believe is not only healthy but essential for the continuing development of any cultural form. Thus it is in our own roles as teachers, musicians, and scholars that we come to this project with passion, energy, and love. The creation of this book has been a collaboration across many disciplines, countries, and media. We have played together, called and responded to one another in both music and in writing, as we have developed this volume. The essays in this book have often stemmed from dynamic public discourse, in the form of interviews, panel discussions, and paper presentations at music festivals, academic conferences, and other forums, including the Guelph Jazz Festival and Colloquium (one incarnation of the festival gave us the theme for the entire book).

Histories and Mysteries

The resonances that accumulated as we assembled the various pieces of this book were happy coincidences. Though we don't want to overplay the musical metaphors, suffice it to say that the book works in a way similar to a musical improvisation. Each collaborator brings to the table his or her own set of skills, interests, and styles, with the intention of trying to collaborate in a discrete (though not necessarily "cohesive" or "unified") process. That process is replicated to the best of our abilities in the pages of the book you are now reading.

Part one of this book, "Beyond Categories: Histories and Mysteries," begins, appropriately, with a Sun Ra-ish paradox: an essay titled "Now Is the Time," by Aldon Lynn Nielsen. Nielsen traces part of two important histories that are still ongoing: the lives of Joe McPhee and Cecil Taylor. The subtitle of Nielsen's essay, "Voicing against the Grain of Orality," reminds us of the paradox of talking about music, even as he examines the important and complex intersections between speech, text, music, and history in the work of two seminal—and still very active—figures in improvised music. Finally, Nielsen's essay offers some brief sketches of a city not often associated with free jazz: Washington, D.C. As does fellow D.C. native Greg Tate, also featured below, Nielsen emphasizes the importance of cultural networks and locations central to free jazz that have been deemphasized in standard narratives.

John Szwed, himself no stranger to the mysteries and histories of Sun Ra, tackles another cosmic figure (and also a Washingtonian) of jazz in his essay, "The Antiquity of the Avant-Garde: A Meditation on a Comment by Duke Ellington." Szwed's intervention into both how the avant-garde in jazz has been defined and how Ellington's relationship with music outside the purview of "straight-ahead" jazz has typically been understood turns our own understanding of the whole history of jazz inside out.

The mystery of music-making and how it can model meaningful human relationships is given expert analysis in "Listening Trust: The Everyday Politics of George Lewis's 'Dream Team.'" Ellen Waterman's and Julie Dawn Smith's collaborative essay is itself an analysis of collaboration, a reading of, and listening to, identity, intercultural interaction, and sonic and social change in a performance by a group of important contemporary musicians: George Lewis, Marilyn Crispell, Miya Masaoka, and Hamid Drake. Waterman and Smith combine detailed analysis of the event (including interviews with the musicians) with insights from cultural studies, psychoanalysis, and anthropological theory to present a provocative picture of what "politics" and "music" might mean to a particular group of musicians in a particular time and place.

Rounding out the "History and Mystery" section are two essays focusing on lesser-known but equally compelling aspects of post-1960s improvised-music culture. "Jeanne Lee's Voice," by Eric Porter, provides a trenchant analysis of the career and techniques of the singer Jeanne Lee. Like Nielsen, Porter points out the literary connections between free jazz's sonic explorations and the avant-garde "sound poetry" stemming from Fluxus and other movements not usually associated with (and sometimes explicitly "against") jazz. He demonstrates the kind of boundary-breaking that was at once aesthetically interesting and implicitly forced on Lee by virtue of her position as a female singer in a masculine jazz culture. Just as Szwed's portrait of Ellington does, Porter's version and vision of Lee results in an illuminating transformation of standard categories—in this case, of jazz, music, and gender.

Smashing categories is the explicit project of the essay "Kick Out the Jazz!" Rob Wallace's meditation on two supposedly disparate genres, free jazz and punk rock. Riffing on Lester Bangs and Greil Marcus, among other commentators, Wallace provides insight into the complex historical relationship between the social and aesthetic dimensions of punk and jazz.

Part two of this book, "Crisis in New Music? Vanishing Venues and the Future of Experimentalism," includes, appropriately, more questions than answers, many of them posed by musicians working, to paraphrase one of the contributor Vijay Iyer's band names, "in the field." This section also includes some of the most unique and timely material found in our volume, addressing the actual lives of musicians in a way that the heroic nostalgia in canonical jazz narratives often neglects. The fields of music-making and money-making have long been at odds in jazz discourse and practice, as guitarist Marc Ribot makes clear in his essay, "Days of Bread and Roses." Musicians working in jazz and its associated genres of music have historically encountered difficulty in terms of financial compensation, and this lack of compensation has been significantly affected by racist attitudes toward the value and merit of black creative practice. Yet even in a potentially more egalitarian era than the early years of jazz, it is clear that musicians from a wide range of ethnic, racial, socioeconomic, and other backgrounds continue to face a lack of popular and financial support for their efforts. In the realm of jazz and music involving improvisation and other links to jazz, this lack of support often remains a determining factor in the social and economic status of the musicians themselves. Ribot's provocative thesis on these issues, revised and updated for this volume, has already sparked debate within its original context (the creative-music community of New York City) as well as abroad (at, for example, the Guelph Jazz Festival in 2007, where Ribot appeared on a panel with fellow contributors Scott Thomson, John Brackett, and Tamar Barzel). We present Ribot's work in conjunction with pieces responding to his original essay in hopes of drawing out the continuing relevance of his polemic as well as the varied ways musicians, academics, and policymakers are currently thinking through the problems of living music. John Brackett offers one direct counterargument, putting critical pressure on some of the assumptions underlying Ribot's belief that the market has failed experimental musicians. The outspoken Canadian trombonist Scott Thomson offers a third perspective, one that provides a ground-floor account of how creative music venues have functioned in Toronto, and of how they reflect a set of priorities somewhat different from those identified by Ribot. Indeed, Thomson and Ribot both elucidate the ways jazz is decidedly not (and never was) an "American affair," but from very different viewpoints and for different reasons.

Tamar Barzel's piece, also riffing on Ribot's thesis, additionally offers an analysis of the public face of "experimental" music, focusing primarily on the Lower East Side, New York. Barzel poses important questions about how musicians self-identify, how academics categorize "experimental" music, and how such issues bear on the spaces and places of the music: Where is it performed and who performs it, and for whom is it performed? And who gets paid?

Such thorny issues are further explored, in the context of public-policy planning and arts administration, by Alan Stanbridge in his essay "Somewhere There: Contemporary Music, Performance Spaces, and Cultural Policy." Focusing on the Toronto venue Somewhere There (again, a phrase by Sun Ra) in order to explore the issues somewhere here (that is, in most capitalist economies), Stanbridge offers a cautiously optimistic view on the current state of creative music in the modern metropolis.

Another vital and unique feature of our volume is found in the original photographs by Thomas King, "Sound Check." "The truth about stories," King writes in his Massey Lectures, from 2003, "is that that's all we are." In this section of our book, King brings his storyteller's gifts to the art of photography, to reframe and refocus our understanding of the stories we might tell about jazz and creative improvised music. Although best known as an award-winning author and commentator on Native issues, King also has a long (if sorely under-documented) history as a photographer. "Sound Check" is a selection of Thomas King's jazz photography. For over a decade, King has been chronicling the history of jazz and improvised music through his photographs at the Guelph Jazz Festival, an organization that has sought to have as a core part of its mandate a commitment to unsettling customary assumptions about the past, present, and future tenses of the music. While many of King's jazz photos have previously been published in magazines and used on CDs, "Sound Check" is the first public display to collect King's jazz photography.

"I do not do performance photography," King explained to us when we asked him for an artist's statement. "The photographs I look for are candid moments, back-stage practices, sound checks, green-room conversations, quiet moments, for the most part. Oddly enough, being a writer and a photographer are not all that different. When I get behind the camera, I'm always looking for the story, and when I write, I write what I see. Light and shadow are, for me, storytelling strategies, and what I capture on film or on a digital chip, I also try to capture in my novels, and what I learn from telling stories, I apply to my photography."

From the photos of the public lives of musicians, we move to an important meditation on the meaning of jazz lives, yesterday, today, and tomorrow. "Black Jazz in the Digital Age," the essay opening the fourth part of the book, "Get Ready: Jazz Futures," interrogates the future, past, and present of jazz, and develops an ethics of improvised music in a moment when "jazz" seems undervalued by the African American culture that produced it. Greg Tate investigates these themes from his own situated perspective as critic, bandleader, and Washingtonian. As is done in many of the essays in this volume, Tate insists that we rework our notions of category, history, and aesthetics, in order to gain a more useful, ethical, and funky understanding of where we've been and we're going (and whether we have to go), and, for that matter, who "we" might be.

The next selection, "Improvising Digital Culture," presents a discussion between two living artists who are engaged in shaping our understanding of the future of the music in genuinely compelling ways: pianist Vijay Iyer and DJ Spooky (Paul D. Miller). Their conversation ostensibly ponders the relationship between technology and music, but like many of the essays included here, intersects with many other issues addressed above. Iyer and Spooky chart the differences between the digital and the analogue, between improvisation as artistic practice and artistic practice as life, and the myriad ways digital culture offers us both access to and distraction from the histories and mysteries that have come before.

Further emphasizing the important links between past and future, we include a roundtable discussion encompassing a variety of important musicians' voices. Living history and historical lives are pondered and discussed in the roundtable panel, originally assembled for the Guelph Jazz Festival and Colloquium of 2005, and transcribed here in "Ancient to Future: Celebrating Forty Years of the AACM." Perhaps the most wonderful aspect of this discussion is the fact that multiple generations of musicians are brought together, highlighting both the endurance of the AACM as well as its contemporary vitality and relevance. This roundtable serves as one important example in an ongoing history of a "power stronger than itself"—a phrase spoken during this event by the drummer Famoudou Don Moye and subsequently used by George Lewis as the title of his history of the AACM. The history of jazz is a history of social change wrought not by one person alone, but by a collective, stronger than any one individual.

Finally, time and space take another Sun Ra-ian shift by way of Buddhist philosophy and poststructural theory—and humor—in Tracy McMullen's "People, Don't Get Ready: Improvisation, Democracy, and Hope." McMullen offers a critical assessment of some of the assumptions underlying both this book (and its key terms) and various strands of post-1960s philosophy and aesthetics. Along the way, she connects the potential insights of Buddhist practice with the spiritual pursuits inherent throughout jazz history, focusing in particular on jazz musicians who are Buddhist (including Herbie Hancock and Hamid Drake).

People Get Ready

"Avoiding artificial separations," as William Parker writes in the liner notes to his Curtis Mayfield project CD, "is the key to understanding the true nature of the music." So, people get ready. Get ready for the collapsing of historically institutionalized categories. Get ready for idiosyncratic admixtures of categorically disparate forms of cultural expression. Get ready for "inside songs" that move with ease into the music's outer regions. Get ready, as Henry Threadgill might have it, to learn (really learn) how to talk about (and listen to) "everything," and to do so with genuine curiosity, attentiveness, and openness. Parker, again: "Curtis Mayfield was a prophet, a revolutionary, a humanist, and a griot. He took the music to its most essential level in the America of his day. If you had ears to hear, you knew that Curtis was a man with a positive message—a message that was going to help you survive." If the future of jazz is now, as indeed we believe it is, then the pertinent question, to rephrase Parker, is whether, in fact, we have the "ears to hear."

Notes

Our thanks to Jesse Stewart, Mark Laver, and Sara Villa for their comments on an earlier version of this chapter.

1. Our distinction here riffs on Vijay Iyer's comment: "Beware of the prevailing view of 'jazz' as some kind of history lesson that you have to sit through because it's good for you. . . . Understand that this is a living art form whose most esteemed practitioners are continually evolving and engaging with the world around them" (Vijay Iyer, qtd. in Lipsitz *Footsteps* 86).

2. As we were preparing this volume, Bill Frisell also released an album titled *History, Mystery*. While Frisell does not play a large part in the essays in this book, he is undoubtedly one of the figures who is constantly developing interesting and fresh ideas within the various worlds of improvised music. The history-mystery distinction also constitutes something of a signifying riff on Graham Lock's notion of "Blutopia": a dual impulse in Afrological forms to remember the past (history) and to envision a different future (mystery) through music.

3. See Howard Mandel's *Future Jazz* 66.

4. See, for instance, British jazz writer Stuart Nicholson's argument, in *Is Jazz Dead? (Or Has It Moved to a New Address)*, about Europe as the last great hope for jazz.

5. Atkins discusses the "post-national" in his introductory essay, "Toward a Global History of Jazz" (*Jazz Planet* xi–xxvii).

6. Hughes's essay, "The Negro Artist and the Racial Mountain," can be found reprinted in many places, including the essential volume of jazz historiography, edited by Robert Walser, *Keeping Time: Readings in Jazz History* (55–57).

7. See chapter three of *The Great Gatsby* for a good example of Fitzgerald's melancholic depiction of jazz. It should also be noted that the band at Gatsby's party is presumably a white band, further complicating Fitzgerald's ambivalent notions about the music. White or black, however, it would seem that Fitzgerald's attitude toward the Jazz Age reflects a loss of faith in the potentially transformative power of jazz—even on the level of pure entertainment. Jazz, for Fitzgerald, is the music at the party, and the party is clearly over once the Great Depression hits.

8. See Paul Gilroy, *The Black Atlantic: Modernity and Double Consciousness*.

9. We would like to thank one of our anonymous peer reviewers for this insight.

10. Penny Von Eschen, *Satchmo Blows Up the World: Jazz Ambassadors Play the Cold War*.

11. See, for example, Derek Bailey's arguments in his book *Improvisation: Its Nature and Practice in Music*: "The revolution that was free jazz is long over and a process variously described as maturing, re-trenchment, rationalisation, consolidation—all the usual euphemisms of a period of stagnation and reaction—

has turned much of free jazz into a music as formal, as ritualised and as un-free, as any of the music against which it rebelled. Like the rest of jazz it now seems to have very little existence outside the perennial festivals at which it presents its stars demonstrating whatever it was that made them stars. But in these situations free jazz seems to fulfill a somewhat peripheral role and has never managed to integrate in any way with the main body of jazz which, after first greeting the free development with scorn and vituperation, has ever since contrived to ignore it" (56). Ironically, it is precisely Bailey's advocacy of a genre like "non-idiomatic improvisation" that attempted to channel the freedom—both musically and socially—that he describes as lacking in free jazz. Part of this debate thus centers on the age-old argument surrounding the validity of the word "jazz" itself. Our book thus focuses on music and musicians who are, in Howard Mandel's phrase, "jazz-beyond-jazz."

12. We also want to stress that the present state of affairs for many of these teacher-musicians is by far not perfect; they are often relegated to the margins within the institutions that venerate them publicly, in an ironic replay of the way jazz musicians were hyped abroad and ignored or oppressed at home during the Cold War.

PART I

Beyond Categories

Histories and Mysteries

Aldon Lynn Nielsen

CHAPTER 1

"NOW IS THE TIME"
Voicing against the Grain of Orality

Take 1: "The Cry of My People"

"What time is it?" It's still a good question four decades after the composer and saxophonist Joe Mcphee shouted it into a room at Vassar College's Urban Center for Black Studies, as a kickoff to a burning performance of his composition "Nation Time." Mcphee's question was timely; it
was, to borrow a phrase out of that time, "right on" time, though his performance was, in a sense, before its time. Recorded live, this concert was
seldom heard in its time, circulated as an LP from CJR Records, only to
become more widely known when it was rereleased three decades later by
the appropriately named Atavistic Records in their still more appropriately
named "Unheard Music" series. This particular unheard music comprised a
nineteen minute instrumental extravaganza built around the simple opening riff (a riff growing out of the spoken question, "What time is it?") but
rapidly gathered impetus and fire from the improvisational coauthorship
of Mcphee's small band of jazz giants, including Mike Kull on keyboard,
Tyrone Crabb on bass, and two percussionists, Bruce Thompson and Ernest
Bostic. A review of the later rerelease, published in the *Alternative Press*,
reports that Mcphee "takes his sax to places Maceo Parker never dreamt
of," a judgment that is in no way a negative comment on James Brown's
great collaborator (118). Rather, it is a reminder for any who may need it
that the "out" Jazz of the Black Arts and Black Power years could be every
bit as funky, every bit as danceable, every bit as "relevant," to use another
term of the time, as anything Soul had on offer. And this is important to
recall only because so many seem in need of just such a reminder. At a conference some years ago, when a presenter played a segment from Amiri
Baraka's Motown LP *Nation Time* titled "Who Will Survive America?" poet

Askia Muhammad Touré could be heard to comment from his seat in the front row, "We used to boogaloo to that." Many have forgotten the purchase that the most avant-garde music and poetry had on an energized youth audience in those years. We have been told so often that because Free Jazz (free verse?) somehow turned away from the audience and killed the genre, this music requires a certain amount of rerelease to overcome the negative commentaries that were circulated, mostly (with always the exception of the exceptionally dour Stanley Crouch) by people who had not been there.

An urban center for Black Studies is not the sort of thing most now associate with Vassar, but it was there and it provided time for McPhee to unfold his music. The recording of "Nation Time" happened during concerts in December of 1970, only months after Amiri Baraka had published his chapbook *It's Nation Time* through Don L. Lee's Third World Press. It was work that had quite deliberately not been included in Baraka's last significant collection of poetry from a major commercial press, *Black Magic*, work that he was to perform incandescently at the climax of the Black National Political Convention, in Gary, Indiana, in March of 1972, an enactment of the poem so effective with the massive audience there gathered that even so mainstream a figure as the Reverend Jesse Jackson immediately took up the call and its response: "What time is it? It's Nation Time." Baraka had explained the origins of his poem as coming directly out of the greetings black people offered to each other in the streets back in the day, a way of calling one another to the time. Both Baraka's poem and McPhee's music underscore something too easily and too often forgotten in the intervening years: while it is true that any amount of essentialism could be sensed floating in the air like incense at any such gathering in the late 1960s and early 1970s, nation was not a given. Nation was, to put it mildly, a social construction in time. Like the gathering at Vassar in December of 1970, nation was a constant improvisation within the parameters of the day.

A few years earlier, when I was still a high school student, one of the local television stations in Washington, D.C., sent a camera crew and reporter to cover the activities of the recently established New School for Afro-American Thought. Its founding director, Gaston Neal, explained the aims and aspirations of the new (and too short-lived) institution while standing next to a table obviously organized to give the camera a view of the intellectual equipment for the cultural revolution in progress. There were heaps of books displayed against an African-themed fabric, and in their midst, centered in the camera's shot, was the posthumously released, final recording session of John Coltrane. The New School, located on Fern Place, Northwest, grew out of the activities around the Cardozo Area Art Committee and had links across the continent to the young activists who had formed the proto-Panther organization at Merritt College, in Oakland. I couldn't have known it at that young age, but Gaston Neal and Amiri Baraka had long been friends. The two met when Baraka, who was then named LeRoi Jones, visited D.C. on a reading tour with Allen Ginsberg and Ray Bremser, a visit memorialized in Baraka's poem "One Night Stand." Neal had been part of D.C.'s own black Beat scene and, along with Baraka, A. B. Spellman, and others, had made the political move to a cultural nationalism that found its most efficacious expressions in music, poetry, and drama. Coltrane had already in 1967 come to serve as a synecdoche for all that was summed up in the characterization of the new institution's educative goals. Here was an essential, if one were required. Clearly Coltrane was central to any curriculum in the new consciousness, to any syllabus of new Afroamerican thought.

That confluence of the black Beat with the emergent New Thing in jazz and the new consciousness called for in the seemingly unending series of manifestoes of the day was the key to a remarkable phenomenon that has yet to be fully acknowledged (though it has often been fully questioned), a genuinely popular and populist avant-garde. It was a structure of innovation and collaboration that had been building for many years. While it was certainly the case that poets of the Harlem Renaissance had made much of jazz, and that some musicians befriended the poets and politicians of their day, there was nothing quite like what was to be undertaken by the Black Arts Repertory Theater School and its innumerable progeny. Composers such as Ellington had often made racial politics a core thematic in their work, and poets, including Sterling Brown, had seen in jazz an embodiment of black aspiration and accomplishment. By midcentury, a new constellation of mutual influence was becoming visible. In a posthumous work titled *Don't Deny My Name*, Lorenzo Thomas observes: "The militant attitude of writers such as [Larry] Neal was reflected—and perhaps instigated—by jazz musicians, whose playing matched the intensity of an entire generation of African American intellectuals who were too young to know much about Jim Crow but old enough to see that integration was, at best, a barely hatched chicken if not a bird in the bush" (116). By the time Baraka published his first collection of poetry, Charles Mingus had

already composed the searing "Fables of Faubus." Shortly thereafter, Max
Roach had gone into the studio with Abbey Lincoln, Walter Benton, Julian
Priester, Booker Little, and even Babatunde Olatunji to record his monu-
mental *We Insist! The Freedom Now Suite*. Nearly contemporaneous with
the advent of what can truly be termed "Free Jazz," Roach's work signaled
a rising sense of political commitment among jazz artists following on the
radical heels of the Bop generation, of which Roach had himself been a
featured player (though Roach was an early resister of the Free Jazz assault
upon harmony). Much as there was clearly a new political spirit abroad in
the land, as the resurgent Civil Rights movement gathered force, there was
an evolving sense among the artists that their own creativity was moving
parallel to the creativity of the movement. In his volume *This Is Our Music*,
which takes its title from a landmark Ornette Coleman album, Iain Anderson argues that jazz musicians were coming more and more to view their
work in much the same way as Beats, abstract expressionists, and poets of
the San Francisco Renaissance, seeing the work "not as self expression but
as self alteration" (54). And, as Roach's composition "Tears for Johannes-
burg" demonstrated, tracking closely with the demonstrations of the poets
themselves (one thinks here of Baraka's meeting Touré for the first time, at
a demonstration outside the United Nations), black musicians, poets, and
political activists all saw their work as part of a growing internationalist
development. This was a progressive globalization in the wake of decolo-
nization and the worldwide struggles for liberation.

The self-organizing efforts of poets and musicians were also converging
during these years. The poetic avant-garde of the mid-twentieth century
recognized that there was little point in addressing themselves to the *New
Yorker* and set about the construction of their own national and international networks of publications and readings. This phenomenon in turn
tracked closely with the renewed emphasis among political and cultural
activists on the creation of alternative community institutions, institutions
such as the New School for Afro-American Thought. As jazz musicians developed newer modes of composition and performance, they rapidly out-
grew (and wore out their welcome in) the traditional jazz venues of clubs
and festivals. Recognizing this situation, groups such as the Association
for the Advancement of Creative Musicians in Chicago, the Black Artists
Group in Saint Louis and the aspirationally named Union of God's Musicians and Artists Ascension Foundation in Los Angeles arose to work collectively for the expansion of performing and recording possibilities. In

1964, WBAI, a radio station broadcasting from New York, gathered a panel to discuss the situation jazz artists faced, a panel that included Ornette Coleman, Cecil Taylor, George Russell, Gunther Schuller, and LeRoi Jones. Taylor foresaw that jazz artists would not only create new forms of their art, but that they would be required to create new venues and that new audiences would potentially create themselves. This is exactly what came to pass. Though many continue to argue, conveniently forgetting the changing economies of the club scene and the changing profit motives of club owners, that the New Thing in jazz literally ran audiences out of the room (audiences, it seems, who really just wanted to dance), as Free Jazz became a self-organizing radical activity it began to gather an ever widening and appreciative audience. There is nothing like a free concert to draw a crowd and, once drawn, crowds tend to be more open minded than we give them credit for being. Two key moments in this evolution involved Amiri Baraka. The first, known as the October Revolution in Jazz, was a stellar concert that included poets and jazz artists, held in downtown New York. Baraka was one of the prime organizers of the concert. The concert was recorded, and a subsequent LP, *The New Wave in Jazz*, released on the Impulse label, brought the best of the new music to a large audience outside the New York epicenter. Not long after, Baraka made the transformative move to Harlem, and the series of outdoor concerts and theater events sponsored by the Black Arts Repertory Theater/School (BARTS) program during his tenure there provided a vibrant counter to the much-discussed reluctance of Harlem club owners to sponsor any of the newer musicians. While BARTS imploded quickly, its example was emulated at new arts centers around the country, and even by official government efforts such as New York State's popular Jazz Mobile, which brought music on flatbed trucks to communities around the state.

The key here is that most of the more radical young writers and painters had grown up listening to the innovations of Bop. When they moved into the bohemian communities of America in the years after World War II, they shared those spaces with the younger musicians who had found their way to the city. In the same way that a Cecil Taylor would lend a hand at the mimeo machine to help LeRoi Jones and Diane di Prima get out the next issue of their newsletter, *The Floating Bear*, the writers were more and more likely to become the new critics that the new music required. Jazz criticism was an enterprise that, in at least its most visible form in publications such as *Down Beat*, had been dominated for decades by white enthusiasts. Now a new generation of bohemian black artists took to the field, arguing in favor of the most recent and most radical experiments in the music, often doing battle with the moldy figs and hobbyists who viewed the defense of the tradition as their calling, much as a contemporary generation of traditionalists, though themselves African American this time around, have taken to the airwaves and print media for yet another round of retroactive denunciations of the avant-garde. Then, too, a greater proportion of the new jazz musicians of the post–World War II years than in past generations saw themselves as interdisciplinary artists. Cecil Taylor was a poet and was engaged with modern dance. Archie Shepp was a poet and playwright. Joseph Jarman was a poet. Herbie Nichols was a poet. Not surprisingly, these composers and performers felt a comradeship and common cause with the now politically charged avant-garde among black writers.

None of which should come as a surprise to anyone. Had you attended any large antiwar rally in the late sixties, chances are you would have witnessed, in addition to the unending speeches of the rally organizers, poetry by the likes of an Allen Ginsberg and rock music that was straining the boundaries of the form. In an era of widespread popular experimentation in all the arts and sciences and politics, it would have been curious had black artists not done what they in fact did do. What we are still in need of recognizing these many years later, though, is the extent to which African American artists generally, and those associated with the Black Arts Movement in particular, played a leading role in taking the most experimental art to a broad and attentive audience. Whether in college concerts, at Black Arts-oriented community theaters, in venues such as skating rinks and parking garages that had been appropriated for the occasion, or in open air concerts in parks and at block parties, the Black Arts era played host to a general flowering of popular engagement with music that tested the limits of listening. When Joe McPhee asked his audience, "What time is it?"—in that very asking bringing musicians and audience together in a new collective time—he was answered with that same sound that moved Calvin Massey four years earlier to compose the Ellingtonian "The Cry of My People." The piece was recorded by Lee Morgan in the same year as McPhee's "Nation Time," and reappeared two years later as the title track on an LP featuring Archie Shepp; Shepp, who wrote poetry and plays, lived in the same building as Amiri Baraka. The LP carried liner notes by Bill Hasson, coordinator of the Institute of Pan-African Culture and a poet who appeared on an LP by Marion Brown, the same Marion Brown whose conversations with Baraka and Shepp aided them in their thinking through of the relationships between the American jazz avant-garde and African musical traditions, and who had stood next to Shepp among the orchestra Coltrane had gathered for the recording of his *Ascension*. All were artists joined in time, joined together as they put into play the question, "What time is it?"

Take 2: Cecil Taylor: Sounding the Poetics of Black Voice

In 1929, the year of the great stock market crash, the year that marked the end of the "Jazz Age," RCA acquired the Victor Talking Machine Company, acquiring at the same time the Victor company's famous "Nipper" logo, that seemingly ubiquitous figure of my listening youth (mine, my parents' and their parents'), featuring the dog, whose name I had never known until researching this essay, listening intently, head cocked, to "his master's voice." Nipper had been painted in his striking pose by Francis Barraud three years after the model dog's demise. Barraud had at first titled his painting *Dog Looking at and Listening to a Phonograph*, only later rechristening it with the phrase that was to be so intimately associated with RCA Victor and the sheer act of listening, *His Master's Voice*. The British Royal Academy rejected the painting when Barraud offered it for exhibition, reputedly declaring that no one would know what the dog was doing. According to Erik Østergaard, whose compendium of Nipper lore I am relying upon here, the painting again met with rejection when Barraud offered it to the Edison Bell Company. Presumably Barraud thought Edison would be interested because it was one of their cylinder recorders that Nipper was depicted attending to. Edison, however, was no more encouraging than the Royal Academy. The company's response was that "dogs don't listen to phonographs." It was only later, when Barraud discussed his painting with a gramophone company, that Nipper became the Nipper of trademark history. The old Edison cylinder machine was replaced as the object of Nipper's attention, in an act of painterly revisionist history, by a gramophone, with its signature bell, and Barraud went on to paint twenty-four versions of his finally successful memorial to the dead dog.

Edison Bell, of course, was right; dogs do not listen to phonographs. Not even, as I can attest, to phonographs of free jazz and poetry. In the end it has to be admitted that the logo struck home for so long with so many for much the same reason that owners of goldfish would like to believe that their pets' rising to the water's surface and mouthing at them are raising a greeting, rather than face the far more likely truth that their fish, crowded into a bowl, are gasping for oxygen. If our voices could truly outlast us, perhaps even Nipper could listen in attentive wonder to our ever replicating calls. *His Master's Voice*, as painting, as trademark, as fervent wish, is after all a dream of fidelity, an aura that still lingers in the age of mechanical reproducibility. It says much of our latent phonocentrism that even in an iPod age we so fervently wish for the return of the voice, and with it the return of our pet audience. But what of voicings set to radically challenge our very comprehensions of voice?

And what of our own infidelity to the full range of voice and performance? What does it say of our attachment to voice that, even while celebrating the turntablist's scratchings and the electronic modulations of human voices heard on recordings from Chaka Khan and Peter Frampton, to Cher, to Danger Mouse, and the gnarliest moments of Gnarls Barkley, we so often turn our ears away from linguistic sounds that lie in wait outside our phonetic frame of local reference? What does it say to us about our love of voice that we hesitate to lend an ear to sounds seen as neither speech nor song? Why is "sound poetry" so often regarded as a white noise, greeted and critiqued in venues seemingly segregated from those staging "slam," "spoken word," "hip-hop," and other voicings inflected, at least to most listening ears in America, as from the neighborhood of blackness? It would seem that the poetry world's response to nonstandard voicings stands in parallel to the trad-jazz world's response to avant-garde soundings in post–World War II new musics. Some four decades ago, the director Dick Fontaine produced a short film titled *Sound??*, the two question marks in the title corresponding to the two central figures of the film, John Cage and Roland Kirk. One point of the film was to follow these two musical experimentalists as they expanded the registers of sounds considered available for musical composition. The camera follows Roland Kirk as he perambulates through a London zoo, then observes him in full performance mode in a jazz club, reworking the soundscapes he had earlier taken in and taped, redeploying them as part of a masterful improvisation within the structures of his own compositions, inviting the audience to join in on bird whistles in the key of "W." In other segments, we see John Cage

build a musical bicycle for a collaboration with David Tudor and his listening to the sound of his own nervous system while he is ensconced in an
anechoic chamber. *Sound??* scores a second point silently. While there is
some interaction between the worlds of Cage and Kirk, as seen in the documentary (Cage can be observed listening to Kirk's sounds at one point), the
two artists never meet on camera. Whether or not it was part of Fontaine's
intention to underscore the generic apartheid at work in the music worlds
of 1966, the fact is that the worlds of sound traversed so productively by
John Cage and Roland Kirk remain largely segregated from one another by
marketing, by habit, and by racial presupposition, forty years after their
momentous, cinematic non-meeting in London.

Which brings us, by a commodious vicus of recirculation, to the re-
appearance of Nipper on the label of one recording by one Cecil Taylor, released just three years after Fontaine's film *Sound??* The recording, which
has appeared in many variant forms, bearing labels other than Victor's,
captures a performance known as "Second Act of A" (so far as I can tell,
there is no recording of a first act), performed by Taylor and his band, in
Paris. Well into the marathon staging of this piece, a sound begins to emanate from the throat of Cecil Taylor. Long-time listeners to such masters as
Errol Garner and Jimmy Garrison have encountered similar phenomena.
Recording engineers taping the John Coltrane Quartet always had to contend with the groaning sounds that Garrison would inevitably make as
he played his upright bass. These are seldom heard on the official studio
recordings, having been obliterated at the board, but recordings of live
performances often feature Garrison's enthusiastic, trademark voicings.
Similarly, one of the most notable things about Errol Garner's best-selling
album *Concert by the Sea*, in addition to the surprise waiting at the concert's end, when the usually reticent Garner actually speaks, is the presence in the recording of not only the ambient sounds of the locale and
the warmth of the audience's response, but the sounds constantly emerging from the body of Garner himself. In neither case, Garner's nor Garrison's, are these sounds the polyphonic singing long associated with Slam
Stewart, popularly known as "the humming bassist," the sounds of guitarist George Benson or Keith Jarrett. Garner and Garrison are not harmoniz-
ing with their instruments, at least not in any familiar sense of the term.
I suspect most listeners, including myself most of the time, regard these
sounds as the spontaneous overflow of emotion in the midst of a not-at-all
tranquil jazz performance. In the case of Cecil Taylor's "Second Act of A,"

however, the audience is confronted with something quite different. This is not Taylor, like a good Baptist in the Amen Corner, spontaneously cheering on his own music, though it is a mode of call and response. Rather, Taylor is inserting controlled human sounds, of a sort not ordinarily encountered in jazz or poetry, within the lineaments of his music's structures. This is a technique he has continued to make use of, as we can witness in the video recording of his performance in Hamburg in 1995.

And this in turn brings me to questions of sound and poetry. In an interview with Chris Funkhouser, conducted just a year prior to the Hamburg performance and first published in Nathaniel Mackey's journal, *Hambone*, Taylor remarks: "I never understood how musicians could play music for poets and not read poems" (19). There are any number of us who might also wonder about poets who don't read poems, but what I want to begin to approach here is a different elision, one by means of which audiences for sound or poetry, or for sound poetry, often separate themselves. There have been several studies now of poetry and jazz; there have been innumerable critical advances into the territories of poetics and hip-hop; and still there has been precious little consideration afforded the sort of works in voice and instruments constructed by Cecil Taylor and recorded in albums such as *In Florescence, Double Holy House*, and *Tzotzil/Mummers/Tzotzil*. The critical and historical work done on sound poetry has grown considerably in recent decades, and yet it has been almost wholly restricted to the works of white artists. If there is any shibboleth extant within the field of African American literary study, by critics both black and white, it is the presupposition of a dominance of performative orality in the formation of black literary structures, and yet the critical literature on black poetry in performance seems unable to bestir itself to move beyond the rather narrow channel it has so far navigated between the sermonic and the slam. Cecil Taylor's works rend the carefully knit fabric of assumptions about jazz and poetry, about race and sound, about singing and signing, about comprehensibility, about time.

For some time, Mike Barnes has been conducting his own variation on the old blindfold tests that *Down Beat* magazine used to engage with prominent jazz musicians. Barnes calls his tests the "invisible jukebox" and, as part of one conducted with Ivor Cutler in 1997, he played a segment of Taylor's *Chinampas*. Listening to this same recording, Fred Moten found a loosening "of the word from its meaning, of the sounds from the word in the interest of a generative reconstruction" (59). That was not quite

Cutler's response. After listening for a couple of minutes, he told Barnes: "I've had as much as I want to listen to. I presume it goes on like that? Well it doesn't communicate with me. There's nothing there for me." After Barnes had told him what he'd been attending to, Cutler responded: "Oh, Cecil Taylor. I thought it was some kind of poetry." Too many listeners, having found the recording equally unassignable to any recognizable category of performance, simply cannot engage the fuller range of the signifying human voice. Despite a long-standing love of such scatting vocalists as Sarah Vaughan and Ella Fitzgerald, many seem unable to transcend the limitations already placed upon what modes of human vocalizing they are prepared to hear within the parameters of music and poetry, this despite the later examples of such scat experimentalists as Jeanne Lee, who worked with the sound poet David Hazelton as well as with Cecil Taylor (Lee's work is discussed elsewhere in this volume, in Eric Porter's essay).

And to this I think we have to add what Melvin B. Tolson characterized as an eighth type of ambiguity, the ethnic and racial type. Just as the critics of Taylor's approach to poetry recital, in his view, operate within a severely restricted range of what can count as jazz, as vocal, as poetic, so too do many listeners operate within certain assumptions about what can or should "sound black." For half a century now, critics who believe that an Ellingtonian swing is a prerequisite for anything termed jazz have lambasted Taylor's music, overlooking his long-standing adherence to other concepts derived from Ellington's orchestration and pianistic voicing.

Similar procrustean views of black writing and performance would have the effect of telling Cecil Taylor that he was, in some sense that is in fact sensible, if not quite visible, not really black. As long ago as the era of the Black Aesthetic, Stephen Henderson argued that "no ideological hangup should prevent black poets from writing 'sound poems,' especially with the model of Bob Kaufman, and Ella Fitzgerald, Louis Armstrong, and the moaning of the black preacher" (143). Melvin Tolson, a poet much admired by Cecil Taylor, had once instructed a Library of Congress audience on the relationships between the rhythms of black preaching and the sound experiments of modernism, a lesson that was not lost on his great predecessor James Weldon Johnson. In his liner notes to *Double Holy House*, Bert Noglik rehearses Taylor's commitments to "the body and the voice." For Taylor, there is a "vocal sound" of a piano. What he learned from Ellington was to "let the group sing" when playing together. So far so good; we are accustomed to apprehending the "vocal" approach to instruments in black jazz and blues. What we are not so accustomed to is the full range of the vocal loosed upon listeners by Taylor. Taylor, Noglik remarks, "above all had always endeavoured to be a poet," whether at the piano or writing words. One jazz musician responded to a question from an interviewer about his music by saying, "Words don't go there," a response that for some reason beyond my fathoming is repeated endlessly in the literature. When we go to Taylor's music, though, we find words have already gone there, that they are, it turns out, as out as anything else in the music. In point of fact, the words have gone "there" prior to the music itself. On a recording like *Chinampas* or *Double Holy House*, we learn from Taylor's interview with Chris Funkhouser, the words have been prepared in advance.

Two elements, on the other hand, are given over to improvisation: the use of the instruments and the use of Taylor's own voice. But just as any good jazz musician will respond to the call of other voices in the mix, Taylor's improvisations leap out from the matter of the text. So, for one telling example, approximately forty-nine-and-one-half minutes into the performance of *Tzotzil*, an especially striking and stressful wordless vocalization is followed immediately by a school-book definition of "synecdoche." Taylor's poem reads at that point, "the substitution of the part for the whole." It would be tempting to literalize this passage, to think of the definition as an explanation of what has just happened. In much the same way that Taylor for many years built his performances around unit structures that could be seen as integrating the furious strands of group improvisation, he could be seen here as in some sense explaining that the wordless passage was a synecdoche for what he is doing in the piece as a whole. And in one strong sense, I suppose that is true. But it is equally possible to read the wordless passage and the definition as existing in a paratactic relation to one another, which still serves as a sort of musical self-instantiation; or might seem to were it not for Taylor's approach to the whole matter of identity and self.

Near the opening of the Funkhouser interview, Taylor explains that one of his aims in both music and poetry is "the possibility of using language to move outside the self." On one hand, this is simply an observation of the social nature of the linguistic, but the particular "out" that Taylor has in mind is not merely a matter of escaping solipsism, nor of moving that which is inner out to a public. Taylor is rather attempting through language to reach a place, a place words do go, that is an outside. In much the same way that Taylor takes Duke Ellington as a model in surprising ways, his identification of a predecessor in this part of his aesthetic is seemingly counterintuitive. Though Taylor has known and worked with Amiri Baraka since 1957, though he has read Eliot, though he has been at the heart of artistic movements now deemed postmodern, it is from the work of Langston Hughes that he draws this particular lesson, from, as it happens, childhood readings of the Simple stories.

Cecil Taylor has always been among the players regarded as out, as working in realms where words don't go. But in his work as a poet, as in his work at the piano, his words do go there and they challenge our ears to follow. In the dance of the intellect, if I might refer to a remark by a recent MLA president, Marjorie Perloff, Taylor's is a dance, as Baraka has it, that punishes speech. Which is to say (phonocentric, Nipper-like essayist that I am doomed to be) that Taylor's percussive poetry is a dance that punishes presuppositions about speech, about the music of black speech, about us, about the aural in the age of mechanical reproducibility.

"A blast of time flooded in upon me," thinks a character in Ralph Ellison's massive, unfinished second novel, "knocking me . . . into a different time" (*Three Days before the Shooting* 393). It's a thought that would serve well as a description of listening to the music of Cecil Taylor; it's as well an apt description of experiencing the full force of the revolutions that brought us the new music and the new politics of "It's Nation Time." The aftershocks of that revolution still propel our thinking and listening today. "So I told myself that I shall think sometime about time," Ellison's character reflects. Cecil Taylor's "Second Part of A" enacts that mode of thinking within a vocal and instrumental improvisation exploding outside time signature, signing time in new ways. The Black Arts taught us to see "nation" as something apart from place, as a collective improvisation within the space of race and time. Joe McPhee shouted out a repeating question, "What Time Is It?"—his band and audience answering together, as a blast of time flooding the nation, an answering rereleased into our own time. Cecil Taylor, now as then, has signed his own answer, echoing Charlie Parker: "Now Is the Time."

John Szwed

CHAPTER 2

THE ANTIQUITY OF THE AVANT-GARDE
A Meditation on a Comment by Duke Ellington

Jazz writers don't normally speak of Duke Ellington as avant-garde. Yet Ellington absorbed and synthesized many of the music styles of his own period and the past, and at the same time also presaged music yet to come. He was one with the twentieth century and deeply entwined with the technology that disseminated and influenced the growth of the music. In addition, he created an orchestra that was so diverse and yet so unique that he was guaranteed to remain at the front of the music for years. Who could be more avant-garde than this?

In an article published in 1973, called "An Open Letter to the Avant-Garde," Charles Mingus recounted a story about running into the Duke at Yale University, at an Ellington Fellowship gathering in October, 1972, where he said, "Duke, why don't you, me, and Dizzy and Clark Terry and Thad Jones get together and make an avant-garde record. Duke replied, 'Why should we go back that far? Let's not take music back that far, Mingus. Why not just make a modern record?'" (119). Mingus thought this was very funny, and it was, but, aside from Duke's sly humor, what did he mean? Mingus had no doubt that Ellington meant that those who were said to be part of the jazz avant-garde of the sixties and seventies were a group of musical amateurs. Specifically, Mingus said that people such as Pharoah Sanders and Cecil Taylor did not know how to play on the chord changes of the canonic compositions ("Body and Soul," "Lush Life," and "Perdido" were the examples he mentioned). But Mingus had a personal stake in this interpretation, and when he added that only a few years back, he, Teddy Charles, and John LaPorta were called avant-garde, it was clear that he resented being passed over by these inept newcomers: "If I was avant-garde in 1954," Mingus asked, "then what am I now? Avant-avant garde?"

Modern-modern, new thing new thing? The new, new thing?" (Mingus 119). His was the kind of sentiment that a lot of modernists called out of their name by postmodernism can empathize with. But is that what Ellington meant? He was loath to criticize other musicians (with the exception of Jelly Roll Morton, for whom he seemed to have saved all his invective), so there is reason to question Mingus's explanation.

We might begin by considering Ellington's comment within the context of his own critique of jazz history—a critique he quietly began near the end of the first two decades of the music's history, and which he continued for the next forty years. Second, we might examine how what we now call the avant-garde—some of the forms of jazz created between the late 1950s and the early 1980s—has been obscured by the way jazz history has usually been conceived, and ironically has also hidden Ellington's pervasive influence on that music.

Ellington Encounters the Avant-Garde in France

Duke's comment about the relative antiquity of the avant-garde is interesting. How far back was "back that far"? If he was speaking historically, did he mean that he did not want to return to the avant-garde as it was understood by young French artists and poets, many of them just back from the surreal trenches of World War I, who began using the term to suggest that artists could function as the small band of elite troops sent out in front of an army? Some of these avant-gardists also proposed using the motifs and materials of African art to rescue what they perceived to be the exhausted art of Europe. They celebrated primitivism, a form of art then considered unschooled, instinctive, physical (here Anthony Braxton's critique of "the phenomenology of the sweating brow" comes to mind), nonreflective, and erotic. This was the era of *negrophilie*, the love of the idea of blackness, that fetishized figures such as Josephine Baker, the featherweight boxer Al Brown, and, incidentally, Duke Ellington, himself.

Assuming that Ellington was aware of Apollinaire, or even only the French idea of the avant-garde, his reaction to being categorized as part of it would make his response understandable. The French art world had gone crazy over jazz from the moment it reached Paris, after World War I, and it was in art magazines that you could first find jazz praised for its exhilaration, its grotesqueness, its physicality, its sources in the unconscious, its raucous loudness—in short, for French critics, it was a delicious mixture of the primitive and the modern. Two of the most important of those writers on jazz in France, both of whom became celebrators of Duke Ellington's music, were Robert Goffin, a Belgian attorney who was also a leading commentator on Apollinaire's work, and Charles Delaunay, son of Sonia Delaunay and Robert Delaunay, each a famous pre-cubist painter with ties to Futurism, and both close friends of Apollinaire.

Although Ellington did not go to Paris until 1933, Jacques Fray interviewed Duke at his apartment on Edgecombe Avenue in 1930, and the art historian and Africanist Michel Leiris reviewed his performances. Both wrote articles that appeared in Georges Bataille's ethnographic surrealist journal, *Documents*, before the Duke reached Paris. Ellington's overseas reception was made complex by the contradictions within his critical reception. While Europe was interpreting Ellington by way of the primitivists and surrealists, in Britain he was being celebrated by those like the British composer Constant Lambert, who saw in Ellington's scores evidence of serious musicianship, evidence of a real composer in the making. These polar interpretations were the basis of a trap that Ellington would find himself in again and again over the years: when he recorded "Reminiscing in Tempo" in 1935, one of his first extended compositions, he was criticized by some for abandoning jazz, if not his race; and perhaps even worse, he was criticized for not swinging. And if he recorded short, programmatic pieces based on, say, current dance fads, some others would treat him as a lightweight, if not a hack.

But Ellington was to face yet other problems by being lionized by the avant-garde. The concept of the avant-garde itself, as commonly articulated, entailed the need for shock and surprise in art, a *frisson*, a thumb in the ear of the bourgeoisie. The history of the avant-garde is strewn with foreign and exotic musics imported into the mainstream, importations that restarted the engines of creativity when restlessness or ennui set in. And more often than not it was some form of black music—be it African, West Indian, Latin, or North American jazz or folk—that was imported. Black music seems to have represented for Western music a kind of distortion before there was electronics, an irruption into the system, a breaking down of the rules of musical order. The music of black Americans thus carried expectations that were not necessarily shared by its creators.

There was even more trouble for Ellington: the usual view of avant-garde artists is that they are alienated from society as well as from the traditions of their art. But this kind of alienation does not seem to work in the same way with African American artists. The stereotyped equation of tradition with the reactionary is not so generally applicable to Afroamerican culture. Archie Shepp once made this point by defining the term *avant-garde* in a "strictly historical sense" and insisting that the tradition was a point of reference for the black musicians of the sixties. The same argument could be made for African American pop music: that is, that black music exists in a broad-based aesthetic that cuts across class, age, and regional differences in the black audience. Recent developments in rap and dance music may have weakened this unified base, but it is still true that African American artists seem not to be in constant search of the alien and the exotic outside of their culture, as are many European and Euroamerican artists. Even when African American free-jazz musicians have drawn on alien musics, they have often done so with the idea that these, too, are "black" musics that are tied to their own music by elements they have in common, such as race or a shared history of political oppression.

To say that African American innovative artists have not conceived of what they were doing as avant-garde in the European sense is, of course, not to say that they have not contributed to various avant-garde movements, or even been initiators of these movements, though to judge by the lack of reference to African Americans in the histories of modern arts, one would think so. Consider, for example, LeRoi Jones's absence from accounts of the Beats, or the failure of art historians to credit the role of black dancers in dance modernism, or the lack of commentary on the influence of jazz in twentieth-century experimental music or, again, in the history of sound art.

In short, there was reason for Ellington to be less than excited by the implications of Charles Mingus's suggestion. Ellington was relatively well-off; he was urbane, fully aware of himself and his importance, and none of this had to do with pulling down the barricades, or the adolescent mode in which rebellion so often takes shape. For him, the avant-garde was not a style. One imagines that for Ellington, music was about intelligence, the freedom to create, the revelation that his music offered, and a way of making a living.

What I've said should not be understood as suggesting that Ellington's music had no elements in it that the avant-garde would not recognize as "theirs," so to speak: in fact, his music was consistently experimental, embodying new forms and transforming old ones; playing with exoticism (not the exoticism of the avant-garde, but of his own people, his own past), transforming it into the modern; and using more fashionable and already publicly accepted exoticisms, such as chinoiserie in the 1920s, Latin music in the 1940s, Asian music and rock 'n' roll in the 1960s. Ellington's was a music that embodied swing, but could just as easily avoid swing altogether, a music often laden with screams, rasps, buzzes, honks, and all the vocalized inflections that his instrumentalists could muster (and which a Tricky Sam Nanton, a Cootie Williams, a Cat Anderson, or a Paul Gonsalves could take over the top on any given day); and it also contained the urban and industrial sounds of an Afro-Futurism of his own invention. What makes Ellington especially interesting here is that he had tapped into a strain of black folk culture that is seldom acknowledged, the deep commitment to technology and modernity. It's something one can hear in the blues—praise songs to wandering and to cities, to automobiles, buses, trains, and airplanes, to record players and automatic transmissions—a celebration of African American postagricultural mobility within their optimism about the future. That is part of what Ellington was accomplishing: he went back to the future, so to speak, as black intellectuals and artists so often have done, and creativity, combined with long memory, brought forth a vision of a future.

None of this means that what Ellington would create would ever be received as he conceived of it—that much is always true in the arts. But when African American artists create within Western society, especially during the period when what they created was primarily for other black people, the spread of their music to a larger audience is often fraught with the danger that their primary meanings will be lost or seriously distorted—particularly by those of avant-garde sensibilities, looking for the new. For white Americans, black American music has often served as an alien code to be used in order to reject and contradict their own tradition. (As an example, just what Ellington intended by his "jungle music" is not entirely clear, though the white public's titillation with his Cotton Club presentations was more than clear.)[1]

The difference between African American and white interpretations of black music often has disturbing, if not disastrous, consequences. Speaking of the responses of whites to black soul music in the early 1970s, Ian Hoare wrote, "This often means that black music is appropriated by way of a series of crude (and false) antitheses. Toughness is espoused because it is preferable to sentimentality; repression is opposed by license rather than liberation, bodilessness by brainlessness, and a highly developed musical technique by an almost calculated technical incompetence" (193). It was by means of such gaps between cultural expectations that the spiritual came to be reductively seen as nothing more than songs of sorrow, New Orleans jazz as good-time music, the blues as self-pitying, break dancing as a peaceful means of settling gang problems, and house music reinterpreted as acid house. Such narrow aesthetic readings have had the effect of constraining African American performers and artists, of often holding them to social roles that are at best stereotypically benign. African American music has typically been seen as exclusively social in function, albeit within a very restricted sense, because much of it is a music that is developed in interaction, through performance, rather than through solitary composition. Yet it is this very process of aesthetic-through-performance that makes the music not just a style but an ethic. Many musicians have struggled against these narrowed perspectives imposed upon them, sometimes by demanding the same respect given to classical music; sometimes by broadening musical terms to include dimensions such as spirituality, soul, and metaphysics, or by reaching for deeper historical and cross-cultural ties (in ancient Egypt and other parts of Africa), sometimes even by denying the existence of the imposed categories, including the existence of jazz itself as a specific form.

Duke Ellington found all musical categorization distasteful, so it's no surprise that avant-garde was one of the categories he dismissed. Over the years, he changed the way he referred to what he played and wrote—from Negro music, to jazz, to swing, and then just music. In 1959, Ellington wrote: "I don't want to be modern . . . futuristic . . . and neither do I want to be hung by the plaintiveness of something we might have done years ago, even with success. I don't want to have to feel obliged to play something with the same styling that we became identified with at some particular period. I have no ambition to reach some intellectual plateau and look down on the people. And by the same token, I don't want anyone to challenge my right to sound completely mad, to screech like a wild man, to create the mauve melody of a simpering idiot, or to write a song that praises God, if I so desire" ("A Royal View of Jazz" 83).

No doubt he was correct to be suspicious (though in that last sentence he sounds like the arch avant-gardist, Antonin Artaud). He understood that genres, styles, and categories conceal and obscure differences even as they claim to discover and recognize similarities (Ellington once suggested that rock 'n' roll was a form of jazz, and even said that he had written several rock 'n' roll pieces). But more to the point, I suspect that he had lived long enough to know that musical styles in America do not die. They continue to exist and evolve and change at different rates; in fact, they influence each other, and consequently they often have more in common than their differences would imply. Yet many writers and even musicians have preferred to construct a kind of evolutionary, or even Hegelian, model of musical change, where one style opposes another, until a new one is generated and the old ones die, or where a single line of historical development is postulated as aiming toward some projected goal or imagined state of complexity. Such a theory of progress can lead to many problems: it may overvalue the present, merely because it is an evolutionary result; or it may overvalue the past, because it is the real, the authentic, the pure, the original. Such a theory can lead to efforts to rule some styles out of musical history because one doesn't like them, or because some styles lead the evolutionary line somewhere that one doesn't like; or a theory of progress may lend itself to efforts to limit and control the contributions of individual musicians by disregarding their own personal evolution when it doesn't fit one's tastes or sense of how musical history should look. Thus, great figures are said to go wrong and fall from grace, and the history of jazz becomes a kind of tragedy, or a ritual in which new kings or queens are enthroned to replace the fallen. Or so it goes with those who we sometimes call the Jazz Police.

It is within this existing paradigm that all of the new, nonrevisionist musics since the 1940s became problems—namely bebop, third-stream, free jazz, fusion, and jazz/rock. Every new style has been greeted as decadent or a wrong turn by someone, but when bebop appeared, many thought it to be such a radical break in the jazz tradition that it was either nonjazz, the apex of where jazz had been heading all along, or a new beginning that was itself authentic and pure.[2] On the other hand, third-stream jazz appeared to some to be a wrong turn toward Europe, or a pretentious, attention-grabbing search for dignity. And free jazz and fusion were dismissed as the last refuges of scoundrels, incompetents, and vulgarians.

Ellington and the American Avant-Garde

Free jazz was seen as the avant-garde at the time of Ellington's remark and was never a widely popular music. Besides rock 'n' roll, the two other kinds of music that were popular at this moment were music of the folk revival and soul jazz. The folk revival was primarily a white phenomenon. White musicians were learning to play and sing in the styles of both white and black folk musicians, yet at the same time, many older black musicians were having their careers rejuvenated by the revival, and the styles of music they played were being exposed to people who had long forgotten them or had never heard them in the first place. Soul jazz, on the other hand, was primarily a black musical phenomenon, and gospel music and later versions of the blues were both being given new life through this form of late 1950s jazz played by Horace Silver, Jimmy Smith, and others. Mahalia Jackson virtually became a crossover star singing the same gospel songs she had always performed for black audiences, and Ray Charles adapted elements of gospel music to his own pop-blues style. So when free jazz began to appear in the early 1960s, it should perhaps not surprise us that it would incorporate many traditional elements of African American music, given that these elements were found in all three of the most popular musics of the day. In addition, any number of free jazz players—Ornette Coleman, Frank Wright, and Albert Ayler, for example—had previously played in rhythm 'n' blues bands.

It is difficult to say who first played free jazz or when the first free-jazz record appeared, and perhaps even more difficult to say what free jazz is. The chronology of this music is also far more complex than commentators usually allow: it begins in the 1950s, not the 1960s; new waves of musicians with new styles entered in the 1960s and again in the 1970s, especially in the lofts of New York City; it appeared in places like Chicago, the West Coast, in downtown New York and Harlem; and there were parallel but quite different developments in Europe and elsewhere. A closer look at the music would show that it was really a number of substyles, perhaps even different styles, that have been treated as only one music by critics and music historians. There was a very experimental group, what to some seemed an almost academic wing (Bill Dixon, Leo Smith, Jimmy Giuffre, and Cecil Taylor); a spiritual or religious group (Sun Ra, Frank Wright, Albert Ayler); a nationalist or political style (Archie Shepp and Charlie

Haden's Liberation Orchestra are perhaps the best examples, producing a music that sometimes mixed poetry, song, and political manifestos in their performances), and a bebop-revisionist (or "freebop") style (Don Cherry, Ornette Coleman, John Coltrane). Some took jazz so far back to its beginnings that it might be called a form of folk jazz (Jimmy Giuffre's trios, and at least some of Albert Ayler's, Frank Wright's, and Ornette Coleman's musics). Others—such as Sun Ra, in his re-creations of early swing—were neotraditionalist for at least a part of their performing lives. And for still others—like Don Cherry—there was a convergence with the musics of the world that literally made them the beginnings of world music as we understand the term today. Since such a list shows that some of these musicians played in several of these styles, sometimes simultaneously, it makes discussion of this period all the more difficult.

But one style or many, free jazz included (and includes) those who seek to move jazz even further away from the constraints of harmony, rhythm, and the forms of pop song and blues than bebop had been able to accomplish. This new sense of freedom affected every level of the music. Ornette Coleman pushed tonality so far that it became a matter of conscious choice among many listeners: no longer could one simply dismiss players by saying that they played out of tune; now the question was whether one liked that kind of playing or not. The element of swing became even more difficult to define than it had been before, and to say that so-and-so didn't swing now demanded some explanation. New words were brought in to explain the goals of the music, and *energy*, *spiritual*, and *structural* began to replace terms of the past. *Freedom*—the word that covered the whole movement—carried intense religious, political, as well as musical meanings. And just how free this music was became a subject for continued debate.

Avant-Garde Jazz as a Traditional Music

Today free jazz is often thought of as the music that broke all the rules, sometimes because it borrowed from modern European experimental music, sometimes because it was played by musicians who were not really comfortable with the jazz tradition. But much of free jazz was based on some of the oldest and most basic of African American musical characteristics, and one might even want to argue that in some ways free players redeemed these traditional characteristics for jazz yet to come. Such features include speech-inflected articulation and tonality; collective improvisation; the use of older jazz styles and musical forms as a basis for new compositions and as a reservoir for quotation and citation; call and response; African, Caribbean, and Latin American rhythms; a bodily mode of performance (playing while dancing, marching, or using horns as surrogates for the body); foreign or domestic folk instruments; "folk" or foreign scales and modes; acoustic instruments; spirit possession as a mode of performance; and the use of rhythm 'n' blues tunes and stylistic devices.

In *Blues People*, LeRoi Jones (also known as Amiri Baraka) says that the vocalized, speech-inflected qualities of instrumental music found in the blues, New Orleans music, rhythm 'n' blues, and bebop, are the most basic of all black musical characteristics (28). This might be something of a baseline for a definition of jazz. This speech quality, above all else, characterizes free jazz. One of Ornette Coleman's most quoted comments is his claim that he wanted to make every note sound different from every other: "The C in one piece should not sound like a C in another." Equally famous was Albert Ayler's announcement that "it's not about notes anymore, it's about feelings" and Sun Ra's assertion that they were playing tones, not notes (thus escaping from the systems that underlay the concept of "notes"). In fact, many free players actually played notes so uniquely and so distinctly that it made unison playing sound strange. But most of the time they did not play in unison: instead, there was a return to collective improvisation, heterophony, and even hocketing, forms of collective playing that had not been widely used since before the swing era.

These were only a few of the older devices and styles that free players consciously drew on. They also borrowed older elements that were sometimes used for parody or comedic effect, and at other times in homage, but they were seldom played in an imitative fashion. Lester Bowie, for example, insisted that his version of "Hello Dolly," with its growls, swoops, and smears, was a tribute to Louis Armstrong, not a parody. In any case, free-jazz players sometimes pasted together these older styles with the newer techniques and elements they were using. Many of Albert Ayler's pieces, for example, begin as marches ("The Truth Is Marching In," *Albert Ayler in Greenwich Village*, Impulse 9155), but quickly become freely phrased collective improvisations. (Ayler insisted that older New Orleans music was his model.) Archie Shepp's "Portrait of Robert Thompson" (on *Mama Too Tight*, Impulse 9134) moves in the opposite direction, starting free and ending with a long version of "King Cotton," the old marching-band tune by Sousa. And Ornette Coleman used elements of folksong, blues, and even children's songs for many of his pieces: "Ramblin'" (*Change of the Century*, Atlantic 1327) and "Little Symphony" (*This Is Our Music*, Atlantic 1588) are examples.

Call and response made a comeback in free jazz, both as an organizing principle when two or more players were playing together and when used by a soloist, who answered herself or himself, echoing one figure with another, treating different parts of the horns or the drum kit as if they were being played by different musicians. John Coltrane and Archie Shepp were especially known for this technique, as was Eric Dolphy (who incidentally named his music company Split Music).

Many of the newer drummers—like Ronald Shannon Jackson—studied African, Caribbean, Brazilian, and Haitian drumming, and worked new rhythms and techniques into their playing; Denis Charles had actually come from such a tradition. Free drummers also experimented with all of the elements of the drum kit, and a few tried to reach back to a time even before the kit had been invented: Milford Graves, for one, did not use a standard drum setup and sometimes hit the bass drum with a stick or kicked it instead of using a pedal, or he played the snare with a tree branch with the leaves still intact. Jerome Cooper added a balafon and horns to his kit (*The Unpredictability of Predictability*, About Time 1002) so that he could play like an old-time one-man band (though the results sounded more African than African American). Denis Charles sought to get a cymbal sound that approximated the light, ringing touch of the triangle players of the Caribbean quadrille bands in which he had played.

White folk revivalists were drawn to the slide guitar and the fiddle, instruments commonly identified with America, though often played with African American influence, and the banjo, an African instrument. Many of the black free musicians distanced themselves from Southern folk music—even the parts that their ancestors had created (one of the few musicians to actually use or imitate American folk instruments was the pianist Stanley Cowell, on "Shimmy She Wobble" [*Regeneration*, Strata-East 19765], his version of an old-time, Southern, black fife and drum band). Instead, they sought out African and Asian instruments—the mbira, various flutes, gongs, whistles, and drums. It was not unusual for whole records to be long jams on a variety of rhythm instruments from Africa and Latin

America. Marion Brown's *Afternoon of a Georgia Fawn* (ECM 1004) was typical.

Other free musicians began to play on homemade instruments. Don Moye, of the Art Ensemble of Chicago, developed a percussion instrument that looked and sounded a bit like a gamelan, but that was made of old hub caps, like those used in spasm bands, the homemade rhythm groups still found on the streets of New Orleans. Some musicians pieced together instruments from scraps of old instruments: Marshall Allen, of Sun Ra's Arkestra, used the wooden body of a shakuhachi flute with a clarinet mouthpiece and called it a "morrow." At the same time, many free musicians used folk or foreign scales or melodies, or at least tried to sound as if they did. John Coltrane was especially drawn to Indian classical music. Don Cherry used Swedish, Turkish, and African folk scales in his work.

Free players were especially concerned with finding new sources of inspiration, and they often spoke about playing "in the spirit," an idea that derives from African American Protestant possessional states (but perhaps also connects to surrealist ideas of finding creativity in the subconscious). Most free players were very physical in their playing, and some, like Sun Ra's musicians or Albert Ayler and Frank Wright, marched, jumped, pogoed, or danced while they played. Again, some of this physicality is derived from religious states of worship, but also from a willingness to allow physical motion to affect the music and become part of it. Their horns were given bodily form as well, by rattling the keys, thumping the pads, and breathing, crying, talking, and shouting through them.

Free jazz had posed a problematic for jazz: it raised questions such as What are the limits of creativity? What can be collectively improvised? Yet instead of considering these questions, jazz history has treated free jazz as a problem, and attempted to restore the evolutionary model by treating free jazz as a failed attempt, and giving it Neanderthal status on the flow charts. Here, jazz historians failed miserably. Such an effort in any other art would have been seen as philistinism: imagine art historians' arguing that Cézanne virtually wrecked art by leading people away from the impressionists.

Though free-jazz musicians searched for novelty in their music, there was a very conscious avoidance of amplification and electronic technology. Presumably this was part of a response to the rapid rise of rock 'n' roll, the largest movement in pop music since the swing era of the late

1930s and early 1940s, and one that partially overshadowed bebop, the first real innovation in jazz in ten years. But as free jazz advanced, some performers—such as Archie Shepp and Albert Ayler—began to modify their music not toward rock 'n' roll, but back toward rhythm 'n' blues, an older and more African American form. In a famous essay of the time, "The Changing Same," LeRoi Jones argued that there was unity and continuity between these two musics, and that swing and cool jazz had been European-influenced detours from the real black tradition. (Twenty years later, Wynton Marsalis would argue that swing and bop were the real African American tradition, and that free jazz was a European-influenced aberration.)

By the time Ellington made his comment about the avant-garde to Mingus, the first wave of new players was getting a fair amount of attention, some of which was extremely negative. Duke's comment might have reflected a fear that the 1960s avant-garde was reintroducing primitivism in its most basic form, though he might have been equally suspicious of the kind of scholasticism, high modernism, and American exceptionalism that one hears today, where it is assumed that the modern is a question of craft and technical perfection, and where terms like *refinement, development,* and *nuance* are the new aesthetic slogans.

The irony is that Ellington was himself a model for a new kind of avant-gardist, one who avoided the traps of early twentieth-century avant-gardism by opening his music up to every conceivable source of influence and freeing himself from the constraints of rebellion. In fact, Ellington became a primary influence on the development of the avant-garde in the 1960s and 1970s, and remains a central figure for what now some call our permanent avant-garde. Much of his influence in the late 1950s and 1960s was communicated to younger musicians through Charles Mingus's music; and Mingus was never shy about his debts to the Duke. This influence was evidence, however, that Ellington's work had not yet been fully assimilated by musicians, and was, in a way, too complex a message to have been absorbed so quickly. Mingus was the last jazz musician to have worked with the most important figures in the music at that time—Armstrong, Parker, and Ellington—and he had the Duke's arrangements transcribed from the records note for note, only to find that they didn't sound right when his band played them. But he nonetheless incorporated the details and characteristic gestures of Ellington's language into his own work.

A partial list of figures associated with the jazz avant-garde who showed the influence of Ellington would include Hannibal Peterson, Julius Hemp-hill, Anthony Braxton, Don Pullen, Carla Bley, John Carter, Sam Rivers, Steve Coleman, the World Saxophone Quartet, Ran Blake, Muhal Richard Abrams, Henry Threadgill, Steve Lacy, and Sun Ra—who had, as a young man, discussed the Duke's arrangements with him, and was thrilled to see Ellington's use of dissonance, which, Sun Ra said, never sounded disso-nant. When these musicians displayed their Ellingtonian influences it was not by doing literal recreations of Ellington's arrangements—that had al-ready been done by the likes of Charlie Barnet and Harry James in the late 1930s and the 1940s, sometimes even using Ellington's musicians.

Three of the most important figures in the 1960s and 1970s avant-garde, Roswell Rudd, Archie Shepp, and Cecil Taylor, were deeply interested in Ellington's music. In 1961 bassist Buell Neidlinger asked Rudd to transcribe and orchestrate two tunes by Mercer Ellington, "Things Ain't What They Used to Be" and "Jumpin' Punkins," for a recording session that included Rudd, Archie Shepp, Cecil Taylor, Clark Terry, Steve Lacy, Charles Davis, and Billy Higgins. Afterward Rudd continued to work on Ellington-based arrangements on his own, until he had a book that included "Rumpus in Richmond," "KoKo," "Take Love Easy," "Searchin'" "Johnny Come Lately," "Red Carpet" (from "Toot Suite"), "Clementine," "Squatty Roo," "Goin' in the Back Way," "Shout Aunt Tilley," "Blue Serge," "Don't Get Around Much Anymore," and "What Am I Here For?" He assembled a rehearsal band to play them: with himself on trombone, Steve Lacy on soprano sax, Charles Davis on baritone sax, Archie Shepp on tenor sax, Kenny Davern on clarinet, Ralph Rost on bass, and Denis Charles or Dan Varela on drums. With clarinet on top and baritone on bottom, Rudd said they got a good facsimile of the Ellington sound. "We played all the parts—trumpet sec-tion, sax section, and followed wherever they went in the original arrange-ments. Then we broke them down and took them elsewhere." It was an interesting combination of musicians: Lacy, Davern, and Rudd had all played in dixieland bands, and Charles Davis had just come from the Sun Ra Arkestra. Shepp had started as a rhythm and blues player, but once he had turned to free jazz, he often played Ellington songs and made melodic allusions to Ben Webster and Johnny Hodges. But Rudd's band was not the end of these musicians' fascination with Ellington. The Archie Shepp Sextet of the 1960s included Rudd, who wrote arrangements for them that used the characteristics of Ellington's music to frame John Coltrane's com-positions, such as "Naima" on *Four for Trane* (Impulse AS71). And three of

Cecil Taylor's first four recording sessions also included Ellington compositions. When Taylor told the *Saturday Review* in 1963 that Ellington was the only prophet he recognized, he also said: "The problem is to utilize the energies of European composers . . . and blend this with the traditional music of the American Negro, and to create a new energy. That's what I did. And was it unique? No. Historically not. Ellington did it" (Goldberg). Taylor reminds us by example that Ellington's long distrust of categories should also be given heed by jazz scholars. What Duke called "category intolerance" ("A Royal View of Jazz" 83) still plagues the way jazz history is written and thought about.

Let Ellington have the last word: "Jazz continues the pattern of barrier breaking and emerges as the freest musical expression we have yet seen. To me, then, jazz means simply freedom of musical speech! And it is precisely because of this freedom that many varied forms of jazz exist. The important thing to remember, however, is that not one of these forms represents jazz by itself. Jazz means simply the freedom to have many forms" ("Interpretations in Jazz").

Notes

This essay is indebted to many rich conversations with Robert O'Meally.

1. For a discussion of different meanings of Ellington's "jungle music," see Graham Lock's *Blutopia* (80–88).

2. For a discussion of the breakdown of the jazz history paradigm in the early 1950s in the face of bebop, see Scott DeVeaux's "Constructing the Jazz Tradition: Jazz Historiography."

Julie Dawn Smith and Ellen Waterman

CHAPTER 3

LISTENING TRUST

The Everyday Politics of George Lewis's

"Dream Team"

We're bringing the music outwards, we're trying to put it in a
different space. We don't see a context in which it doesn't fit,
because it's so close to everyday human experience.
—George Lewis (interview)

By examining improvisation through the two lenses of performative and
psychoanalytic theories we can begin to articulate a creative practice that
speaks to a "politics" of improvisation embedded in the experience of the
everyday. In each of the two interconnected essays that follow, we trace
one such improvisational environment created by the collective improvisations of George Lewis's "dream team"—Marilyn Crispell, Hamid Drake,
Miya Masaoka, (and of course George Lewis)—from different trajectories,
with an eye toward mapping the group's "listening trust." Ellen Waterman,
following Judith Butler, examines the performativity of improvisational
music, while Julie Dawn Smith draws upon the psychoanalytical work of
Julia Kristeva, to explore ideas of listening and repetition in improvisational practices. Both are concerned with the revolutionary potential (too
often unrealized) of improvisational practices to model ethical social relations. Indeed, the quartet of Lewis, Crispell, Drake, and Masaoka offers
a resonant case study for thinking through some key issues related to how
we might hear the future of jazz, particularly in terms of gender and intercultural understanding.

The idea of a "listening trust" underlines the quartet's emphasis on values
that are often associated with a diverse set of improvisational musics performed after the 1960s (including free jazz, free improvisation, and the

AACM-derived creative improvisation), in which collaborative and dialogic musical processes are privileged. Performative and psychoanalytic frameworks may be utilized to challenge formalist musicological frames of reference by considering performance techniques, player interaction, the role of listening, community, notions of agency, difference, and ethics as integral elements of improvisational music.

The performance we have chosen as a case study for our analyses took place at the Vancouver International Jazz Festival on June 28, 2003, at the Vancouver East Cultural Centre, in front of an audience of about 380 people. Our work is based on interviews with the musicians, and on digital video and audio recordings of the concert, as well as our own experiences as audience members at the event and our ongoing dialogue about the performance.[1] Each of these sources of information provides a different, and limited, set of data through which to examine the performance. Together, they form a useful set of tools for developing a critical understanding of improvisational performance dynamics.

For several theorists (George E. Lewis, Ajay Heble, Daniel Fischlin, Alan Durant, and Jacques Attali), improvisation's location at the edge of representation and theory marks it as a political force. By challenging the authority of the text, improvisation disrupts the expectations of codified music, a challenge that in turn disrupts established musical rhetorics. Embedded in the aesthetic, psychical, and political disruption potentially generated by improvisation are questions concerning how music functions in society, especially in relation to power.

Here we want to acknowledge the importance of Lewis's articulation of historically and culturally emergent responses to improvisation, embodied in his critical terms "Eurological" and "Afrological." As discussed in his important essay "Improvised Music after 1950," these terms point to the power dynamics embedded in academic musical discourses on twentieth-century composition and improvisation (Lewis compares, for example, the respective valorization in, and erasure from, texts on the avant-garde music of John Cage and Charlie Parker). Lewis is not suggesting that particular musical forms are inherently linked to ethnicity or race; rather, he intends to "historicize the particularity of perspectives developed in culturally divergent environments. These terms refer metaphorically to musical belief systems and behavior that, in [Lewis's] view exemplify particular kinds of musical logic" ("Gittin' To Know Y'all" 1).

We consider the aesthetic and political performance practice embodied in the quartet of Lewis, Crispell, Drake, and Masaoka as a response to complex historical narratives that tend to set up and maintain binaries between written and improvised music; between work and process; between authority and collaboration; and between art and everyday experience. But we do not claim that improvised music is inherently ethical; indeed, power imbalances cloud many avant-garde jazz narratives (even those concerning revolution).[2] If jazz is to fulfill its potential to articulate what Robin Kelley has called "freedom dreams," it must be made audible through everyday human experiences of respect for gender, sexuality, and cultural difference.

We have drawn strategically from critical theory as a way to consider improvisation beyond the confines of musical belief systems and behavior that exemplify particular kinds of musical "logic." We argue that, like the feminist, queer, psychoanalytic, and performance theories we are utilizing, improvisation operates in the "spaces in the margins of hegemonic discourses" (De Lauretis 26). Similarly, we suggest that improvisation is concerned with the relationship of bodies and imaginations within social communities, much as the theories we employ. And, as Theresa De Lauretis reminds us, it is "the micropolitical practices of daily life and daily resistances that afford both agency and sources of power or empowering investments" (26)—a claim we also make for improvisation. Applied to the study of improvisation, this interdisciplinary approach offers new insights into the aesthetic and social effects of its practices, because feminist, queer, psychoanalytic, and performance theories interrogate contingent subjectivities and acknowledge the circumstances (social, historical, political, and psychical) by which they are bounded and within (and against) which they signify.

Our collaborative research and writing process has emulated the dialogical nature of musical improvisation. While the two sections below stand as independent essays, they were written in conversation with one another, informed by our respective positions as performer-scholar (Waterman) and presenter-scholar (Smith). This dialogue and our own self-reflexive comments are retained in the texts and are themselves in dialogue with the musicians.[3]

EW: A Performative Analysis of George Lewis's "Dream Team"

The quartet of the trombonist George Lewis, pianist Marilyn Crispell, drummer Hamid Drake, and koto player Miya Masaoka was originally formed for a single performance at the Guelph Jazz Festival in 2002. Artistic director Ajay Heble asked Lewis to choose a group of musicians to perform with him at the festival, and Lewis described this particular quartet as his "dream team." My experience of that performance was of participating in a particularly spacious and thoughtful conversation among four highly compatible and supportive people. Curiously, given that few words were spoken and the music was in a highly abstract, free-improvisational mode, the performance appeared to me to have a peculiarly ethical dimension—to articulate a politics of balance, equality, and exchange through embodied musical sounds and gestures. Indeed, the moniker *dream team* is reminiscent of Kelley's "freedom dreams," a term that expresses the urgent need for equitable race, gender, sex, and class relations within society. Kelley's idea that "the most radical art is not protest art but works that take us to another place, envision a different way of seeing, perhaps a different way of feeling" (11) captures my experience of hearing these musicians' sensitive interactions within a gender-balanced and racially diverse ensemble.

The opportunity to study the quartet more closely emerged at its second (and to date only other) performance a year later at the Vancouver International Jazz Festival. Julie Smith, a scholar and associate producer of the festival, was able to arrange for digital video and audio recording of the performance.[4] The musicians kindly gave us interviews, and Julie and I began our extended exploration of a performance that, like their first one, appeared to enact a highly sensitized, cooperative aesthetic and political stance, which Julie has aptly termed a "listening trust." Our analysis takes account of individual histories and personal narratives as well as the particular performance situation.

The "listening trust" expressed through the quartet's Vancouver performance draws on the concept of performativity, a theory concerned with the "construction of identity in both a discursive and material sense" (Price and Shildrick 413). Embodied and citational musical performance provides a rich ground for thinking about both the aesthetic and the social effects of improvisation, a musical form that calls on each player's personal history of skills, influences, style codes, experiences, intuition, and sensitivity to make music in community.

Performativity and Musical Performance

The doubled concept of performativity is a powerful tool for assessing how identities are articulated in improvisational musical performance through both material and discursive operations.[5] Material operations encompass all on-stage interactions: among the musicians, between musician and instrument, and between musicians and audience. Discursive operations include the articulation of style codes, the assertion of instrumental personalities (for example, through timbre, volume, or accents), and the intertextuality that occurs in ensemble, often characterized by musicians as dialogue (Berliner). Such musical elements are performative at the level of creating musical structure, signaling shifts in direction, and establishing and maintaining dynamic and emotional tension; furthermore, as Ingrid Monson has shown, it is often through such musical signs that the dynamics of gender, race, and community are articulated.[6] As Andrew Parker and Eve Sedgwick have neatly put it—performativity asks the question, "When is saying something doing something?" (2).

Performativity has perhaps been most influentially deployed by the philosopher Judith Butler in her analysis of the social construction of gender, in which, arguably, the discursive and material senses of performativity merge. For Butler, "Gender is an identity tenuously constituted in time, instituted in an exterior space through a *stylized repetition of acts.* The effect of gender is produced through the stylization of the body, and hence, must be understood as the mundane way in which bodily gestures, movements, and styles of various kinds constitute the illusion of an abiding gendered self" (*Gender Trouble* 191). The notion of a stylized repetition of acts (known as citation) is central to Butler's understanding of performativity. As Terry Threadgold succinctly states, "Butler, following Derrida's reading of Austin on the performative and using now the metaphor of rehearsal, argues that the performative utterance (one which produces the effects of which it speaks) is not, in fact, tethered at all to an originary context, but may produce radically different effects in different contexts" (65–

66). Locating citation's efficacy within specific contexts resonates strongly with the discursive and material aspects of musical (and other types of) performance.[7]

Indeed, Threadgold reminds us that "for Butler, the agenda was to . . . offer a new set of metaphors for talking about social change and remaking the self, to make the self 'sound' differently" (64). By exploring the roles of context, and material and discursive performativity in the quartet, we can better understand the relationship between the aesthetic, social, and political dimensions of improvisational musical performance.

Context: Improvisation and the Performance
of Identity

One of the primary contexts for this analysis has to be George Lewis's position as an artist and scholar whose work may be said to straddle both Eurological and Afrological musical perspectives. He is recognized both as a composer and as an innovator in computer music, and as an internationally regarded jazz trombonist, subject positions that Lewis views as part of the "complexity of experience that characterize[s] multiple, contemporary black lives" (*A Power Stronger than Itself* 368). Deeply influenced by his education in the Association for the Advancement of Creative Musicians (AACM), Lewis has called urgently for an analysis that adequately "historicize[s] the particularity of perspectives developed in culturally divergent environments" ("Gittin' to Know Y'all" 1) and recognizes the social and political force of improvisation.[8] Indeed, Lewis's definition of improvised music as a "social location" ("Improvised Music after 1950" 149) has become a touchstone for many scholars in the emerging field of improvisation studies. Lewis distinguishes the improviser from the composer and the performer, marking what he sees as a distinct set of characteristics involved in the act of improvising music: "Working as an improviser in the field of improvised music emphasizes not only form and technique but individual life choices as well as cultural, ethnic, and personal location. In performances of improvised music, the possibility of internalizing alternative value systems is implicit from the start" ("Improvised Music after 1950" 149–50).

When interviewed, the members of the quartet made explicit connections between the social and the aesthetic processes involved in their improvising. In the context of "playing free" it was important to Lewis to be able to choose a group of musicians he knew and trusted, and who would be empathetic on both a musical and a social level (Interview). Lewis told Julie and me that the distinctive thing about Crispell, Drake, and Masaoka "is that they're not invested in themselves as stylists. They can sort of reach out to everyone else, and their music starts as a form of reaching out; it's embedded in the method of playing. Which is a sense of empathy, and a sense of looking at the larger picture and trying to see what's happening at this moment and with these people, both in terms of what the sound is and how I respond to that—what we might call a purely musicological sense—and also how you might look at it emotionally. The part of it that people just do every day, where they sort of read intentions" (Interview).

All four equated good musicianship with maturity and sensitivity. Marilyn Crispell stated matter-of-factly that "the people in the group are master musicians and there's also a great sensitivity there." As Miya Masaoka put it: "Well, just because they're all such great players, the antennae are up just a little bit higher and the sensitivity is up just a little bit higher." Hamid Drake expressed the importance of musical maturity, which allows the players to be "spacious around each other. . . . I feel that's what this group is really about, being vulnerable, and everyone being proficient on their instrument, but also not knowing necessarily what we're going to do, it causes us to really go deep to really bring out something that's really meaningful and worthwhile to listen to."

For these musicians, empathy is an explicitly musical skill vital to the process of making music in community, and it is deeply embedded in a network of shared histories, training, and performance experiences. George Lewis and Hamid Drake have known each other since about 1973, through playing with the venerable AACM saxophonist Fred Anderson. Their common connections to the aesthetic ideals of the AACM (such as those discussed in the panel transcript of the AACM, elsewhere in this book) made both players adept at what Lewis describes as the "code switching and fragmented narratives and multiplicities" that allow a musician to reach outside him or herself and connect with others (Interview).[9] Marilyn Crispell may have absorbed similar concepts through her long association with the AACM's Anthony Braxton, whom she met in 1977.[10] However, Drake, Lewis, and Crispell also had common training through the Creative Music Studio of Karl Berger and Ingrid Sertso, in Woodstock, New York, where jazz and world music traditions were combined.[11]

Taken as an ensemble, these musicians model jazz's potential to unsettle customary assumptions of fixity and to challenge rigid taxonomies. The koto player Miya Masaoka was described by Crispell (who had not previously played with her) as "the wild card" in the group (Interview); however, Masaoka and Lewis have long collaborated and recorded together.[12] Masaoka has created, as has Lewis, a number of technology-driven multimedia installations, and she has also developed innovative digital interfaces with her instrument. Drake and Masaoka share the experience of undertaking the serious study of traditional non-Western musics. Drake is proficient on the tabla, and was a founding member of the Mandingo Griot Society (Kennedy, "Drake, Hamid"). Masaoka studied the koto in Japan and then went on to develop her "own approach to technique and musical vocabulary" (Minor 21). In 1990, Masaoka formed the San Francisco Gagaku Society (traditional Japanese court music). Finally, Lewis and Masaoka have formal training in composition, and together with Crispell, they identify as composers as well as improvisers.[13] Indeed, all four musicians embody complex and multiple subject positions that vex traditional (and still remarkably stubborn) binaries such as composition and improvisation, east and west, and black and white.

In being invited to form his dream team, Lewis was able to express not only an ideal of musical empathy, but to articulate a resistant politics of representation. For Lewis, the gender balance and racial diversity of the group (one white woman, one Japanese American woman, and two African American men) was a positive and purposeful response to the long history of the underrepresentation of women and people of color in improvised music. In describing his experiences as a performer in the European free-improvisation scene in the 1970s, Lewis noted, "I began to notice . . . that I was always the only black person. And I began to think 'I don't want to be the only black person' . . . And then I began to realize that except for Joëlle [Léandre], she was always the only woman or maybe they'd have Irene [Schweizer] . . . overall it just didn't have the dynamic I was interested in on a number of levels" (Interview).

Because the quartet was presented on a double bill with the Susie Ibarra trio (also multiracial and featuring two women), this representation of racial and gender balance was reinforced at the Vancouver concert, coding the event as a celebration of cultural as well as musical diversity.[14] However, in the context of George Lewis's scholarly and creative work, this performance context might be read as a comment on the need for a frank engagement with issues of race, gender, and class in experimental music, including improvisation. Much of Lewis's scholarly work "concerns the ways in which not only music scholars, but also musicians themselves, have either confronted or avoided engagement with issues of race in experimental music. . . . This general erasure of race seems at variance with experimental music's presumed openness, its emphasis upon resistance, and its excavations of subaltern and marginalized histories of sound" ("Gittin' to Know Y'all" 1). Lewis's dream team clearly constitutes a performative manifestation of his scholarly concerns. Here, gender and race are foregrounded as performative elements that carry a certain amount of transgressive power in the context of experimental improvised music in which there is a systemic underrepresentation of women and people of color.[15]

Embodied Performance and Material Performativity

The Vancouver East Cultural Centre is a small, 380-seat theater (a former church) with wooden seats, wraparound balconies and front rows that are very close to the stage. While the stage has a traditional proscenium, Julie Smith notes that of all the venues used by the Vancouver International Jazz Festival, "the Cultch" is the most relaxed and intimate.[16] During their concert the quartet reinforced the sense of intimacy by their onstage behavior.

Each player was dressed quite differently, further highlighting the diversity in the group. Marilyn Crispell wore concert black (she came on stage holding her purse, which she tucked under the piano), Hamid Drake wore a hat and shirt that referenced African culture, Miya Masaoka wore a formal silk skirt, and George Lewis appeared in his ubiquitous academic's shirt and trousers. They arrived on stage casually, seemingly without taking notice of the audience.

The players were configured in a bow shape on the small stage, with George Lewis slightly in front and to the side of Hamid Drake—which seemed to set him up as the leader of the group. (At Guelph, on a larger stage, they were arranged in a continuous bow, with no discernible "leader.") Lewis's leadership was further reinforced by his communication with the group and with the audience. During the concert he was the one who talked to the audience, and in a quiet, informal voice that only those in the first couple of rows could clearly discern. He strongly signaled his collaborative working process with the group through words such as "y'all done?" and body language—turning to each musician, looking at them directly between pieces. He sometimes made use of an exaggerated and deferential shrug before playing as if to say, "Well, somebody has to start."

Between each piece the players chatted among themselves, tuned their instruments, rearranged clothing, and generally behaved as if at a rehearsal rather than in a formal performance; this was noticeable even within the relatively informal context through which free improvisation is often coded. For example, between the second and third pieces the musicians spent a protracted amount of time discussing the lint on the towels they'd been given, tossing them around the stage, shaking them, joking—enacting a small comedy. The musicians' casual, "natural" behavior had the effect of drawing the audience into the performative event. Rather than playing *to* the audience, the group behaved as though they were playing *with* us.

Christopher Small has made a radical call for a new definition of music not as a noun, but as a verb, not music, but musicking. As he understands it, "music is not a thing at all but an activity, something that people do" (2). Small's emphasis is on music-making as a collective activity (including all the musicians involved, listeners, and those who have supporting roles in production). Taken with the musicians' comments about musical and social ethics, their casual onstage behavior worked to blur the separation between performers and audience members, making musicking explicitly a listener's business as well as a musician's. The group's own commitment to empathetic listening was signaled by a circular swaying motion that all the players demonstrated continuously, in different degrees, throughout the concert. Closed eyes were often, but not always, a feature of this motion and it often occurred in conjunction with more prosaic movements such as adjusting an instrument or rolling up sleeves.

Ritualistic gestures, by which everyday actions are framed as performance, are known as restored behavior—a concept that is closely related to citation. Richard Schechner (drawing on the work of Erving Goffman) defines restored behavior as "living behaviour treated as a film director treats a strip of film. These strips of behaviour can be rearranged or reconstructed; they are independent of the causal systems (personal, social, political, technological, etc.) that brought them into existence" (28). Restored behavior "emphasizes the process of repetition and the continued awareness of some 'original' behaviour" (Carlson 52). In a performance, restored behavior is "marked, framed, and separate," and therefore subject to transformation and transmission (Schechner 28). Through such transformations, heightened meanings may be conveyed by seemingly simple actions.

In musical performances one form of restored behavior is seen in the small rituals of onstage behavior, such as the circular, swaying movement mentioned above. During the quartet's performance, individual musical and personal identities were reinforced by the ritualized gestures that are specific to preparing to play particular instruments, for example: choosing mallets, greasing the trombone slide, tuning the koto, and adjusting the piano bench. From time to time throughout the performance, these ingrained individual gestures (born of long association with a particular instrument) were repeated as a player's attention was drawn momentarily away from the ensemble and toward his or her particular needs. Notes were played that were clearly meant for the performer only; for example, while the others played, Masaoka would bend her head close to the koto and pluck strings to adjust the tuning. In the context of performance, these gestures were performative in the sense that they transmitted information both between musicians and to the audience. Musicians routinely telegraphed their intention to play several seconds before doing so. Particularly noticeable was Drake's elaborate preparation with a pair of soft mallets in the second piece; at one point he moved them around on the drum head fully thirty seconds before making a sound. These strips of restored behavior are precisely performative gestures in that they signal the body's preparation to play. They are the embodied expression of musical intention, and while they differ among players, they are always present in some form and are as integral to producing the sound that follows as a wind player's intake of breath.

Citation and Discursive Performativity

Lewis, Crispell, Drake, and Masaoka told us that they did not rehearse or plan elements of their performance either in Guelph or Vancouver; yet, revisited in audio and video recordings, the Vancouver performance has a purposeful flow and the pieces are distinctly shaped. The hour-long performance contains four distinct, highly structured pieces of music. Briefly, they are characterized: piece one, motivic variation in a fluid ensemble structure; piece two, stylistically different duos that slowly weave into a thick quartet; piece three, an intense, quiet, experimental study in timbre; and piece four, a groove-oriented jazz "parody" with an enigmatic koto solo to finish.

At the beginning of the concert, it appeared that Lewis's leadership was signaled through musical timbre as well as body language and words. As the only wind instrument, with a primarily melodic orientation (albeit an extraordinary timbral range) the trombone automatically emerged in the foreground; however, the overarching texture and formal organization were clearly group efforts. For example, during the fifteen-minute long first piece, Lewis took four solo moments, each only a few seconds long. Late in the piece, he played an extremely active passage in counterpoint with piano and percussion. As he finished, the audience began to clap, but the complex, interweaving musical texture continued to unfold, so that the applause soon faltered. For the rest of the set, the audience clapped only at the end of each piece. To clap during the music meant to miss the next crucial bit of information. Within the quartet, individual virtuosity was downplayed in favor of ensemble expression, so that the audience was encouraged to listen to everything in the texture.

Silence was a strong structural element in the ensemble. Solo passages were fleeting for the most part, and the musical texture moved fluidly and spaciously among duos, trios, and quartets. Drake told us that playing with the koto encourages him to work with very low volumes, but with great intensity, while Masaoka noted that "if you're a very soft instrument you have to plan, strategize." Crispell spoke of "not being afraid of the [musical] space." Lewis thinks of silence as a sign of shared responsibility within the group that opens up new creative possibilities: "It's like any kind of conversation. If you start talking and keep talking then certain things are . . . just naturally not going to be possible because you're there. But if you get out of the room or be quiet—it happens all the time. You go out so that two people can have a conversation and find out something about themselves that they wouldn't have found out if you were there" (Interview).

Citing silence equates to respect and trust, but it is also an important discursive strategy in the structural evolution of this particular music, which could not be articulated without it.

Discursive performatives may also be heard in the distinct elaboration of style codes that occurred within and between the two duos, performatives that structured the second piece of the set. For Masaoka, duos are "always a very good kind of configuration because [they] bring out the interaction of each [player] very clearly" (Interview). In their second piece, the quartet built a dialogic structure in which each duo's "conversation" was established through different playing strategies, and then articulated within a cohesive quartet formation.

The first duo was initiated by a melodic trombone solo. Marilyn Crispell waited until she heard a distinct pause—the end of a phrase—then placed her hand on the piano. Lewis shifted slide position and the two reentered in unison—on the same note—as if playing a precomposed, rehearsed piece. Both musicians continued to play in a close, intertwining, melodic texture that was most often heterophonic (two very similar melodies or gestures closely shadowing one another). Subsequently, Lewis performed another gesture that seemed to hint at a compositional structure already in place, created just moments ahead of playing it. He had to stop midphrase and adjust his trombone, which he did very quickly, entering again on a catch breath precisely in the manner of a musician concerned not to miss his next cue. Lewis has described the improviser's art as one of making compositional decisions in real time, within a collaborative process. "The thing about improvised music is that in the ideal case you have to internalize someone's input without your real consent. I mean, you're consenting to do it, but you're not telling them what to do and you don't know what they're going to do" (Interview). In Lewis's view, the improviser's art is a kind of amplification of everyday processes of decision-making: "You have to look at all the modalities, and there's many of them, and grasp them within a certain period of time . . . and improvisers are very good at seeing that big picture" (Interview).

The second duo was initiated by Drake, who signaled his intention to enter with a series of three rolls on the tom, causing the trombone and piano to resolve their duo in a series of imitative tremolos. The duo between Drake and Masaoka was in a completely different sound world than the previous one, with Masaoka making use of explicit references to traditional Japanese koto technique and tuning, a style code she did not reference at any other point in concert. Texturally, the interplay between the two instruments consisted of reactive accents (for example, in the cymbal's responding to low notes in the koto), mutual strumming and rolling gestures (in which Masaoka emphasized the percussive aspect of the koto by knocking on the bottom of the instrument), and pitch bending (a standard koto technique, which Drake echoed faintly by rubbing a mallet over the head of a drum). At no time did the drum overpower the koto in this quiet mimetic duet. The chief process at work here may be described as trans-literation, "the action, process, or result of converting one set of signs to another" ("Transliteration").[17] For Masaoka, playing with percussion pro-vides a certain kind of freedom from the fixity of pitch: "I like to try to . . . find certain kinds of techniques that don't reference pitch in such an obvi-ous way, and it gives me more freedom to do more activity in a non-pitched environment and then the pitches don't define the areas of where it has to go, . . . There's more freedom if you're a percussionist" (Interview).

I hear these two distinctive duos as emblematic of the musicians' stated investment in fractured narratives and code switching. A free-jazz and a "world" music feel were articulated by the two duos, respectively. Each duet allowed for an intimate intertwining of two musical lines—familiar codes and shared histories are evident here. And each exhibited a fine bal-ance between the musicians involved, a balance characterized by mutual respect, with no attempt by one player to dominate the other. The cita-tion of discursive gestures (a roll, a pitch bend, a flurry of notes) was nu-anced by individual timbral qualities, timing, and expression. The fact that the two duos could then intertwine in a cohesive quartet texture shows remarkable adaptability—what Masaoka characterizes as "thinking as a group" (Interview), a model of the "listening trust."

When Is Saying Something (Not) Doing Something?

In considering both the Vancouver performance of the quartet and our interviews with the musicians, there seems to be no doubt that their im-provisations made audible the social and political potential of jazz. But what are the limits of the music's performative effects? To what extent do performers' aesthetic and political intentions translate into social change? And to what extent do performance contexts work to enhance or dilute performers' messages? What difference does it make, performatively, if a performance is framed as multicultural or experimental, as a headlining act or a workshop, as art or entertainment? It is all too easy to fetish-ize improvisation as somehow inherently ethical, simply because it allows for individual agency within collective expression.[18] As Butler reminds us, the transgressive possibilities of performativity are constantly challenged and limited by regulatory discourses (for example, discourses of race, gen-der, sex, aesthetics) that, through citation, work anxiously to materialize particular subjectivities: "That this reiteration is necessary is a sign that materialization is never quite complete, that bodies never quite comply with the norms by which their materialization is impelled" (Butler, *Bodies That Matter* 2). Arguably, the performative force of improvisational performance is found in the everyday politics of resistance practiced by at least some musicians and listeners—De Lauretis's micropolitical practices, Butler's transgressive performance, and Kelley's freedom dreams.

Lewis pointed to the limits of music as activism (something that Crispell, Drake, and Masaoka also expressed in our interviews with them). Improvisational music, Lewis suggests, has an inherent "potential for challenging and questioning." But, he contends, "That's as far as I can take it" (Interview). However, as the epigraph to our essay suggests, he is explicit about the "ambassadorial" function of his own musicking: "We're bringing the music outwards, we're trying to put it in a different space. We don't see a context in which it doesn't fit, because it's so close to everyday human experience" (Interview). The performative dimension of improvisation is that of reframing everyday human experience, creating new possibilities for awareness and empathy in musicians and listeners alike. As Lewis said toward the end of our interview, "We've been talking about politics for quite a while. But it's a politics of improvisation that is really not that separate from any other experience."

JDS: Psychoanalytic Notes on George Lewis's "Dream Team"

Like performativity, psychoanalytic theory has a great deal to say about aesthetic, political, personal, and collective identities. As well, it offers insight into the workings of memory and repetition and can therefore be productively utilized to examine particular contexts and point toward future possibilities for jazz and creative improvisation.

The encore performance of George Lewis's dream team, at the Vancouver International Jazz Festival in 2003, was presented without reference to the Guelph Jazz Festival concert or to the circumstances that first brought this amazing group of musicians together. Because each performer had a strong connection to the Vancouver music community, or had played in various contexts in the festival over the years, or had done both, the configuration seemed a natural fit.

Yet, for those who heard (or heard about) the group's performance at the Guelph Jazz Festival, the repetition raised some interesting questions. What are the limits of repeatability in improvised music? Should improvised performances be compared? Can improvisation be expected to be new, fresh, and innovative—surprisingly different—with each incarnation? What are the politics of repetition and surprise? What are the politics of listening twice? In an interview with Ellen Waterman and me the day of the performance, George Lewis voiced the inner dialogue he was experiencing with respect to playing with his dream team a second time:

> I've tried to forget everything about the last event. I don't want to be in the position of trying to recreate that [Guelph] experience. I want to be in the position of having to look at it again and say, "Well, what am I figuring out here, what can I find out?" It's not like I want to forget those histories. Because I can't do that, they're too deeply embedded in who I am as a person. I can't forget my histories with these people, but I do want to forget that particular substantiation of it because it might be . . . Well, I have this tape and I was thinking I should sit down and listen to it again, and I realized I was avoiding listening to it because I really shouldn't listen to it. Don't do it! Don't get into the stage of critiquing it and saying what worked and what didn't work. You can do all that critiquing right while you're playing. You don't have to do it afterward or before. (Interview)

What surprised me about the concert was that on a certain level, it did not surprise me. I don't mean to imply that the performance was predictable or common by any stretch of the imagination. To the contrary, it was relaxed yet engaging, humorous yet intense, dynamic yet delicate. Perhaps it is more accurate for me to say that the performance was what I had expected—an amazingly nuanced and powerful interaction between four of the best improvisers in the world. Yet it was startlingly different, combining unexpected sounds, contours, textures, and gestures, detours never before experienced in quite that way. I had heard each musician in a variety of different contexts, in a variety of different cities, over a number of years, and I knew their individual histories, where they intersected, where they diverged. Yet I had never seen them in this particular formation, in this particular context, and the anticipation of hearing a compelling and attentive conversation between these four musicians was truly exciting.

I trusted that the spaciousness Ellen described in the Guelph performance would indeed be present in this performance. This was confirmed throughout the concert itself, but also by Hamid Drake in an interview the next day: "There was a general kind of tone and feeling that was the same . . . the respect, the humor, I think both concerts had that."

There was no trepidation on my part that the improvisations would fall short or that they wouldn't "work," as is sometimes the case when improvisers are brought together in an ad hoc situation. Nor was I concerned that this would be a "repeat" performance. Of course the group was not exactly ad hoc, either, given that George Lewis had put a concerted amount of thought into assembling this particular combination of players for the original performance and there were strong histories connecting the musicians on various levels.[19] I noticed a palpable excitement in the audience before the performance and recognized familiar faces as I looked around the venue. Not only were many audience members devotees of improvised music, they were avid followers of these particular musicians—listeners who were knowledgeable about each of the performer's musical histories and aware of their interconnectedness—listeners who recognized the astounding possibilities of this combination. And there were those who were about to encounter these musicians for the first time, an exciting prospect for me as a presenter, whose job it is to bring musicians and listeners together in the best possible performance situation. For professional arts presenters, working to bring players together with a substantial and appreciative audience in an optimum setting is performed out of respect for the musicians and their work—part of the politics of presenting.

Gathering these four players together in the same place, at the same time, for a second performance was considered a coup of sorts, given their busy schedules, the active music season, the specificity of their first group performance, and the enormous demand for each person's participation in myriad other projects around the world. I must admit I can no longer attend any concert without my presenter's hat on, as certain considerations loom large the moment I walk into a venue—capacity versus attendance, production, sound, lighting, staging, signage, hospitality, and so on. When I sat down to listen to this particular performance, all these factors, combined with fatigue, thoughts about the interviews, and monitoring the video and audio recordings, clouded my mind. Yet my own history with these players as a presenter, as a listener, and as a friend, along with the comfort I felt with the festival's production team, the vibe of the venue, and the potential for interaction between the performers and audience in that particular moment, enabled me to engage in this "listening trust," indeed to settle into the improvisation and improvise from my own listening position.

The Drive to Improvise

Derek Bailey proposes that improvisation is the oldest form of music-making and that all music is in fact propelled by the "drive to improvise" (ix–x). This statement interests me from a psychoanalytic perspective, and I would like to suggest that on some level the drive to improvise points to the role of the unconscious in improvisational practices, for both performers and listeners. The theorist Alan Durant makes the same connection between improvisation and the discourse that takes place in psychoanalysis, mentioning the possibility that improvisation finds its alter ego in the psychoanalytic technique known as free association (273). These comments invite me to "psychoanalyze" improvisation—that is, to look at the creative processes of improvisation through a psychoanalytic lens—and to suggest that, much like the psychoanalytic method, improvisation traces a journey, communicates a story, and affirms agency by producing a sonic narrative of lived experience. Furthermore, psychoanalysis provides an expanded view of improvisation as both a deep well of cultural memory and a horizon that hints at the music's revolutionary potential.

The psychoanalyst and literary theorist Julia Kristeva explains in *The Sense and Non-sense of Revolt* that when Freud asked a patient to say whatever came into her mind—that is, to free-associate—he was inviting a kind of speech that affects thought and perception, body and mind. He was not interested in intellectual arguments and vague abstractions, but in the patient's stories (36). The concept of free association thus requires a complex and heterogeneous concept of language, one that challenges language's authority as the "solid terrain that leads to truth" and allows for the machinations of dreams, the unconscious, and other elements that often escape linear time and representation (49). Kristeva tells us that in the process of free association "language constitutes an intermediary zone, an interface between the unconscious and the conscious" and "unconscious representations are distinct from verbal representations but capable of being associated with them and, as a result, capable through language, of reaching consciousness" (48). In other words, language acts as a structuring principle for unconscious drives and articulates them at the conscious level. The medium of sound is just such an intermediary zone during the course of improvisation, acting as an interface between the unconscious and the conscious manifest in music.

The extemporaneous narration of a story or journey in free association and improvised music, then, creates a "fantasmatic narrative," a mythic blending of conscious and unconscious elements that produces a third component, an ontology Kristeva calls *signifiance*. This is a space of psychic excess, a "process, dynamic and movement of meaning" (37). Signifiance constitutes an in-between state, an extrapsychical moment in which the capacity of a speaking and sounding being to signify creates "a horizon of being outside the psychical where human subjectivity is inscribed without being reduced" (59). Free association narrates the struggle of the psyche, which Kristeva describes as an encounter with "the dynamic and the dichotomy between *act* and *representation*" (46). This dynamic dichotomy recalls the tension inherent in Christopher Small's statement "music is not a thing but an activity," quoted earlier in Ellen's text. According to Kristeva, it is this tension that is the catalyst for a politics she refers to as "revolt."

In a contemporary psychoanalytic context, Kristeva argues that revolt is articulated in the narrative process of free association. In this configuration, revolt becomes a performative act, breaking free of the one-dimensional struggle between prohibition and transgression it is often thought to represent, to become a more complex, layered, and dynamic encounter with self and other. Indeed, the concepts of change and transformation are embedded in Kristeva's nuanced notion of revolt, and her theory offers an expanded, polyvalent configuration that incorporates notions of movement—cycle, return, memory—with notions of time and space, that is, change, mutation, and duration. Revolt ceases to operate in the arena of dated dialectical forms and becomes more concerned with "topologies" and "spatial configurations," a nuanced way of working through the cycle of desire and repression. "Revolt here is not an advance toward 'singing tomorrows' but, on the contrary, a return and a process" (50). She characterizes revolt as a renewal rather than a rebirth, a heterogeneous process of repetition and recollection, a calling to and a retrieval of subjectivity. In this configuration, revolt is intimately related to the notion of citation and repetition.[20]

Living Revolt

Kristeva claims that if society is to avoid stagnation "[t]here is an urgent need to develop the culture of revolt starting with our aesthetic heritage." The theorist James Snead echoes her statement: "The important thing about culture is that it should not be dead. Or, if dead, then its transformations must continue to live on in the present" (213). If we think of improvisation as a sonic telling, a free association that sounds the dynamic unfolding of conscious and unconscious processes, (an expression of signifiance), we are keeping this aesthetic heritage alive and connecting it to the culture of revolt.

The creative text along with the analysand's narrative are, in Kristeva's words, "animated by a desire to overturn the world, oneself, the Other, love and death" (51). In this way the improviser dwells, as does the writer and the analysand, in a strange and mobile space, inhabiting the liminality and paradox of the "prior future" that is the stuff of free association. Improvisation, as a narrative process, is not merely driven by exact repetition, a redundant reiteration of the same old story, but instead enacts "a question, a rupture, a sub-version, a re-volt" (10).

This means improvisation is a discourse in which time and memory are repeated but never sound the same, a discourse in which "notions of personhood are transmitted via sounds, and sounds become signs for deeper levels of meaning beyond pitches and intervals," to quote George Lewis ("Improvised Music after 1950" 156). In this way, the improviser engages with the same creative struggles encountered by all revolutionaries.

Hamid Drake stresses the importance of improvisation as a workshop or a laboratory that can be creatively used to observe the limitations within ourselves, with an eye toward transformation: "For me that's what the music is all about, it's a commitment to my growth and in some ways a commitment to the growth of those who are listening also" (Interview). For Marilyn Crispell, the give and take of conversation is key: "It's like having a conversation and someone is talking to you and you listen, and based on what they say you answer" (Interview). George Lewis emphasizes the significance of personal narrative that references historical, cultural, and gendered contexts in the everyday: "The music being an expression of not only immediacy but also of personal histories and collective histories, becomes this political space. But not necessarily in the sense of 'I'm articulating a particular agenda.' But certainly you have to think about the politics that are inherent here. And in that sense, thinking about it and really kind of documenting it and theorizing it, allows you to deploy that understanding of the music as well. And the people who are thinking on that level about it . . . you know when they are doing it, because you can hear it in the sound" (Interview).

These insightful observations by improvisers in the quartet remind us that improvisation traces a journey, communicates a story, and affirms agency by producing a sonic narrative of lived experience. Contained in the improvisatory moment is a space of risk and excess, a space of creativity, and of politics. Improvisation is indeed a revolution of, in, and through sound.

Improvising Memory, Sound, and History

Miya Masaoka simply but profoundly described the connection between improvisation and lived experience to Ellen and me when she paraphrased Charlie Parker's adage: "What you live comes out of your horn." Masaoka's "horn" is of course her koto, an unlikely instrument to appear alongside the drums, pianos, and trombones in an improvising quartet. Even the mere introduction of this instrument into jazz and free improvisation can be seen as revolutionary, because it introduces a surprising layer to improvisational language.

For example, the day after the quartet performed, Hamid Drake spoke of the effect the koto had on his playing:

> The quality I would say it brings out is, you can still play very soft and gentle but with intensity and passion. I think that's what that particular instrument brings out in me, to play sonically at a much lower level but at the same time still bring forth a lot of strong intent and passion and intensity. I don't think the intensity level has to be lessened and I don't think volume always means intensity. I feel the koto is a very intense instrument and even its use of space within the form—its use of emptiness within form—is very, very, very powerful because sometimes I think with that instrument the silences are just as strong as the actual sound. So I would say that is one of the qualities playing with Miya in this particular group brings out for me.

Having studied traditional Japanese music with two sensei, in combination with her music studies at San Francisco State University and Mills College, Masaoka reinvents both ancient and contemporary approaches to the koto, as two aesthetics are blended together and transformed into a personal language. In an interview with Bill Minor, she speaks of her musical hybridity: "I've done two tours of Japan, and they view my music as being very much both Japanese and American, just as I am" (21). Similarly, in her candid interview with Ellen and me, Masaoka expressed the materiality of her doubleness:

> At different times it's very trendy to be Japanese—I remember when all of a sudden it was trendy to be Asian sometime in the 80s and it was so bizarre because I would get teased as a child when I brought chopsticks, or sometimes I would have sashimi and sushi in my lunchbox and people would make horrible fun and horrible remarks and it was just the worst. So I refused to let my mom pack me anything like that. And then ten years later, the children have grown up . . . and everyone is going to sushi restaurants and it's completely different.
>
> And then also of course the whole generation of my parents being in the concentration camps in the United States—these camps were also in Canada—was a really different experience of what it was to be Japanese in the 40s. And it certainly wasn't trendy, and cool, and chic, and exotic. They were in these prison camps for four and a half years and all their property was taken away. So there are such different experiences of what it means to be exotic and how that is beneficial or detrimental depending on what decade you're in. (Interview)

Masaoka's playing contains the embodiment of this aesthetic, cultural, and personal memory, as she improvises her story over and over. In the different laminar depths of her narratives, generations of Japanese musical traditions are present, as are the changing technologies of music; the sorrow of internment camps passing through the generations; the surprise of the unorthodox; the embarrassment and the hipness of her Japanese American "difference"; and the fierce, creative independence she exudes, all resounding in her koto, as she reiterates: "And certainly that's always true that you're playing what you've been formed with in your whole life musically and every way else" (Interview).

Improvising Difference

By drawing from "difference," improvisation deploys a politics described by Kristeva as an "outlaw aesthetics" that creates strategic and complex discourses of identity.[21] Here, the AACM's notion of "sonic personality" or "finding one's own sound," as described by George Lewis, is applicable: "In the context of improvised musics that exhibit strong influences from Afro-logical ways of music-making, musical sound—or rather, one's own sound" becomes a carrier for history and cultural identity. "'Sound' becomes iden-tifiable, not with timbre alone, but with the expression of personality, the assertion of agency, the assumption of responsibility, and an encounter with history, memory and identity" ("Gittin' to Know Y'all" 4). What both Lewis and Kristeva are alluding to is that our identity (or self, or personal sound) is inextricably linked to the identity of the "other." Kristeva argues in *Strangers to Ourselves* that otherness is the space of strange or foreign aspects within ourselves that each of us must come to terms with. Con-fronting the other within is crucial to our encounter with "history, mem-ory, identity"—indeed to developing the sonic personality Lewis speaks of.

Kristeva describes the other as the stranger, the foreigner, the wanderer, an embodied presence that cannot be reconciled simply by the acceptance of "otherness" or the other into the social fabric. The foreigner, as other, confronts us with our own otherness—the repressed other that lingers in our own psyche. This is an encounter with the ambiguity of our boundaries that throws us slightly off balance, revealing the fragility of our identity and the other within—a subjectivity that is never fully decided but fluid, constantly in motion. Our sound and our identity embrace this fluidity.

Kristeva associates this psychic and sonic fluidity with difference, the point at which the "fragility of representation" is revealed. The encounter with difference—initially, as the difference within us—triggers a loss of boundaries of self. We sense that the line separating imagination from reality has been erased (*Strangers to Ourselves* 188). Thus, the fear of the other we experience when confronted with difference is ultimately a fear of our own repressed otherness, of the stranger within ourselves: "The for-eigner is within me, hence we are all foreigners. If I am a foreigner, there are no foreigners" (*Strangers to Ourselves* 192).

For Kristeva, the commitment to an ongoing encounter with the exter-nal other must be coterminous with the commitment to the ongoing en-counter with the other within, a journey "toward an ethics of respect for the irreconcilable"—not only an apt description of improvisation but of the articulation of identity through improvisation (*Strangers to Ourselves* 181–82). This ethics also contains a politics that reaches beyond "brother-hood, paternal law and divine authority" to cut across economic, ethnic, political, gendered, and national borders. To reconcile the irreconcilable is to create a "paradoxical community" that is, musically speaking, akin to the "transcultural sociomusical environment" George Lewis articulates with respect to improvisation and the "empathic communication across time" described by Ajay Heble and Daniel Fischlin in their analysis of the improvisational process (7). In Kristeva's words, paradoxical community is based on respect for "a mankind whose solidarity is founded on the *consciousness* of its unconscious—desiring, destructive, fearful, empty, impossible" (*Strangers to Ourselves* 192, emphasis added). This solidarity can be worked through at the aesthetic level—in the revolutionary sounds of improvisation.

Improvising Listening

There's definitely a feeling of what's happening from the audience.
You can tell if people are listening . . . and paying attention and they're
thinking about things. You can feel that. You can also feel when you
have the audience with you.—Miya Masaoka (Interview)

With respect to the interpreter of improvisation (or free association)—that is, the analyst, the critic, the scholar, and the listener—Kristeva suggests that the reception of an improvised narrative must be approached not only from the standpoint of fixed codes but with "a certain openness in one's own psychical apparatus, a flexibility that ultimately represents an aptitude for revolt" (*The Sense and Non-Sense of Revolt* 51). Hamid Drake notes, "You always meet people who will speak about improvised music and they'll say they heard some concert and it changed their life; you know, it really changed their life. And it got them to think about things that perhaps they wouldn't have access to" (Interview).

The listener, too, is decentered and ceases to interpret from the position of "normative truth." Following Helen Deutsch, Kristeva proposes that the interpreter should position herself not only as "the subject thought to know" but also as an "eternal adolescent," a revolutionary listener: "This may sound odd, because we know that the eternal adolescent is immature and capriciously fragile, moving from depression to hysteria, from amorous infatuation to disappointment." Yet she observes that with this volatility comes "a certain suppleness of agencies, an adaptability, a capacity to modify oneself according to the environment and the other, as well as against them" (*The Sense and Non-Sense of Revolt* 51). Hamid Drake speaks of his hope for revolutionary listening: "There's so much emotion involved and when you're dealing with something that's as subtle as emotion—there's so many emotions in the atmosphere—if the artist is really sensitive they're going to pick up on that and it can't be ignored. So, if one is an artist, I feel they have a great responsibility, and if one is a listener there's a great responsibility. So it's a shared thing and hopefully if one enters the door and settles, my hope is that one day we'll reach the point where all expectations are dropped" (Interview).

It is important to note that revolutionary, decentered listening is especially pertinent to the music critic who approaches the improvised performance from the position of paternalism, a judgmental father figure who values the sound of his own diagnostic voice over that of the creative artist. In this scenario, the improviser is treated as the patient, the improvisation as the symptom, while the critic prescribes the cure. The composer-improviser Anthony Braxton comments extensively in his *Triaxium Writings*, on the problems inherent in a hearing-impaired approach to the music, arguing that a paternalistic attitude is part of the white critical response to jazz, a response that contributes to the oppression of African American musicians as it primitivizes and exoticizes them (quoted in Lock 173–84). Braxton notes, "One of the most sophisticated weapons that white people have come up with would be language—words—a mono-dimensional language used to evaluate and distort a multi-dimensional music" (quoted in Lock 219).

The analogous effects of sexism can be found in critical responses to women improvisers, such as the de facto gendering of women's performances as "feminine" (and thus lacking), noted by Susan McClary in her book *Feminine Endings*, the reiteration of the limiting trope "you sound good for a woman," recounted by several female musicians interviewed by Val Wilmer in her classic book *As Serious as Your Life*, and the deployment of the ambiguous compliment "you play like a man," recounted by Jane Bunnett in the liner notes accompanying her CD *Spirits of Havana*. "I thought it was really funny," Bunnett recalls of her association with the Cuban master musician Guillermo Barreto, "because what he'd said was, you play like a man! But he always meant that in kindness" (Palmer).

The image of the critical listener as eternal adolescent, offered by Kristeva, is an alternative description of the participant-interpreter of improvised music who is willing to take the risk of displaced listening that unauthorizes herself. I use the term *risk* because the decentered listener embarks on a journey for which she has no map or compass, pouring herself into the contours of the sounds and gestures of the performance, allowing for detours into unfamiliar territory and possible encounters with the unknown, the unconscious, self, and other. This kind of revolutionary listening is the basis of a critical stance that locates itself strategically off center, an ability to hear beyond the readymade judgment of fixed and immobile musical "truths." Like improvisation itself, this is a position of criticism and analysis that is fluid, receptive, and wise. "Then and only then," Kristeva writes, "will texts appear not as fetishes or dead objects corresponding to definite states of history or rhetoric but as so many experiences of psychical survival on the part of those who have engaged in the struggle and on our part as well" (*The Sense and Non-Sense of Revolt* 51).

Listening Trust

In the course of improvisational performance, the feedback, responses, and interpretations of "others" are an integral part of the dynamic and mobility of the music's free association, occurring as improvisations at the moment of improvisation. The simultaneity of creation and interpretation that takes place in the improvisatory space constructs a polyphonic antiphony, as multiple listeners in a multiplicity of listening positions—on the stage as well as in the audience—engage within individual and collective levels of stratified listening. From moment to moment, layers of listening are added to layers of sounding to create interactive discourses that run parallel to one another, circumnavigate each other, collide, and disperse. "There is a piling up of otherness: the addressee is an other-being: 'I' is an other-being: these others are altered by contemplating each other ... this interlocking of alterities can give subjectivity an infinite dimension of creativity" (Kristeva, *The Sense and Non-Sense of Revolt* 67).

Improvisation generates a creative, interactive dimension through sound: a boundless engagement with our own revolutions and the revolutions of the other. George Lewis notes that empathy plays a role in the improvisational listening experience when he states, "It seems clear that the listener also improvises, posing alternative paths, experiencing immediacy as part of the listening experience" ("Improvised Music after 1950" 148).

This is the "listening trust," a pact among performers and listeners that they will listen and be listened to; an agreement to engage in an "empathic communication across time" and to employ an "ethics of respect" for the performative journey with which and in which they engage. Marilyn Crispell sums it up: "There's a kind of relaxation that happens when you trust the other people on stage with you—that they will do what's appropriate, and if there's space where something needs to or should happen, or might happen, that they have the ability to enter that space and do something good" (Interview). Lewis's dream team improvises powerfully in the paradoxical moment of seemingly quotidian yet revolutionary spaces where, if we listen carefully, we will hear the future of jazz, in the sounds of equality, respect, and empathy.

Notes

1. We are grateful to the quartet and to the Vancouver International Jazz Festival for allowing us to record the performance, and we wish to thank Marlene Madison for her sensitive videography.

2. See Heble, *Landing on the Wrong Note*, especially chapters 5 and 7; Julie Smith, "Playing Like a Girl"; and McMullen, "Identity for Sale."

3. Earlier versions of these essays were presented at the Guelph Jazz Festival Colloquium (September 2003), and at the conference New Perspectives on Improvisation, at McGill University, in Montreal (May 2004). We have benefited greatly from the feedback of our colleagues, including Ajay Heble, Eric Lewis, George Lewis, and Tracey Nicholls.

4. Smith later became the executive director of Coastal Jazz and Blues.

5. Here I endorse Stuart Hall's nonessentialist understanding of identity, whereby "identities are constructed within, not outside, discourse [and are therefore] produced in specific historical and institutional sites within specific enunciative strategies" (4). A theory of performative language is found in speech-act theory, classically defined by J. L. Austin. For detailed discussions of performativity, see Parker and Sedgwick, "Introduction: Performativity and Performance," and Schechner, *Performance Studies*.

6. See Berliner on "The Collective Conversation of Jazz Performance," and Monson on the discursive qualities of rhythm sections in jazz ensembles in her *Saying Something*.

7. For example, see Carlson, *Performance* (170–86), for a discussion of Butler's influence on performance art.

8. The Association for the Advancement of Creative Musicians was founded in Chicago in 1965, and includes such influential figures in creative improvised music (or Great Black Music, in AACM terminology) as Muhal Richard Abrams, Lester Bowie, Fred Anderson, and Anthony Braxton. The AACM was created to foster innovations in great black music while offering a positive coopera-

tive aesthetic and political model for African Americans. Lewis has been associated with the AACM since 1971, when he studied composition with Abrams and trombone with Dean Hey. Lewis has also written a book about the organization: *A Power Stronger than Itself.*

9. While Drake is not listed as a member of the AACM, his early musical training and performance experience were with the seminal AACM saxophonist Fred Anderson. Anderson introduced Drake to Lewis.

10. Throughout her career, Crispell has also performed extensively with other AACM musicians, including Roscoe Mitchell, Leo Smith, Joseph Jarman, Fred Anderson, Kalaparusha Maurice McIntyre, and Fred Hopkins (Kennedy, "Crispell, Marilyn").

11. The Creative Music Studio (CMS) was founded in 1971 by Karl Berger, Ingrid Sertso, and Ornette Coleman. Active full-time until 1984, and with a continuing presence as a foundation, the CMS was a pioneer of hybrid styles involving jazz and various non-Western world-music traditions.

12. *The Usual Turmoil and Other Duets* (Music and Arts CD-1023, 1997).

13. Crispell has published a booklet entitled *Some Information about my Compositions.*

14. Jennifer Choi, violin; Craig Taborn, piano.

15. In addition to Lewis's comments above, see Lewis, "Improvised Music after 1950"; Oliveros, "Harmonic Anatomy"; and Julie Smith, "Playing Like a Girl." It is also worth noting that Masaoka has a background in union activism (Interview), and that several of Masaoka's compositions are explicitly political. For example, *What Is the Difference between Stripping and Playing the Violin?* (1997) is a site-specific piece, originally performed on a street in San Francisco, inspired by the brutal killings of prostitutes in Masaoka's neighborhood. The show included performances by exotic dancers and a panel discussion on sex workers, in conjunction with a performance by the sixteen-piece Masaoka Orchestra, which features Western and Eastern instruments, and combines compositional, improvisational, and conduction techniques (Masaoka Orchestra). Drake articulates his musical practice in terms of his spiritual practice in Tibetan Buddhism. In our interview, he spoke at length about the responsibility of the artist, saying, "You have to be responsible for what you put out into the world. . . . And it's no different than any other social project; I feel it has to have the same kind of intention and integrity as any other social thing that is put out to other people." Crispell is reticent to connect political and aesthetic processes in her work.

16. The Vancouver East Cultural Centre was renovated in 2009.

17. Masaoka has also explored this technique in her Transliteration Trio (Miya Masaoka, koto; Samir Chatterjee, tabla; and Amir ElSaffar, trumpet), which performs "compositions and improvisations of transliterated sound symbolism of the tabla or koto based on the development of a new vocabulary for transferring tabla techniques to the Japanese koto, and conversely, koto techniques for tabla" (Masaoka, "Ensembles").

18. The limits of this analysis (confined to performers' histories, intentions, and actions, for the most part leaving out audience's reaction and critical reception) mean that these questions can only be answered from the players' perspectives. I'm increasingly convinced that a truly performative analysis must include an audience-reception study. Julie's essay discusses the social and political dimensions of listening to improvised music.

19. Ellen has discussed George Lewis's purposeful articulation of a resistant politics of representation in the formation of this group.

20. The concept of citation was discussed in Ellen's earlier text.

21. This statement is also true of free association.

Eric Porter

CHAPTER 4

JEANNE LEE'S VOICE

On 52nd Street I realized Jean [*sic*] Lee is clothed and fed by her
voice. That's the same street my aunts and uncles were born and
black on, so 52nd and 10th means something to me—like a people
who come out with what they can carry: love, sweat, blood and
song. Though everything we know is wonderful and rich, we, as
a people, hide, to keep it safe. Jean Lee don't. . . . Aretha ad-
dresses God, Billie Holiday seduced him. Tina Turner made the
devil think twice/but Jean Lee is mingling among us. . . . She is
not afraid of all this body that moves so sweet I dare you/and
isn't this more than you ever imagined; her body is song. . . . We
got a woman among us who isn't afraid of the sound of her own
voice. She might lay up nights, wondering how are we staying
alive 'cause we didn't hear what she just heard/or sing it. Well.
Did I hear the congregation say Amen.
She sings.
Jean Lee/She sings

Ntozake Shange's review of a performance at Soundscape, in New York, in
1981 (quoted above), sets the stage for understanding Jeanne Lee's extraordinary voice. Noting the function of song in a society defined by its slave
past, placing Lee among a tradition of black women vocalists, referencing
the way she fused the aesthetics of dance and vocal art in performance, and
suggesting that she was invested in a politics of the everyday are all relevant tactics for making sense of Lee and her music. Despite the force of her
voice, Lee was not fully audible to various interpretive communities over
the course of her forty-year career, because of her position as a woman,
working mother, black person, and, as she described herself shortly before her death, in 2000, "a jazz singer, poet/lyricist, composer/improvisor,

who since the 1960s [had] extended the vocal jazz tradition to keep pace with the innovations made by instrumentalists . . . [and] extended the jazz song into a foundation for multi-disciplinary (music, dance, slides, film) performance" (Lee, "Overview of Artistic Achievements"). Shange's analysis, however, begins to fill in the gaps in the textual record and makes Lee and her music more intelligible by balancing documentation and recuperation with a creative historicization of her work.

Following her lead, I seek here to engage Jeanne Lee's life, art, and ideas within the contexts Shange identifies. Moreover, the scarcity of published and archival information on Lee, her genre-bending artistic legacy, her sometimes cryptic remarks about the significance of her work, and the occasionally explicit but often subtle ideological codes permeating the production and reception of improvisational practices suggest the value of drawing inspiration, as Shange does, from Lee's unorthodox, multidisciplinary practice while making sense of her project.

By adopting such an approach, I hope, on one level, to begin to recuperate the legacy of an important artist whose work has gone largely unnoticed by scholars, and to address the cultural politics of Lee's work, within the music world in which she operated as well as within the broader discursive field imbuing improvisational music with meaning. Using Lee's performance in 1979 of her poem "In These Last Days" as a point of reference, I examine the ways her multidisciplinary artistic practice extended the parameters of improvised vocal music and articulated utopian social goals. Building both from long-standing histories of African American cultural practice as well as from her own immersions in the jazz world and intermedia arts scene, Lee expressed a unique vision while participating in the development of the hybrid aesthetic orientation and the postnationalist and postcultural, nationalist, social imaginary that informed the creative and intellectual work of other African American improvisers during the 1970s and that has helped define experimental, improvised music through the present.

Lee's performance of gender in the piece (and its performativity) addressed issues pertaining to the material and discursive terrain female improvisers had to negotiate. Lee's rearticulation in a new context of the performance practices in which she had been immersed enabled her both to carve out space for herself in the improvised music world and to implicitly comment on its gendered exclusions. In other words, the social and aesthetic vision Lee voiced through her words and the performance of them on "In These Last Days" was a kind of repetition with a difference of the modes of raced and gendered imagining evident in the work and reception of the improvising communities with whom she had been in dialogue.

"In These Last Days" may be reread, in somewhat trans-historical terms, as a meditation on the writing of jazz and improvised music history and the power embedded in such narratives. When we listen to Lee's unorthodox and multidisciplinary creative project, her troubling of gender conventions, and her postnationalist and postcultural, nationalist orientation, we not only gain a better sense of the cultural politics of often ignored experimental improvisations from the 1970s, we also hear a response to some of the familiar, politically compelling, yet somewhat restrictive narratives of jazz and improvised music history in the present. Her work encourages us to rethink jazz and improvised music history in ways that are consistent with her project. As Daniel Fischlin and Ajay Heble remind us, "Improvisation (in theory and practice) challenges all musical orthodoxies, all musical taxonomies, even its own" (*The Other Side of Nowhere* 31).

We Got a Woman among Us Who Isn't Afraid of the Sound of Her Own Voice

Born in 1939, Lee said her creative sensibility early in her life was deeply influenced by her father, the concert and church singer S. Alonzo Lee, as well as by the education she received at the Wolver School, a private institution that followed the pragmatist philosophy of Henry David Thoreau. Lee graduated from Bard College in 1961, where she studied literature, psychology, and dance, choreographing along the way pieces to music by Bartók, Bach, Charles Ives, Schoenberg, and Zoltán Kodály, as well as that of jazz composers and improvisers. Soon after graduating from college, Lee recorded the album *The Newest Sound Around*, with pianist and fellow Bard alumnus Ran Blake. Although her work with Blake was popular in Europe—which led to a successful tour in 1963—the duo never caught on back home. Almost a year after the recording of *The Newest Sound Around*, Lee and Blake had yet to get a nightclub gig in the United States (Coss).

Lee more or less disappeared from the jazz scene in the mid 1960s, and instead devoted more of her time to collaborations with people in other artistic movements. She developed over the decade a multidisciplinary approach to improvisation that took her beyond the parameters defining much jazz singing. We may understand her approach as an outgrowth of her existing immersion in jazz, poetry, and dance, which recombined already mutually constitutive "Afrological" and "Eurological" (G. Lewis, "Afterword" 168) cultural practices, and a product of her involvement with the intermedia arts scene developing in the San Francisco Bay Area and elsewhere during the 1960s.

Lee was briefly married to and collaborated with the sound poet David Hazelton and worked with other artists affiliated with sound poetry, Fluxus and Happenings. She became interested in sound poetry's dedication to conveying emotional meaning through intonation, communicating via nonverbal utterances, and connecting poetry to bodily movement and sensation. Lee was also drawn to the experimentalism, ritual, audience participation, and iconoclasm associated with Fluxus and Happenings.[1] Lee claimed that her interest in these artistic movements stemmed in part from her recognition of the limitations of jazz singing, although she clearly brought her own skills as an improviser and a composer to these movements. Lee described this phase of her development: "As an improvising singer, there was always the option to scat, thus imitating the jazz instrumental sounds. There were also jazz lyricists who set words to instrumental solos. Since neither of these options allowed space for the natural rhythms and sonorities or the emotional content of words, I started composing music for the sound-poetry of Dick Higgins, Alison Knowles, Dieter Rot, Ian Hamilton Finlay and Henri Schaeffer, first at the Open Theater in Berkeley, California, as part of a multi-disciplinary company of musicians, painters/slide projectionists, sound poets and dancers (1964–1966)" ("Narrative of Career").

Once asked about the influence of instrumentalists on her singing, she said, "I'm more interested in what the voice is in itself." She suggested that it was in the mid 1960s when she realized she "was moving away from the conventional idea of music. [She] could take music out of musicality, add space and silence." One way she achieved this was to integrate her own poetry and music into improvisational performances. But rather than merely read poems over musical accompaniment, she began, as she put it, to "take poetry as a point of departure for improvisation" (Riggins 4). She explored the tonal possibilities of verbal poetic utterances, repeating words, syllables, and vowel and consonant sounds and fusing them with grunts, clicks, screams, and other vocalizations not necessarily related to speech. Lee was also interested in vocal performance as a process in which meaning located in the body could be communicated to the audience, and she drew upon her training in dance to develop this technique. As she described it: "The voice is a very important instrument, it's part of the body and can emulate bodily feelings. . . . so using the psoas muscles and the diaphragm together you can take it into dance or voice or both . . . you learn to work with the dynamics of the feeling . . . you learn to work with the emotions. . . . when your body is working you don't have to think of a horn but you can think of body movement" (Riggins 5).

After beginning a creative and romantic relationship with the German multi-instrumentalist Günter Hampel, in the late 1960s, Lee reestablished herself as a major voice in African American and European improvised music circles. And from this period forward, she regularly integrated aspects of poetry and dance into her musical work. In addition to working regularly during this period with Hampel, she recorded and performed during the late 1960s and 1970s with Carla Bley, Anthony Braxton, Marion Brown, Andrew Cyrille, Sheila Jordan, Rahsaan Roland Kirk, Jimmy Lyons, Grachan Moncur III, Archie Shepp, Cecil Taylor, Reggie Workman, and a number of other American and European improvisers. She participated in several performances of John Cage's bicentennial composition *Renga with Apartment Building 1776* — an experience that inspired her to compose her own extended works. Funded in 1976 by a grant from the National Endowment for the Arts, Lee combined poetry, music, and dance in her two-act, ten-scene jazz oratorio *Prayer for Our Time*, based on "Conference of the Birds," a poem by the thirteenth-century Persian poet Fariduddin Attar. In the decade preceding her death, her primary performing outlets were the Jeanne Lee Ensemble, which combined poetry, music, and dance, and her duo with Mal Waldron.

Lee also maintained a commitment to arts education, and she spoke of the influence on her educational vision of theorists such as Carl Jung, the choreographer and ethnographer Pearl Primus, the dance therapist Irmgard Bartenieff, and the percussionist Badal Roy (Foote). She received an M.A. in Education from New York University in 1972 and subsequently developed her own curriculum and taught classes, conducted workshops, and held residencies in various educational institutions in the United States and Europe, ranging from elementary schools to universities. Educational writings included short features on music and folklore for the *Amsterdam News*, curricular plans for elementary schools, and short stories for children. In 1999 Lee published *Jam! The Story of Jazz Music*, a textbook for grades four through seven.

Like a People Who Come Out with What They Can Carry

Lee's multidisciplinary project foregrounds vocal art as an embodied process, and echoes Lindon Barrett's comments about the African American singing voice as a mode of expression through which "African Americans may exchange an expended, valueless self in the New World for a productive, recognized self" (*Blackness and Value* 57). As an alternative to Eurocentric ideas of literacy (or "signing voices"), through which exclusive definitions of humanity have been produced, the "singing voice provides the allowance for African Americans to enter or subvert symbolic, legal, material, and imaginative economies to which we are most usually denied access" (57). African American singing voices accomplish this, Barrett argues, through their "disturbance," by means of various vocal techniques, of the systems of signification through which the social order is scripted and by "foreground[ing] and play[ing] upon bodily dimensions of vocal action usually taken for granted . . . a signal cultural moment and revision for those who would be confined, according to dominant wisdom, to the supplemental role of the body" (78–79). By collapsing the dichotomous parsing of mind and body, literacy and orality, Barrett suggests, the African American singing voice has drawn attention to a black social and imaginative presence while producing alternative, less exclusive conceptions of "human value" (85). Barrett's conceptualization provides a useful, general frame for understanding the recuperative, disruptive work that African American singing voices may accomplish, but it raises the question of how this story has played out in distinct ways, in different times and places. Lee's voice announced her presence and reinscribed human value, given her methods of performance, the distinct positionalities she articulated, and the different modes of exclusion she encountered.

    Lee's poem-composition "In These Last Days" written in 1973 and recorded in 1979 with the drummer Andrew Cyrille and the saxophonist Jimmy Lyons on the album *Nuba*, helps situate the development of Lee's multidisciplinary project in its historical context, referencing the social struggles and political and economic dislocations of the 1970s. It provides insight, as well, into an aesthetic vision that included a commitment to social change through creative endeavors, in general, and improvised music, in particular. But analysis based on content alone would remain incomplete without an attention to how Lee improvises the poem in performance, for it is her intonation, her repetition and elongation of words and syllables, her screams and nonlinguistic utterances, and her interactions with the other instrumentalists on the piece that allow us to better understand how her improvising voice and body may also have been engaged in a less evident kind of tactical work both in its social moment and in relation to the wider system of meanings embedded in improvisational practices.

> *In these Last Days*
> > *of Total*
> *Dis-in-te-gra-tion,*
> > *where every day*
> *Is a struggle*
> > *against becoming*
> *An object in*
> > *someone else's*
> > > *nightmare:*
> *There is great joy*
> > *in being*
> *Naima's Mother*
> > *and unassailable strength*
> *In being*
> > *on the Way*

Lee's performance of "In These Last Days" expresses a social vision that dovetails with the utopian aspirations she expressed in interviews and her arts-education projects during this period. The words "these Last Days / of Total / Dis-in-te-gration / where every day / Is a struggle / against becoming / An object in / someone else's / nightmare" are improvised and repeated in different registers, across varying ranges of intervals. There is particular focus on the word "struggle," which is elongated and distorted, ultimately becoming a scream. All of this conveys a sense of urgency that situates the poem in the crisis that resonated within various communities in the United States during the late 1960s and early 1970s, in the wake of the limited gains and very real failures of the ethnic mobilizations of the previous two decades, the embrace and rejection of various forms of identity politics, the repressive backlash against these movements, the divisive and violent war in Vietnam, and the political and economic crises of the 1970s. It was indeed a moment when the collective, utopian dreams had for many turned into living nightmares, and human beings struggled against their objectification both within various repressive apparatuses and in light of the limitations of oppositional, identity-based movements.

Yet, Lee maintains a sense of optimism, evident in the concluding lines: "There is great joy / in being / Naima's Mother / and unassailable strength in being on the Way." "The Way" may be read as her commitment as a practicing musician to social change. During the 1970s, Lee focused on creativity and imagination as tools in social struggles and suggested on more than one occasion during the decade that encouraging creative thought and activities might well provide an antidote to the alienation that human beings experienced in deindustrializing, capitalist societies. She emphasized the general importance of rituals that would allow people "to stay alive" and "rediscover the places where we are human" (Terlizzi, Martinelli, and Archangeli 7–8). As an educator, Lee held a particular interest in the pedagogical possibilities of ritual. She viewed dance (particularly, African dance) as a refinement of the rituals of everyday life, which, in turn, could convey a sense of collective identity, history, and purpose. During this period, she developed a nonprofit corporation, Earthforms Rituals, which promoted concerts and educational programs revolving around participatory rituals conducted by her and others, and she at times performed using the stage name Earthforms. Lee's rituals fused her own poetry and music with the work of "other contemporary non-classical composers and poets," grounding them in a "thematic, rhythmic and kinetic genesis in our daily lives." The ritual "People and Places," for example, was "a musical and choreographic study of climatic and environmental effect on survival habits and their evolution into rituals of people around the world" ("Compositions and Arrangements"). Lee performed some of these rituals on her 1974 recording *Conspiracy*, released on the short-lived, "artist-owned" record label also called Earthforms.[2]

Lee's activist and educational vision falls within a genealogy of black surrealism that Robin Kelley begins to chart in his book, *Freedom Dreams*. Kelley defines surrealism as "a living, mutable, creative vision of a world where love, play, human dignity, an end to poverty and want, and imagination are the pillars of freedom. . . . It is a movement that invites dreaming, urges us to improvise and invent, and recognizes the imagination as our most powerful weapon" (158–59). Recognizing that avant-garde, future-oriented imagining is no substitute for protest and social activism focused on present-day economic and political needs, Kelley stresses the complementary importance of a vision that imagines a "total transformation of society, . . . new social relationships, new ways of living and interacting, new attitudes toward work and leisure and community" (5).

More specifically, Lee's work can be situated in the postcultural, nationalist, intercultural, internationalist, and therapeutic humanism that defined the projects of other members of the African American musical avant-garde during the second half of the twentieth century. Like the multi-instrumentalists Anthony Braxton and Wadada Leo Smith, Lee maintained a commitment typical of those in the Black Arts Movement to community-building through creative educational projects, while recognizing the limitations of narrowly conceived identity politics and the necessity of creative exchanges across cultural and national boundaries. The movements of improvising musicians across national boundaries (primarily between the United States and various European countries) and their attempts to define socially relevant roles for themselves have to be understood in part as a response to their critical denigration and financial exploitation at that moment. Lee herself found no shortage of difficulties trying to earn a living as a performer. Yet she tried to maintain an optimistic take on the possibilities inherent in an immersion in multiple communities of performers, on the cross-cultural influences that helped shape her own creative vision, and on the technologies that facilitated these exchanges. As she put it in 1979: "This country is just building a culture, the culture to sum itself up is coming out of the new 'Jazz' musicians . . . the shapers of the culture . . . fountainheads of the culture, I look at my own work as a bridge. . . . The music has been borrowing from all cultures and sects . . . laying the mandates from which the culture will grow" (Riggins 5).

She believed, as well, that "technology is not an evil in itself, although it has to be used in the proper way. For the first time in the history of the world it is possible to have all the knowledge that has always been growing in every place, accessible to everybody. No one place should dominate the system of knowledge" (Terlizzi, Martinelli, and Archangeli 8).

Lee conceptualized a cultural politics that sought to center the "work of the imagination" at a moment, as Arjun Appadurai argues, when the globalizing forces of new electronic media technologies and the movement of bodies across national boundaries were beginning to create "diasporas of hope, diasporas of terror, and diasporas of despair." He continues: "These diasporas bring the force of the imagination, as both memory and desire, into the lives of many ordinary people, into mythographies . . . [that] are charters for new social projects, and not just the counterpoint to the certainties of daily life. They move the glacial force of the habitus into the quickened beat of improvisation for large groups of people" (Appadurai 6).

Like Braxton, Smith, and others who were theorizing the practice of improvisation during the 1970s, Lee conceived of a new social imaginary that was attuned to human liberation. Her vision exceeded the limitations of nation and race. It maintained an ethical and political commitment stemming from her immersion in her artistic communities, foregrounding the role that improvisation could play in building new social groups.

In addition to theorizing this imaginary, Lee enacted it in performance. During the late 1970s, Lee sometimes described herself as a "voice environmentalist": "I look at myself as already an environment, the environment is there and it comes through me in sound. In turn the music is created as a total environment to the audience. I'm always trying to allow the environment to manifest itself through me . . . when I'm working with a musician I'm trying to deal with the sound. When I want to direct the music I create a poem and then there's a more deliberate environmental frame and we all work within that" (Riggins 4).

On the one hand, this concept suggests a commitment to human interactivity during the creative process that creates nonhierarchical relationships among performers and audience members and invites the audience to participate in the creation of meaning around the performance. It is an ethos that can be found in the work of Fluxus and Happenings, as well as in that of African American improvisers such as members of the AACM and the multi-instrumentalist Marion Brown, on whose *Afternoon of a Georgia Faun* Lee performed.[3]

But we can also locate in Lee's commitment to a more democratic performance through voice environmentalism an articulation of her vision for a more democratic social order performed through, and ideally enabled by, rituals incorporating improvisation. Lee spoke of jazz as a "very fine microcosmic demonstration of democracy" and of the need for performative flexibility and collectivity to enable its production (D. Lewis 6). Voice environmentalism may be read as a mechanism for refocusing Lee's utopian, futuristic longing on everyday acts of survival through improvisation. In an eloquent gloss of the work of Michel de Certeau that is geared toward understanding multidisciplinary performance, Susan Foster describes his project of locating in the often erratic, "thought-filled gestures" of everyday life "a vital reservoir of resistance to the overwhelming force exerted by dominant orderings of the social." Although such "tactics" are generally sustained only momentarily and do not express the "cohesiveness" necessary for implementing substantial social changes, "they are a perpetual source of resistance to the normative" that is overdetermined by multiple "strategic structures." As a means of making his points, de Certeau, "imbues action with thought. . . . extend[ing] to all bodily articulation, whether spoken or moved, the same capacity to enunciate" (Foster 5–7).

Foster's observations have profound implications for improvisational performance practices, which often replicate, transform into art, and ritualize the unscripted thoughts and activities of everyday life. They help us understand the work improvisational projects implicitly and explicitly do by responding to (and encouraging responses to) social orderings of power. Returning to "In These Last Days" with Foster's analysis in mind, Lee's interactions with her fellow improvisers Lyons and Cyrille—nonhierarchical, mutually generative, and committed to exploring the sound of being on "the Way"—appear to be a restaging of a world where performing and listening bodies (if we consider the audience for this recording) interact with one another in a tactical negotiation of the strategic structures conspiring to make "objects" of human beings at that moment. In addition to performing a utopian, democratic future through Lee's utterances of its lyrics, "In These Last Days" links sounds, bodies, and minds through Lee's voice environmentalism in an everyday project of allowing people "to stay alive" and "rediscover the places where we are human" (Terlizzi, Martinelli, and Archangeli 6–7).

She Is Not Afraid of This Body That
Moves So Sweet

"In These Last Days," in its lyrical content and its articulation, may also be read as a negotiation of the linked politics of race and gender in the world of improvised music of the 1960s and 1970s; gender being one of the modalities, to paraphrase Paul Gilroy's paraphrasing Stuart Hall, through which politicized and redemptive black music has articulated race and class (Gilroy 85). Clearly, some of Lee's male colleagues in the community of African American improvising musicians were aware of the problems stemming from the exclusion or devaluation of women musicians. Braxton, for example, insisted that a successful cultural politics coming out of this community must not only include women but also address legacies of sexism within it (Braxton 3: 429–441). Still, the practice of and critical discussion around improvised music, even when radically oppositional along other axes, was often shortsighted when it came to gender.

Lee's reference in "In These Last Days" to her "great joy in being Naima's Mother," performed on record calmly and melodically in the lower registers of her voice, asserts her identities as an improvising artist *and* as a woman with a child (she had two more children after writing the poem). This assertion of identity speaks of the way Lee's work negotiated, if not necessarily transformed, gendered definitions of improvised artistry and looked toward a kind of musical synthesis that other women in music were striving for at that moment. As Dana Reason suggests, the marginalization of women in improvised-music circles stems, in part, from a lack of attention to their existence (that is, "a myth of absence") and from an attention that recognizes their existence but, because of gendered conceptions of artistry, deems their work substandard or distinctive in a sense that otherwise limits their full participation in the improvised music world.

Lee's performance of "In These Last Days," then, recorded at a moment when women were making some inroads into jazz and the larger world of improvised music as business people and instrumentalists, may be seen as a negotiation of this two-pronged system of exclusion. She makes herself visible and intelligible as a black, female improviser by presenting herself in her social role as mother—something she also accomplished by bringing her children onstage from time to time—and engaging in a mode of performance (and explanations of performance in contemporaneous interviews) that draws attention to itself as an emotional and embodied practice.

Such performance clearly conforms in some ways to long-standing prejudices against vocal music in musicians' and critics' circles, because vocal music has often been linked with women and the female body, which in turn have been associated with emotions, irrationality, and sexuality, rather than with the masculine mind or heroic romanticism assumed to be the generative force for serious improvised art. Yet, this presentation of self also calls attention to the difficulties of balancing careers in music and family commitments, precisely because of such gendered expectations. Lee confirmed this near the end of her life, when she attributed the relative paucity of recordings under her own name to the fact that she had been busy raising children (D. Lewis 9–10).

Moreover, thinking about Lee's performance in terms of performativity, as a kind of repetition with a difference of gendered modes of performance and assumptions about the same, makes intelligible the disruption in this piece. As Judith Butler writes, "Performativity describes this relation of being implicated in that which one opposes, this turning of power against itself to produce alternative modalities of power, to establish a kind of political contestation that is not a 'pure' opposition, a 'transcendence' of contemporary relations of power, but a difficult labor of forging a future from resources inevitably impure" (*Bodies That Matter* 241). Lee, in a sense, creates an "alternative modality" of both performance and self-empowerment by drawing from, synthesizing, and destabilizing the gendered (and raced) improvisatory traditions in which she was immersed.

George Lewis has identified two fundamental, "opposing tropes" that have been used to make sense of late-twentieth and twenty-first century improvised artistry: "(1) the image of the heroic, mystically ego-driven Romantic improviser, imprisoned by his own will; (2) the detached disengaged, ego-transcending artist who simply lets sounds be themselves" ("Afterword" 169–70). These tropes have been applied to what Lewis calls, following Braxton, the post-Bird and post-Cage (that is, the African American avant-garde and the European and European American) aesthetic traditions. Although Lewis's primary concern in this particular analysis is the way such tropes reinforce racialized assumptions about art—and consequently the marginalization of and "furtive" appropriation of the Afrological tradition—they may be considered products of both raced and gendered modes of performance and interpretation. In other words, these tropes marginalize female improvisers, while reinforcing a racial hierarchy in their opposition. As a multidisciplinary performer, Lee drew from aesthetic traditions that were in part defined by these tropes. As she synthesized sonic experimentalism, a decentering of the will via voice environmentalism, emotion, and embodiment, she developed a vocal practice that exceeded the restrictive definitions of female vocal art through a rearticulation of these forms.

Lee's earliest work as a professional jazz singer and her work in intermedia performance in the 1960s provide the method for such synthesis and anticipate the later project through their own cultural politics. Lee's performance on *The Newest Sound Around* (1961) simultaneously builds from and exceeds conventions established in jazz vocal practice. One of the striking things about the album is Lee's engagement with Abbey Lincoln's music. Lee's vocal inflections resemble Lincoln's, and she builds upon Lincoln's explorations of the instrumental qualities of the voice through improvised, nonverbal vocal lines. Lee also performs at the session material written or included by Lincoln on her own album *Straight Ahead* (1961): Thelonious Monk's "Blue Monk," for which Lincoln had written lyrics; the Billie Holiday-Mal Waldron composition "Left Alone"; and the title track, with words by Lincoln and music by Waldron.[4]

Lincoln's work on *Straight Ahead* represented a critical moment in her flight from the musical and ideological baggage associated with material available to jazz singers. During the late 1950s and early 1960s, Lincoln made an effort to move away from romantic ballads that spoke of abusive and dysfunctional heterosexual relationships; she began performing material that described healthier relationships between men and women, provided varying degrees of social commentary, and demanded a more "instrumental" approach to singing. Moreover, Lincoln's shift in material also spoke to her commitment to the mutual liberation of black men and women in the political context of the black freedom movement (Porter 149–90).

Although the extent to which Lee shared Lincoln's political commitments is unclear, Lee remembered that Lincoln's work allowed her to move beyond the limitations of jazz singing and pointed her to a more poetic and social sensibility. Looking back on the early part of her career, Lee said, "The person who left the most impression on me in terms of life-situations as well as what she was doing with her voice was Abbey Lincoln. From the credibility of her craft and her own reality and not so much as a 'style.' It was like using the energy as a painting. Billie Holiday too, but she comes from another era, Billie has the same kind of thing musically, but Abbey advances that type of understanding, . . . Abbey is more human, it's not just a woman who's a victim of her role" (Riggins 4).

Again speaking about Lincoln, Lee said, "This woman made it possible for me to have faith in the fact that I am a poet and I did not have to sing standards in order to be a Jazz singer. I could find a way of putting my own perception into musical terms" (D. Lewis 12).

By disrupting the close relationship between jazz singing and the feminized sphere of popular vocal music, and by bringing a level of technical virtuosity to their work, Lincoln and Lee challenged the idea that female vocal-jazz artists, while an important element of the jazz tradition, did not quite measure up to the artistry and genius of male instrumentalists and were a secondary class of performers. That Lee was able to disrupt this dichotomous juxtaposition of female vocalist's bodies with male instrumentalist's minds is evident in the critical responses to her by some European jazz writers who commended her improvisational skills. As one of them put it: "Miss Lee, as far as I know, is the first to fulfill 100 percent what most jazz singers wish for in their dreams—namely a complete disregard of the former borderline between the human voice and an improvising horn" (Williams 16).

We see a somewhat different negotiation of modes of exclusion in Lee's participation in the intermedia arts scene, which may be read as rejecting, at a symbolic level at least, the art world's erasure of black culture-based improvisational practices as well as the belief that an immersion in such communities would produce a better kind of black artist. As George Lewis suggests, members of this art world often theorized improvisation as a human or mechanical spontaneity in ways that sometimes denied the influence of African American cultural practices or that acknowledged them only as an incorporative other to be transcended ("Improvised Music after 1950").[5] Lee negotiated this exclusion simply through her presence, while her performances sometimes retooled the formal mechanisms of erasure and denigration into vehicles for the rearticulation of black cultural priorities.

In 1966 Lee's Town Hall performance with Jackson Mac Low of his composition "The text on the opposite page may be used in any way as a score for solo or group readings, musical or dramatic performances, looking, smelling, anything else &/or nothing at all" provides an example. Drawing upon Buddhism and following the lead of John Cage (with whom he had studied), Earle Browne, and other experimental concert music composers, Mac Low was, by the 1950s, using "systematic-chance operations, regulated improvisation, and indeterminacy into the compositions and performance of verbal and theatrical works." "The text on the opposite page" exemplifies this approach. The piece was created by assigning two-digit numbers to the keys of a typewriter and then depressing the keys in an order determined by the occurrence of random-digit couplets in the RAND

Corporation's table *A Million Random Digits with 100,000 Normal Deviates.* The Town Hall performance had Mac Low and Lee holding negatives of the score in front of a blinking red light, creating sounds suggested by characters they chose at random during the periods the score was illuminated. Playing in the background was a manipulated audiotape of an earlier performance of the composition by the electronic composer Max Neuhaus, who subsequently lowered the pitches of the voices on the tape to produce "thunderlike (or oceanlike) waves of sound" (Mac Low, liner notes).

Lee's and Mac Low's performance upholds the "systematic-chance operations, regulated improvisation, and indeterminacy" that structure the piece by both the random selection of the characters they read and the deadpan tone with which they produce the sounds indicated by these characters. Yet at various moments, Lee brings a sound poet's attention to repetition and nonverbal utterance that begins to make new meanings. She speaks the punctuation marks * and ' first as their verbal signifiers (that is, as "asterisk" and "apostrophe") but then voices them in nonverbal ways through a series of clicks and grunts. Lee speaks the word *comma* and then she employs it to explore the various sounds that can be extracted from the aural signifier. Most notably, comma becomes *mama*, itself a signifier of, among other things, the black—and, with her on stage, black female— vernacular vocal practice of the blues. Also notable is Lee's introduction of syncopated rhythmic conception into her reading.

Lee thus fuses a jazz-based ethos of improvisation with an improvisational approach grounded in sound poetry, and in so doing she creates a new vocal technology that disrupts the logical structure of a piece that, intentionally or not, participates in an art-world conceptualization of improvisation that distances it from its black antecedents. Although Lee does respond to the score's instructions to improvise randomly and adheres to a poststructuralist suspicion of cultural or linguistic determinacy, the particulars of her improvisational performance exceed the "score." Through intonation and phrasing, she references and expands upon the art of scat singing, thus disrupting the deracinating tendency of the postwar American art world that was radical in other ways and reinscribing black women's vocal art within its practice.[6]

Lee then emerged from the 1960s as someone whose work had challenged the exclusion of female jazz singers from the category of genius in jazz and challenged the elision of African Americans from art-world aesthetics for being the wrong kind of genius. She accomplished this by drawing upon, synthesizing, and rearticulating the codes that defined these oppositions. Later in her career, as we can see with "In These Last Days," "tak[ing] poetry as a point of departure for improvisation" and exploring "the natural rhythms and sonorities or the emotional content of words," as Lee put it, allowed her to further negotiate and disrupt raced and gendered definitions of improvisational artistry (Riggins 4; "Narrative of Career").

Lee's performance of "In These Last Days"—her use of huge intervals, screams, groans, melodic passages, dramatic changes in the timbre of her voice, and especially her repetitions of such techniques—defines her work through the emotions inflected in her utterances and in the liruption of the syntactical order of her text. And it is within this embodied verbal excess that Lee blurs gendered distinctions of improvised performance, as she moves beyond the limitations of voice imposed by genre and standard techniques (not to mention everyday speech). Lee presents herself, to build upon Carla Peterson's phrase, as an "eccentric black female [voice and] body," expressing a "freedom of movement stemming from the lack of central control and hence new possibilities of difference conceived as an empowering oddness" (xii).

As she communicates with Andrew Cyrille and Jimmy Lyons in a sonic exchange beyond the limitations of words, she builds a more egalitarian creative ethos between improvising male instrumentalists and female vocalists on the bandstand. Lee is not so much being backed by the other musicians as she is fully integrated into the ensemble. As she put it in an interview that year, her goal was to "live the spaces in the music fully" and "to work with the people as musicians and not just as 'fill-in'" (Riggins 4). We can also locate in Lee's repetitive fusing of voice, dance, and poetry into excessive performance tactical disruptions of normative ideas about gender and race that were brought to bear on improvising musicians and embedded in discourses around improvisational practices. Rearticulating through fusion and repetition the assumed codes of masculine and feminine improvisations collapses their distinction, not only challenging the idea that male improvising instrumentalists engage in a musicianship superior to that of female vocalists but also threatening the very logic of the categories as well.

In other interviews from the period, Lee validated spaces where improvising women could get together to make art, while looking toward a kind of gendered synthesis that her improvised work on "In These Last Days" suggests. When asked to comment about her participation in a salute to women in jazz, she remarked, "There's something to be shared in female sensibilities, with men and women. I think each person has an individual balance, and how that balance manifests is due to the individual. Some women want to use a driving, masculine force and some go through another type of thing. It's all like a dance with everyone trying to get the right balance and configurations" (Riggins 4).[7] Although arguments like this clearly tread on dangerous ground by naturalizing essentialist notions of gendered modes of creativity, they do reflect the way that women in experimental music, caught between the dual problems of invisibility through the "myth of absence" and invisibility through stereotype, tried in some ways not so much to seek inclusion in a masculine sphere but to transform the cultural and discursive spaces in which they operated as a means of negotiating the gendered constructs imposed upon them.[8] It parallels, as well, the technique we hear on "In These Last Days."

She Might Lay Up All Nights Wondering How Are We Staying Alive 'Cause We Didn't Hear What She Just Heard or Sing It

Jeanne Lee's artistic and intellectual project also suggests we step back and think in historiographic terms about the implications of placing this artist, who traveled in and out of jazz, into the popular and scholarly enterprises of jazz and improvised music history. Lee's historical grounding and future imagining suggest that her unorthodox project may be productively analyzed in its temporally and spatially immediate surroundings and be read against the exclusionary narratives that continue to make sense of the music in the present.

Lee's multidisciplinary and experimental artistic and intellectual project encourages us to challenge the gendered exclusions in jazz and improvised music history, paying close attention to the diverse experiences of women artists and to center gender as a category of analysis in jazz and improvised music studies (Tucker). Lee's work also highlights the importance of often-understudied improvisational practices developed during the 1970s, in which artists from various cultural and geographical backgrounds drew upon multiple histories and experiences, while developing their work across various genres and media, in dialogue with the social transformations and identitarian social movements of the period. As such it affirms George Lewis's "optimistic" championing of the perspective that American experimentalism in music would "grow up and assert its character as multicultural and multiethnic, with a variety of perspectives, histories, traditions, and methods" rather than "remain an ethnically bound and ultimately limited tradition that appropriates freely, yet furtively, from its presumed Others" ("Afterword" 170).

But Lee's work also challenges us to interrogate and complicate the very narratives affirming black humanity through music from which we might draw more sustenance. We may see Lee operating within, made intelligible by, and sometimes working against, to invoke and augment Ronald Radano's argument, a "discursively constituted black music standing between as it embodies the textual and musical as resonance." This textual, sonic dialogic, he suggests, with its roots in the white-supremacist ideological projects accompanying slavery and colonialism, continues to "give shape to resoundingly racialized [and gendered] constructions of difference" but also holds within its contours the power to disrupt such orthodoxies (11–12).

Returning, then, to Lee's disruptive, eccentric vocal performance on "In These Last Days," and situating it again as an extension of her social vision and her insistence on the embodied aspects of improvisation, we can hear this piece speaking against the disciplining, imperial projects that jazz has sometimes been asked to serve. During the 1970s many straight-ahead and avant-garde jazz projects alike were increasingly wedded to the project of nation through recuperative terms like "America's classical music" or "Afroamerican classical music." Musicians and other commentators had long inscribed onto elements of "black music" (including improvisation) values that located black citizen-subjects within the national imaginary, in the face of various forms of racist exclusion, as a means of garnering respect for the music from the guardians of high culture, and, beginning in the 1970s, for tapping into the limited funding available from government agencies. The most obvious and perhaps successful outgrowth of this strategy may be found in the "African American exceptionalist" (and masculinist) vision of Wynton Marsalis, Stanley Crouch, and Albert Murray, deployed in the development of Jazz at Lincoln Center and as the central narrative of the Ken Burns *Jazz* documentary.[9] Similarly, the U.S. House of

Representatives' determination in 1987 that jazz was a "rare and valuable national treasure" stemming from African American experience and reflecting "the highest ideals and aspirations of our republic" (Walser 332–33) speaks of the influence of various trajectories of musicians' activism and attempts by critics and scholars to define it as such.

Although a necessary move in many respects, given the precarious position of jazz artists and black people in U.S. society, the long history of Cold War-era State Department-sponsored tours of jazz musicians has shown that this celebration of improvised music on the grounds of its consistency with American values, as well as its symbolic incorporation of black people into the national body politic, could be consistent with the version of American exceptionalism that has underwritten U.S. imperialism at various moments during the post–World War II era (Von Eschen). The United States' role as a "virtuous" source, and guarantor, of human freedoms has been predicated in part on the nation's ability to emphasize its transcendence of its own history as a slave society and its desire to include at least some of its racial subjects into its citizenry. Promoting jazz as a national art form has been one way to do this.

In a recent meditation on representations of African American women's singing voices on the national stage—Marion Anderson at the Lincoln Memorial in 1939, Fannie Lou Hamer at the Democratic National Convention in 1964, Chaka Khan at the Republican National Convention in 2000, etc.—Farah Jasmine Griffin suggests that such voices have often been called upon to serve a kind of "mammy" function by "healing" and "nurturing" the majority culture in times of crisis. Such representations stand in contrast with others, wherein black women's voices speak clearly to and for "disenfranchised black people, as a voice that poses a challenge to the United States revealing its democratic pretense as a lie." In other words, "representations of the voice suggest that it is like a hinge, a place where things can both come together and break apart" (104, 108).

By improvising the lyrics "an object in someone else's nightmare" in disruptive intervals and augmenting them with nonlinguistic utterances, Lee both reproduces and exceeds the literal meanings of these lyrics and speaks for and against this project of national unity to which jazz in general and black women's jazz voices in particular have been asked to sing. In its excess, Lee's performance enacts the experimentalism and communication beyond language that has defined black women's vocal art and invokes a particular history out of which such art developed. Lee's insistent embodiment interrogates the decorporealization and depoliticization of the black (female) voice and thus bears traces of a moment of origins (that is, slavery) for both her improvisational practice and for the condition of being an object in the present. By improvising objectification in this way, Lee bridges past and present and comments on the long and global history of black and female bodies being treated as material objects, and she comments on the ways history anticipates how other laboring bodies at this postindustrial moment were increasingly treated like replaceable machine parts by the economic regime of flexible accumulation. In other words, Lee's voice refuses the erasure of the role of slavery in the production of black (and black female) bodies and improvised music, and it demands that this history be connected to those of people living under the then-emergent conditions of globalization.

Performing these lyrics through an improvised aesthetic of excess, which had rejected both the deracinating indeterminacy of the art world and the masculinist prescriptions of improvised music, troubles the role of "jazz" in the recuperative humanism that would reclaim black people merely as national citizen-subjects or participants in a triumphant multiculturalism and the role of jazz in its somewhat different position as one of a variety of place-based ethnic exotica that have been used to sell a neoliberal political and economic order to workers and consumers. Lee's conception and performance, then, simultaneously postnationalist and postcultural nationalist, yet beholden to an originating African American moment, speaks to a kind of cultural politics that is resistant to ethnic particularism yet also attentive to the specifics of local struggles and experiences. It is a move beyond the racial prescriptions of the present, but not one of racial amnesia. It calls on musicians and their allies to move toward a progressive, humanist vision that is still concerned with the particulars of lived black experiences and creative projects across the globe.

Notes

The author would like to thank the following individuals and institutions for making this publication possible: the UC Humanities Research Institute, the UC Santa Cruz Institute for Humanities Research, and the UC Santa Cruz Committee on Research, for financial and infrastructural support; fellow members of

the 2002 UCHRI Global Intentions residence group (Georgina Born, Renee Cou-
lombe, Susan Leigh Foster, Adriene Jenik, Anthea Kraut, Antoinette LaFarge,
George Lewis, Simon Penny, Jason Stanyek), for many lively discussions about
improvisation; audiences at the 2004 Guelph Jazz Festival symposium, 2002 Association for the Study of African American Life and History meeting, and 2003
UC Santa Cruz popular culture symposium, for comments on presentations of
this work; Torie Quiñonez, for assistance with the research; Clare Moss, for gen-
erously sharing her own research on and enthusiasm for Lee and her work as
well as for comments on this piece; the editors of and anonymous readers for
CSI/ECI, for their insightful critiques and welcome suggestions for improve-
ment of an earlier draft; and Catherine Ramírez, as always, for insightful readings and everything else. Any and all errors of fact, judgment, or analysis are
entirely my own doing.

1. Documentation of these movements indicating similarities with Lee's work
can be found in Higgins, *Modernism since Postmodernism*, and "A Taxonomy of
Sound Poetry"; Sandford, *Happenings and Other Acts*.

2. This record was originally made for the label Seeds, which went out of
business during its production. After some legal wrangling, Jeanne Lee acquired
ownership and rights to the album and released it on her Earthforms label.

3. Brown self-consciously drew from West African musical practice to create
an environment for a collective, egalitarian approach to making improvised
music, especially on the piece "Djinji's Corner." He was also invested in depict-
ing the natural environment on the title track. Lee spoke briefly about Brown's
influence in her interview with David Lewis.

4. Neither "Left Alone" nor "Straight Ahead" made it onto the original release
of *The Newest Sound Around*; they are included on the reissue.

5. My thinking here is also influenced by Georgina Born and David
Hesmondhalgh's discussion of "musical modernism, postmodernism, and
others" in their introduction to *Western Music and Its Others* (12–21).

6. For example, Dick Higgins locates a "sound poetry tradition" in African
American music, namely in scat singing, but he presents it primarily as an
antecedent to the self-conscious genre that comes to fruition in the 1950s. See
"A Taxonomy of Sound Poetry" (1–2).

7. Lee speaks briefly about exploring a female sensibility in Weinreich, "Play
It Momma."

8. This performative strategy mirrors comments made by the feminist
improviser-composer Pauline Oliveros, who during the 1970s argued for a kind
of musical synthesis that privileged elements of musical practice culturally determined as "female" (i.e., "receptive" and "intuitive") as a means of validat-
ing the work of female practitioners while simultaneously calling such cultural
definitions of creativity into question. The entry of more women into the world
of composition, she suggests, could redeem the intuitive mode of creativity,
thereby creating a more balanced and potentially liberating creative synthesis

available to all human beings and dismantling the gendered cultural constructs that marginalize women in the music world. See Oliveros, *Software* 132–36.

9. For discussions of the Ken Burns's jazz series that simultaneously understand the value and limitation of its narrative, see Lipsitz, "Songs of the Unsung," and Jacques, "A Roundtable on Ken Burns's *Jazz*."

Rob Wallace

CHAPTER 5

KICK OUT THE JAZZ!

The title of this essay is a punkish pun on the title of the song and album by the proto-punk band, the MC5, *Kick Out the Jams!* (1968).[1] It could also be a rallying cry from an imaginary exchange between the stereotypical punk and the stereotypical jazzbo. Do they have anything to say to each other, beyond mutual outbursts of scorn? Despite the fact that critics and musicians have addressed the nuances of this history for many years, the commonsensical view that punk—or, more accurately, rock music as a whole—and jazz are musically and culturally disconnected even though they share a common African American ancestry is fairly widespread. A recent and hilarious satire of this sort of populist essentialism came in the *Chappelle's Show* skit of 2004, wherein Dave Chappelle ponders the question of why "blacks like drums" whereas "whites love the electric guitar."[2] Such a perspective assumes punk and jazz probably have little to say to one another, and that jazz was dead by the time punk showed up anyhow—and also that jazz, especially free jazz, is black, and punk is white.

Nevertheless, the possible connections between the two worlds provided the title of Lester Bangs's piece from 1979, "Free Jazz/Punk Rock." Bangs heard the banging of the then-burgeoning downtown New York scene as the sound of a new music where the energies of rock and jazz had combined not into the often-vilified genre of "fusion," but a new fusion of free jazz and punk rock. He had heard this sound in earlier incarnations like the Stooges, with their combination of motoric rock and rhythm 'n' blues saxophone courtesy of Steve Mackay. While Bangs's version of the genealogy I'd like to trace here is over thirty years old, it bears repeating, rekindling, rebanging, rebooting, kicking out some new jams, particularly when the legacies of both punk and free jazz remain contested aesthetic and political territory. The virgule in Bangs's title raises the question of just how related these clanging cousins are, whether the virgule cuts them apart or seams them together. How much musical and political force were and are the free-jazz and punk movements capable of delivering, both individually and in an uneasy but nevertheless actual alliance?[3] What historical contexts contributed to these connections?

The following meditation on punk and free jazz focuses primarily on several proto-punk and free-jazz meetings. In the twenty-first century, both punk and free jazz continue to be recontextualized, rehistoricized, and embraced by new generations as valid, vital forms of political and musical expression. Jazz and punk demonstrate a possible diversity of forms and norms—musical, racial, sexual, and political—that threatens the rigid categories placed on popular music even as jazz and punk somehow cohere as categories themselves.

Playing fast and loose with the terms (and chronology of) *punk* and *free jazz*, as I will do in this essay, reflects some of the protean aesthetic and political appeal of these forms. The difficulty of defining jazz and punk is also emblematic of their usefulness as sources of continually renewable energy, and the story of their ongoing, dynamic relationship is one of the most interesting and important examples of jazz history and mystery. This essay, then, should be read both as a call for (future) histories to be written of the encounter between punk and jazz, and as an initial sketch—perhaps more punk rock than jazz in its speculative nature—of how jazz's present is the result of some possibly surprising interactions between two of the twentieth century's most energetic musical forms. The implications for the future of jazz are, perhaps paradoxically, that the revolutions of free jazz and punk represent part of a historical continuum (to paraphrase Tom Roe) where loud music, anarchic passion, and disciplined abandon can potentially always be regenerative in the face of aesthetic, economic, or political stagnation.

Anarchy in the U.K.: The Original Jazz Punks

[J]azz is the assassination, the murdering, the slaying of syncopation. In fact it is a revolution in this kind of music. I even go as far to confess we are musical anarchists . . . our [performances] are seldom consistent, every number played by us eclipsing in originality and effect our previous performance. (quoted in Parsonage 135)

The trumpeter Nick LaRocca made the following statement to a British interviewer in 1920, the year LaRocca's Original Dixieland Jazz Band (ODJB) brought their brand of jazz to England: "Jazz is the assassination, the murdering, the slaying of syncopation. In fact it is a revolution in this kind of music. I even go as far to confess we are musical anarchists . . . our [performances] are seldom consistent, every number played by us eclipsing in originality and effect our previous performance" (Parsonage 135). The ODJB is now generally regarded as an important example of the development of early jazz, although their once-coveted position as the first band to record jazz music has been complicated by recent trends in jazz and popular music historiography.[4] Nevertheless, the ODJB did represent one dimension of a genuinely new sound and cultural transformation that was well under way by the time they recorded in 1917. Furthermore, LaRocca's infamous (and often racist) bravado notwithstanding, pronouncements of anarchy in the early twentieth century were probably more shocking than in 1976—the year anarchy was declared in the U.K. by the Sex Pistols. For it was during the teens and twenties when actual anarchist violence created hysteria comparable to the contemporary specter of Al Qaeda.

Early twentieth-century anarchists, socialists, and other dissenters who were *not* committed to violent overthrow of governments, however, developed a political discourse analogous to descriptions of jazz, such as Rosa Luxemburg's dialectic of "spontaneity" and "organization"—or this depiction of anarchism by Lucy Parsons, one of the few African American anarchists of the early twentieth century: "No barriers whatever to human progression, to thought, or investigation are placed by anarchism; nothing is considered so true or so certain, that future discoveries may not prove it false; therefore, it has but one infallible, unchangeable motto, 'Freedom.' Freedom to discover any truth, freedom to develop, to live naturally and fully."[5]

As we have noted in our introduction to this volume, this experimental, political notion of freedom can be found in jazz discourse, even in the music's early years, when jazz was often perceived by white and black audiences as a form of mere entertainment. While African Americans are not commonly associated explicitly with political anarchism, Parsons's words remind us that the "blackness" often connected with anarchism (in the form of masks, flags, and other symbols) could be creatively viewed as a version of the later Black Power movement, where blackness operated as a provisional, oppositional category—a positive label, whereas before it had symbolized stupidity, laziness, evil, and primitive culture. Blackness, like the blackness of outer space in Sun Ra's mysticism, becomes a strategic essentialism, rather than an essentialist racial designation or "reverse-racism."

Compare Parsons's notion of freedom-in-anarchy to Langston Hughes's vision of freedom, as proclaimed in his essay "The Negro Artist and the Racial Mountain" (1925): "Jazz is one of the inherent expressions of Negro life in America; the eternal tom-tom beating in the Negro soul—the tom-tom of revolt against weariness in a white world" (56). He goes on explicitly to connect this notion of "revolt" via jazz to freedom: "We younger Negro artists who create now intend to express our individual dark-skinned selves without fear or shame. If white people are pleased we are glad. If they are not, it doesn't matter. We know we are beautiful. And ugly too. The tom-tom cries and the tom-tom laughs. If colored people are pleased we are glad. If they are not, their displeasure doesn't matter either. We build our temples for tomorrow, strong as we know how, and we stand on top of the mountain, free within ourselves" (57). The "freedom," then, already sensed within early jazz and erupting in 1959 with the arrival of Ornette Coleman's *Free Jazz*, was a complicated nexus of cultural, musical, and political aspirations. Jazz was always a music of freedom, whether in the form of new and provocative artistic developments or the interconnected political aspirations of the newly hopeful black masses. As Jesse Stewart and other commentators have pointed out, however, the definition of this freedom (like the word *jazz* itself)—anarchic, racial, sexual, capitalistic, liberal, etc.—has also been debated throughout the music's history.[6]

Nick LaRocca's notion of "eclipsing originality," in his comments to the British press, emphasizes that improvisation is always different, always novel, and this feature is an essential reason many jazz musicians and fans have appreciated the music. Although LaRocca was not directly inciting the kinds of improvisational politics that some anarchists and other radicals were ready to kill for, die for, or both, he was ironically expressing a very real threat that mainstream society heard and saw in jazz: the fear of an art form that was provisional, based on collective decision-making, and that would be different every time it was played. Ideally, then, anarchy resisted barriers to human oppression, as jazz resisted barriers to musical expression.

Yet jazz *was* rooted in ethnic blackness, and the African American roots of jazz connected the music with a revolution beyond rhythm and tune. LaRocca's Italian American roots ironically (albeit implicitly) tied him to the feared Southern Mediterranean and Slavic anarchy waiting at America's doorstep; but the more insidious, racialized fear regarding jazz's collective improvisation was the fear of a black planet. It was precisely blackness that LaRocca denied to jazz, even while using the African American art form's liberatory energies, along with his white skin, to become the leader of one of history's most influential jazz bands. LaRocca had it right when he saw the revolutionary potential in the music he was taking credit for; he was wrong when he claimed that he and other white musicians had invented the music. In this respect, Johnny Rotten would later become the Nick LaRocca of punk; like LaRocca and his advocacy of "jazz anarchy," Rotten was an important catalyst for the popular dissemination of the fuck-you wildness associated with punk, while a legion of other performers such as Crass, The Ex, and the Clash attempted to develop the music in a more politically committed manner—despite the fact that, as Stacy Thompson has argued, "the economic need to generate profit or at least sustainability militate[d] against punk's increasingly desperate effort to avoid producing for profit, the effort to create a realm free from the commodity market" (106). *Jazz, anarchy,* and *punk* thus all bear the weight of multiple rhetorical categories, operating as loose yet powerful signifiers for proselytizers and critics alike.

Liberation Music

We could point to a variety of "anarchic" ruptures in jazz history, often connected to the freedom struggles of African Americans: from at least as far back as bebop, to Sonny Rollins's *Freedom Suite* (1958) (it was Rollins, incidentally, who for a time sported a punkish Mohawk), to the sly ways Charles Mingus and other musicians bucked the hypocritical U.S. government's "freedom" rhetoric during State Department-sponsored tours.[7] But if the ODJB represents the stereotype of anarchy—the bomb in the crowd—with their barnyard braying, novelty sounds, and hyperbolic pronouncements about jazz anarchy, then the free jazz of the 1960s onward represents a more nuanced version of anarchy that has taken various forms throughout history. Grounded in ideas of collective decision-making and guided by a spirit of egalitarianism, the best free-jazz groups were more diverse, both in terms of musical sound and physical players, than the typical jazz histories would have us believe. Even in the divided cultural ground of the United States during the late 1960s and early 1970s, jazz ensembles included musicians from many different ethnic backgrounds and nationalities, and at least a few more women than might be in the typical jazz combo.

For example, even independent of its sonic implications, the Liberation Music Orchestra, led by Charlie Haden and Carla Bley, was a striking visual representation of solidarity in diversity, as seen on the album cover of the original Impulse! release in 1969. Held by the two white band-leaders on each end, a banner proclaiming the name of the group (with Haden's name in graffiti letters above) hangs over a truly diverse set of musicians, including the Argentine Gato Barbieri, the African Americans Don Cherry and Dewey Redman, and the Euroamericans Paul Motian (who is of Armenian descent) and Roswell Rudd, among others. The music on the album is the "cacophonous" improvisation typically associated with free jazz mixed with Spanish folk melodies and circus music, all arranged in a suite-like structure by Bley. The album also incorporates a sample of a recording by Carlos Puente performing "Hasta Siempre," mixed into the live music.

What emerges, even over thirty years hence, is a remarkably cohesive, structured, yet organic and varied collection of improvisations and composed sections, performed by a rich mix of musicians. The music itself, incorporating Jelly Roll Morton's "Spanish Tinge" as well as South American and African percussion, and Western orchestral instruments not usually associated with post-New Orleans jazz—tuba and French horn—reflects and amplifies the human diversity of the musicians. Lester Bangs, reviewing the album in *Rolling Stone*, criticized the "somewhat labored New Leftist atmosphere of the undertaking," but praised the album for its "raw multi-voiced cry for the ever-distant prize of true freedom"—foreshadowing his pronouncements about the energy of free jazz, pronouncements that would characterize his favorite punk music several years later ("Charlie Haden" 35). For his part, Haden has continued to tour the ensemble, with a rotating cast of musicians, at key moments of crises connected with U.S. imperialism, most recently in 2007, in the midst of the wars in Iraq and Afghanistan. The group's release in 2005, *Not in Our Name*, recorded in 2004 and responding to that year's continuation of the George W. Bush administration, as a result of the U.S. presidential election, even features a reprise of the original album cover from 1968. Older, wiser, but still stand-

ing resolutely for social justice, Bley and Haden hold the very same banner that was made for the Liberation Music album from 1969. In the liner
notes Haden states, "People sometimes ask us if it makes any difference to
make a recording like this? What is important is that we choose to express
our concerns when the circumstances warrant it and our natural mode
of expression is music" (*Not in Our Name*). Rather than succumb to the
stale notion that art cannot influence "real" life, Haden and Bley assert the
role that artists play in contributing *to* real life. If fraudulent elections and
unpopular wars suppress the citizenry's voices, then their musical voices
become even more necessary. Rather than make politics into art—represented at its worst by the technocratic media empires largely funded by
and disseminating the views of the right wing—Haden and Bley take the
Benjaminian path and make art political.

The Liberation Music Orchestra's musical, ethnic, and gender diversity was not the exception to the rule during the late 1960s and early 70s.
Haden, of course, had made musical and social waves a decade earlier as
the unassuming white bassist who broke ground with Ornette Coleman's
quartet. And as David Ake has perceptively demonstrated, the reactions
of critics and the musical establishment to the quartet were less about the
sound of the music and more about the way Coleman's group challenged
conventional categories of identity.[8] Thus Haden was well suited to create
a multiethnic group, as were many of the members of the Liberation Music
Orchestra. The ensemble is emblematic of the spirit of collectivism that
formed an important and lasting part of the free-jazz movement. Such collectives emphasized the aspects of music-making that cannot be measured
in terms of ticket or record sales.

Throughout the 1970s, an era typically described as the dark times for
jazz in America, these collectives of musicians offered a community both
for music-making as well as wider social organizing, education, and em-
powerment. These collectives also challenged the mainstream capitalist
model of music production, which measured success only in terms of dol-
lar signs. The departure from mainstream capitalism implied an effort to
connect the music to a community of active *listeners* rather than one of
active *customers*. As would the later DIY punk ethos, free jazz encouraged
artists to take control of the means of production. As record reissues and
scholarship on these earlier moments of proto-anarchism in jazz flourish
in the early twenty-first century, we are starting to get a clearer sense of
how the seemingly disparate and small-time collectives like the Tribe, of

Detroit; Strata-East, of New York; Black Jazz, of Chicago; the Black Artists Group, of St. Louis; and others were actually part of a wider network of artists and community activists. The AACM, then, an important model for many of these organizations and discussed throughout this volume, is merely one of many organizations that preceded punk rock's valorization of the DIY attitude.[9]

Although many of these collectives were Afrocentric in orientation, their broad interpretation of what counted as "free" music was a threat to the more conventional notions of black jazz music and defies any simple sonic categorization. "Free" jazz was and is the freedom to reference a variety of different soundworlds from within and without the history of what the Art Ensemble of Chicago called "Great Black Music." The same could be said of Miles Davis's "fusion" projects. Davis scorned the free jazz of his time, but he was likewise scorned for plugging in, selling out, and toking up with the hippies. Yet the "United Nations" of musicians in his 1970s-period bands (which included musicians from throughout the Americas, Europe, and India) and the variety of music they produced were beyond category, resistant equally to mainstream notions of race, ethnicity, and musical aesthetics. Thus "fusion" and "free jazz" were closely allied in their combined revolutionary status, just as the black nationalism of the Black Panther party and the dancing in the streets of the psychedelic hippies were united in their struggle to overcome the repression, paranoia, and militarism that defined Vietnam-era America.[10]

I am not arguing here that these liberating fusions were completely utopian. They were not free from discrimination or hate; as some critics have argued, the frenetic sounds they sometimes produced were possibly indicative of the extramusical social-category shifts they were attempting to enact. Like much of the punk rock that would follow, this was socially and sonically challenging music. Yet the very real connections between different ethnic and aesthetic factions under the labels of free jazz and fusion did offer positive, alternative sites for music and social relationships to occur. And while the more militant forms of black nationalism were also echoed by the free-jazz avant-garde, even the outspoken Archie Shepp noted, "If the esthetic is Black, it need certainly not be exclusive. It simply asks to be taken on its own terms. After all, no one questions the fundamentally Gaelic attributes of Morton Downey, nor the Romantic origins of pizza, though both have become as domestic as apple pie" (5–6). Shepp, who worked with talented white musicians like Haden, Roswell Rudd, and

Perry Robinson, was shrewd enough to know that arguing for Black Power was not the same as desiring a "Crow Jim" Black dominance over whites.[11] Free jazz offered instead a rainbow coalition of bands and musical styles that broke the aesthetic and social boundaries of what was acceptable in jazz, while maintaining the centrality of African American traditions.

Jimmy Jazz Meets the Young Punks

Punk, crashing into the world somewhere around 1970 and developing more formally after the debut of the Sex Pistols, in 1975, held the same kinds of boundary-breaking alliances as free jazz, admittedly sometimes uneasily.[12] A significant reason for punk's explosion was the openness of its DIY aesthetic, which downplayed musical virtuosity and allowed kids from anywhere to form a band. In fact, being in the punk audience was often an important criterion for the formation of a band. The shared experience of hearing live music and even being encouraged to "start your own band" by the band performing (as Mike Watt has been known to proclaim) is a crucial example of the "egalitarian, collectivist agency" that punk could inspire (Phil Dickinson). Sometimes this took the form of mixed-up fellow-outcasts, like the multiracial Dead Kennedys, and the mixed-sex X bands: X-Ray Spex, in London, and X, in Los Angeles. Alliances could be formed based on class, race, or gender, as in the Bad Brains, Afroamerican Washingtonians; the Minutemen, working-class kids from San Pedro; and the feminine punk of the Slits. The specifically Afroamerican contribution to punk rock is traced in James Spooner's documentary *Afropunk* (2003), subsequently launching an Afropunk festival and other expressions of renewed interest in black punk, such as the book that explicitly tackles the complex interracial domain of punk, *White Riot: Punk Rock and the Politics of Race* (2011).[13] Not merely made up of a mob of white dropouts, punk, from its earliest days, encompassed a diverse cast of characters and characteristics, sometimes taking the form of diverse bands or, at the very least, demonstrating a begrudging attraction to racial others.

This more complex picture of punk was noted by some critics early on, as in Dick Hebdige's canonical *Subculture: The Meaning of Style* (1979). Writing of the summer of 1976 and punk's U.K. debut, Hebdige tells us: "Apocalypse was in the air and the rhetoric of punk was drenched in apocalypse: in the stock imagery of crisis and sudden change. Indeed, even punk's epiphanies were hybrid affairs, representing the awkward and unsteady confluence of two radically dissimilar languages of *reggae* and *rock*" (27). It was a similar connection that Bangs noticed on the American scene in the punk and free jazz he heard in the same year, where the mix of black music forms that subsequently informed punk were up for grabs, combined into variously punky, funky, free-jazzy bands like James Chance and the Blacks, Defunkt, DNA, and others.

Indeed, the similarities between punk's sonic and symbolic rupture in the 1970s and the improvised music that, especially in Europe, was turning into a unique new music, are hard to ignore (Mike Heffley incidentally names the emerging British free-improv scene in the 1960s and 1970s "Quiet Anarchy") (Heffley 89–91). Despite differences in aesthetic orientation and political commitment, events like Derek Bailey's Company Week, which brought together musicians from around the globe to play together in sometimes combative, unfamiliar territory, echoed punk's explicit and expletive-filled denunciation of mainstream music. "The symbolism of the first Company Week happening in 1977, The Year Punk Broke," writes Ben Watson, "means little to Derek Bailey. Someone who never credited the Beatles or Stones in the first place was hardly going to be impressed with Joe Strummer telling everyone their day was done. But to anyone who was inspired by the raw situationist disdain of the Sex Pistols and their 'assault on the music industry' in Jubilee Year, the congruence is striking" (222–23).

Daniel Carter, an African American reed player based in New York, who has played in free-jazz and punk groups, has noted that "in hardcore punk . . . you had multiple tempos, really starkly different changes in tempo and character all in one piece, kind of like a history of music compacted into one piece" (quoted in Roe 256). Carter's description of the urgency and frenetic quality of punk articulates the way the sonic catharsis of earlier free jazz could feed the fires of punk while itself being influenced by the developments in punk.[14] One explicit example of this symbiosis is John Zorn's recording from 1989, *Spy vs. Spy—The Music of Ornette Coleman*. Sonically, the album was probably no surprise to fans of Zorn, even though it took the funk and blues implications of Coleman's music and fused them with, as Zorn phrases it in the liner notes, "the New York-London-Tokyo Hardcore Triangle. Fucking hardcore rules." Hardcore punk, that is—and now hardcore Coleman. With two drummers, two saxophonists, and one bassist tying them together, *Spy vs. Spy* is an aural argument for the relevant energies uniting free jazz and punk. It succeeds because the musicians involved are themselves products of the same New York environment that created some of the most significant punk music—growing up with rock and jazz on equal-footing, not as adversaries—and because Zorn saw and heard that the spirit of punk was already present in Coleman's music and attitude before punk existed.

Free jazz, then, was not destroyed by the anarchic bombs of punk (which were targeted at rock music, in any case), but continued to inspire and evolve simultaneously. Generational conflicts, perhaps more than anything, were major factors in the controversy surrounding the genesis of free jazz and punk. Just as Albert Ayler's music, for example, drew on and radically extended the premises of early jazz, the movement of Pink Floyd (a band discussed in greater detail below) from improvising psychedelic explosion to lumbering rock dinosaur mocked by Johnny Rotten hid a nuanced history of rock lineage behind the supposed fundamental break that punk represented. The nature of these musics, however, tends to combine with critical and public amnesia about such connections to instill a sense of permanent rupture associated with both free jazz and punk. As Mike Heffley argues, "The conflict in jazz history is not between racially essentialized cultures, so much as between a given social group and those voices of its own—prophets, shamans, creative artists—that they do not know whether to love or hate, reward or kill" (282).

As jazz was threatened by rock 'n' roll, so too was rock 'n' roll threatened by the arrival of punk. Previously, jazz had encompassed a continual history of supposed death throes—be it the arrival of "sweet," white big-band music; militant bebop; softer cool jazz; or, finally, anarchic free jazz and rock-influenced fusion. As a whole, the histories of jazz and rock encompass a series of generational, aesthetic, racial, and sexual conflicts, seemingly threatening the existence of older forms at every turn. Yet it may be that such conflicts are precisely what keep the music fresh and relevant. As Stacy Thompson has noted, "Punk collectives' failures are the guarantors of these collectives' fidelity to their punk DIY ethics" (106). Similarly, the grim determination and dedication of many free-jazz musicians, who only recently have gained relative financial success and public acclaim, represents a version of credibility that has long functioned in the jazz discourse as a mark of authentic artistry (and sometimes, an unfortunate valorization of the suffering, Romantic artist). Michael Ehlers, head of the Eremite record label, emphasizes that "there's kind of this fantasy among rock music writers that underground rock has resuscitated free jazz. This music never went away. These guys have been playing it all along and have seen everything come and go twice before" (Roe 258). From new sonic combinations to DIY spirit, then, free jazz paved the way for a punk scene grasping for new modes of production, aesthetically, politically, and economically.

Set the Controls for the Heart of the Sun

Given the potential, then, for such analogous terrain in punk and free jazz, from D.I.Y attitude to the diverse forms of musical and social alliances, it is not surprising that the musics shared connections even before punk was punk. The connections between punk and free jazz in England, for example, across aural if not racial boundaries, had been made at least as early as 1967, when the early version of Pink Floyd and especially Syd Barrett, was influenced by, and sometimes shared the same bill with, the seminal free-improvisation unit AMM.[15] Keith Rowe, who was AMM's co-founder and guitarist, was one of Barrett's key models for making music come alive and breaking free from rock cliché. Floyd's chroniclers have marked this connection as a particularly important element of the band's early sound. Nicholas Schaffner, for example, notes that "while never amounting to much in commercial terms, AMM exerted a profound influence on [Pink Floyd]" and that Barrett incorporated "such AMM performance techniques as rolling ball bearings down guitar strings" (29). Rowe notes that the inspiration for AMM's sound—like British rock 'n' roll—was informed by the past while trying to break new ground: "We knew we were not black or American. We had had enormous respect for what black jazz musicians had done. Great jazz musicians who weren't appreciated never slavishly copied the generation before. They developed languages, ideas and forms—a powerful inspiration for us to develop a unique European music" (quoted in Palacios 121).

Pink Floyd was also the house band for the "Spontaneous Underground," a series of happenings set at London's Marquee Club, organized by Steve Stollman. Stollman was the brother of Bernard Stollman, founder of probably the second-most famous record label to promote free jazz: ESP (the most famous being Impulse!). Thus the creation of England's most successful psychedelic rock band (not including the Beatles) was in a real sense a direct result of American free jazz and British free improvisation. Listening to Pink Floyd's early music, then, commentators—in this case, ska-punk keyboardist and Two-Tone Records founder Jerry Dammers—would naturally hear analogies in the Pink Floyd sound (and, for that matter, the music of the Who) to free jazz:

> You're not going to tell me that Pink Floyd weren't influenced by Sun Ra . . .
> all that space imagery they came up with, I'm sure they got it from him. I
> know Pete Townshend was a huge Sun Ra fan—oh yeah, I mean all those hip
> guys knew all about that in the sixties. They probably weren't letting on too
> much, but I'm sure that—I mean, psychedelic music was invented in jazz,
> definitely, and then a sort of bastardized version was taken out in rock. But
> the whole idea of that spacey . . . whatever it was . . . comes from jazz, from
> all those spiritual jazz guys.[16] (Dammers 129)

Pink Floyd's drummer, Nick Mason, describes the band's early gigs with a particularly trenchant sense of the distance between jazz and punk, however: "It was almost a sort of punk thing, very free. It's funny when you're improvising and you're not particularly technically able; it's one thing if you're Charlie Parker, it's another thing if you're us. The ratio of good stuff to bad is not that great" (Schaffner 47). These assessments of Pink Floyd's punk freedom versus the virtuosic skill of bebop highlight the ways rock and jazz, from Charlie Parker to Chuck Berry, Sun Ra to Sonic Youth, have been heard simultaneously as miscreant noise and artistic music. The mark of musical virtuosity has long been a key factor in determining one from the other. Many jazz musicians, even those associated with the original moments of free jazz, such as Elvin Jones, looked scornfully on the developments of the late-1960s improvisers: "The ones I've seen were just fishing around on their instruments and bullshitting the public to a great degree rather than doing anything constructive musically" (quoted in A. Taylor 228).

Disdain for perceived musical charlatanism is still a common feature in jazz discourse, and has historically been directed at rock music as well. In an interview conducted in 2001, the clarinetist Don Byron noted, "It's always interesting to me how much noise people will tolerate on the guitar. If it's on the guitar you can play like no music at all. That guy [from Sonic Youth] can't even finger a scale. And he'll tell you that. But he is one of the heroes of the guitar."[17] In rock music and especially in punk rock, however, this lack of technical skill was flipped on its head and made into a virtue—a marker of authenticity that years of jazz training could only stifle, as the one-time punk-rock drummer Stewart Copeland relates, in typically sardonic fashion:

I was raised to be a jazz musician . . . which is why I am immune to jazz. And my main reason why I love dissing jazz is jazz musicians. The problem with jazz musicians is that they are all crap. It's sort of like jazz is the refuge of the talent-less. If you really want to be a musician and you are prepared to really work hard at it, but you don't have the gift and you don't have any soul and you don't have any talent, jazz is what you should do; because all you need to do is just spend hours training your fingers to wiggle very quickly and you'll be a hero in the jazz world.[18]

Free jazz, however, with its often less-obvious formal features and opportunities for more open, improvisational structures than earlier jazz, tended to be stereotyped as the emperor's new clothes. Yet in a musical tradition that valued virtuosity (something that rock shared to a much lesser degree than jazz), free-jazz musicians who did not explicitly demonstrate a knowledge of older forms were bitterly condemned by critics and fellow musicians alike. Another drummer, Milford Graves, who was highly proficient in several styles of playing but known for his free-jazz drumming, reminds us that sympathetic reactions to untrained musicians were nevertheless part of the particular mystery of free jazz:

How do you explain it when a musician that's only been playing five or six months comes out and plays something on his horn and someone can dig it? Or someone who don't know *nothing* about music, getting up there and banging on the drums and five million people start moving and yelling? And then someone who's been in music for ten years can take every note in the book and play upside down, but when he gets up there, nothing happens? You can't put that [criticizing lack of technique] on a musician who moves the people. You have to ask yourself, "What am *I* doing?" and "Is it really no good?" And I think that's why a lot of musicians were against the new music at first— they saw a lot of people responding to it, and they knew those people weren't crazy. (quoted in Wilmer 22)

Graves's comments remind us that the benefits of virtuosity only go so far in communicating with an audience; the energy of a performance, the spirit behind the sound, is what truly matters. Despite the fact that many free-jazz musicians—and many punk musicians, for that matter—are skilled performers, both punk and free jazz arguably rely on an aesthetic of honesty, even if that honesty is, paradoxically, an honesty of blatant artificiality, an honesty of who-cares nihilism. It is this quality of honesty and directness that punk musicians who value free jazz often note about the music.

For example, Mike Watt, whose electric bass sports a taped-on photograph of John Coltrane, points to the kinship between punk and jazz, in this statement reflecting his first exposure to *A Love Supreme*: "I'd never heard this kind of stuff, and at first I thought it was punk music. I knew these guys were older, but I didn't know he was dead. I grew up in low-income housing, I didn't know about this jazz stuff. The passion that these cats had . . . They were much more schooled than our punk scene with their learning and technique, but I felt a lot of kindred spirits with the enthusiasm and motivation there. That's where I found that empathetic resonance hearing all this."[19] The Clash's Joe Strummer makes a similar case for the "empathetic resonance" between punk and jazz, when he describes the first time he saw the Ramones perform on their tour of England in 1976. According to Strummer, there was "no shambling" in this music, and it moved people in the same way Milford Graves suggests even untrained musicians in free jazz could potentially move audiences: "It was like white heat," says Strummer of the Ramones, "because of the constant barrage of the tunes, you couldn't put a cigarette paper between them . . . you couldn't have gotten tighter if you had been in New Orleans your whole life . . . it was unbelievable" (Fields and Gramaglia).

Strummer's implicitly linking the intensity and, indeed, the discipline of a unit supposedly as ramshackle and untalented as the Ramones with the music of New Orleans—be it funk, jazz, or rock 'n' roll (I believe Strummer is referring to jazz)—is a clear articulation of the sonic and social connections that many musicians perceive in punk and jazz. Interestingly, too, Strummer emphasizes that the typical brevity and fast tempo of punk songs belies the importance of their unity in performance: the live punk concert, Strummer contends, is less a machine-gun scattering of disconnected rants and more a continuous stream of energy, an event not unlike the lengthy, intense forays of a free-jazz performance.

While Nick Mason might not have felt up to the caliber of a bebop drummer like Max Roach or Kenny Clarke (or Sun Ra's drummers Robert Barry or Lex Humphries), the drumming style he adopted early in Pink Floyd's development, featuring lengthy tom-tom excursions, punctuated

by washes of cymbals, complemented by the ubiquitous visual and chemi-
cal aids of swinging London rock gigs, certainly communicated something
vivid to early audiences.[20] It's no surprise, then, that Jerry Dammers who
is now exploring the spaceways with his Spatial AKA Orchestra, would
connect the space imagery and swirling psychedelia of Pink Floyd's "Interstellar Overdrive" and "Astronomy Domine" with the contemporaneous
space-jazz reveries of Sun Ra.

A decade after Pink Floyd thrilled audiences in London's UFO club with
their primitive psychedelic improvisations, Johnny Rotten would use the
post-Barrett Pink Floyd as an example of the worst sort of rock dinosaur
that needed to be driven to extinction, infamously wearing a defaced-Floyd
T-shirt on British television. The emotional directness and improvisational
excitement of early Floyd had apparently been replaced by bloated rock
stardom, which punk needed to destroy. Yet Pink Floyd's initial interest in
the realms of improvised music nevertheless launched one rocket in the
journey of punk rock and free jazz, a moon shot that was echoed across the
Atlantic by at least one band who thought space was the place: the MC5.

It's after the End of the World

Moving from a fast-paced song about a spacecraft and breaking down into
a freely improvised collision of electricity, drums, and intoned poetry, the
MC5's "Starship" blasted into musical space roughly around the same moment that Syd Barrett and company were making AMM-meets-Sun-Ra rock
in London.[21] "Starship," the final track from the MC5's debut album, *Kick
Out the Jams* (1969), is sometimes credited as a Sun Ra composition. Yet
only a portion of the lyrics are by Sun Ra, that portion from a poem originally included on the back of *The Heliocentric Worlds of Sun Ra, Vol. II*.
Nevertheless, with this nod to Sun Ra and their concomitant free-rock experiments, the MC5 were explicitly trying, as the Sun Ra biographer John
Szwed states, to "loosen up the performances of white rockers and assume
the visual and musical interaction of free jazz concerts" (244).

The lead singer, Rob Tyner, had taken his surname from McCoy Tyner,
John Coltrane's pianist. And the guitarists Wayne Kramer and Fred Smith
were interested in adapting the saxophonic bursts of Coltrane, Albert Ayler, Archie Shepp, and Pharoah Sanders, as well as the electric free-jazz
guitar playing of Sonny Sharrock, to their own rock styles. The band even

considered recording an album for ESP records, the label that released Sun Ra's *Heliocentric Worlds* and that included several rock bands, along with a host of free-jazz artists. If the ESP rockers the Fugs wanted to levitate the Pentagon, the MC5 wanted to follow Sun Ra into the cosmos.

The MC5's manager, the White Panther Party cofounder John Sinclair, arranged to have the Sun Ra Arkestra play a show on the same bill as the MC5 in 1967. The relationship between the two groups was rekindled in 2006, with the current members of the Arkestra and the surviving members of the MC5 sharing the bill for several performances. On at least one occasion, the guitarist Wayne Kramer played with the Arkestra. He described the experience in a piece called "My Night as Tone Scientist": "This kind of playing takes a great deal of concentration and my sore wrists reminded me of it later. Marshall was so gracious in granting me a few solo passages. For me, this was Heaven. Of course there were interludes of music that some might call 'free music,' although this is a misnomer. When and how you play in this context is anything but free. This is about discipline, not freedom, which was one of the principles at the core of Sun Ra's philosophy" (Kramer 127). If Kramer's comments here and elsewhere in the piece suggest that he couldn't keep up with the jazz-heads, perhaps we might understand Lester Bangs's initial dismissal of the MC5's free-jazz street-cred back in 1967. His review of *Kick Out the Jams* declared that the album amounted to little more than "scrapyard vistas of clichés and ugly noise" ("The MC5: *Kick Out the Jams*" 34). Instead of free-jazz apocalypse, Bangs heard hippy trips. He saw the MC5's Motor City cousins, the Stooges, as a more completely realized version of the fusion of proto-punk and free jazz. This is possibly due to the largely timbral congruence between Steve Mackay's sax and the tenor madness of free jazz.[22]

Yet the scorn heaped on the MC5 by Bangs also stems from the inherent risk in the provisional, utopian project of *Kick Out the Jams*, and the analogous mission—albeit motivated by different forms of oppression and opposition—of Sun Ra and other black free-jazz players. Improvising on the edge, they risked making mistakes and making bad or boring music in the search for freedom. Their respective methods of liberation, however, were not necessarily interchangeable, despite the MC5's attempts to kick out the free jazz jams. As Dick Hebdige has noted of the contradictions between punk's version of apocalypse, "stock images of crisis and sudden change," and Rastafarian-influenced reggae's version of apocalypse, "the overthrow of Babylon," the MC5's attraction to Sun Ra created an uncomfortable alliance (27). John Szwed relates that "Sun Ra was shocked by their hippie lifestyle—their language, drugs, their state of undress, and the police surveillance which followed them. And to make matters worse some of the Arkestra musicians were drifting over to hang out with the ladies of Sinclair's place" (245).

John Sinclair, and his influence on the MC5, did genuinely represent a white ally of black liberation. Yet the privileged position of white youth— still operating in a largely male-dominated cultural climate—no matter how sympathetic to the cause of their African American compatriots, could often lean toward the revolution of "fucking in the streets" (one of the White Panther's stated goals), rather than the true emancipation and equality of citizens. Kathy Asheton, sister to the rhythm section of the Stooges, pointedly recalled that "John Sinclair was a pig. He really took over the MC5 as far as instilling them with his political garbage . . . They were really chauvinistic" (McNeil and McCain 46). The MC5's own Wayne Kramer reflected, "We were sexist bastards. We were not politically correct at all. We had all the rhetoric of being revolutionary and new and different, but really what it was, was the boys get to fuck and the girls can't complain about it" (47). To the disciplined and authoritarian Sun Ra, the hi-jinks of the White Panthers might have seemed out of line with the kind of musical universe he was attempting to create:

> In an interview he gave to Sinclair in 1966, Sun Ra outlined his views: Now I got the Solar Arkestra . . . But it's not religious, like some people are saying— I'm not the least bit religious, I'm not interested in that. Because churches don't do anything but bring people . . . peace. What I'm talking about is disci- pline—striving for things that will never be, they need to discipline them- selves so they can do something beneficial to people. But they keep talking about peace. Like I say, the only time they'll be peaceful is when they're dead. (22)

Sinclair's commitment notwithstanding, the discipline that Sun Ra play- fully articulates here—and that Kramer noted as he attempted to play with the Arkestra years later—is very different from the wild abandon of the White Panther Party's initial entrée into political and cultural revolution.[23]

The sonic qualities of proto-punk and free jazz were sometimes moti- vated by different impulses, as well. The sonic violence that Ravi Shankar heard in Coltrane's late music, for example, was similar to the violence in proto-punk outfits like the MC5, but in Coltrane there wasn't nihilism or negation just for the sake of it.[24] Nevertheless, there are certainly aural similarities between the music we might generically refer to as punk and free jazz: they are often played at a loud volume, and they can suggest anger, frustration, and paranoia. We usually don't think of free jazz as a genre of "songs"—even the seminal early recording of free music, drummer Max Roach and singer Abbey Lincoln's duet on the *Freedom Now!* suite contains no words, the language having been stripped down to a scream. "I didn't think screaming was music," recounts Lincoln in Ken Burns's documentary *Jazz*, "but it turned out to be." But free jazz does have strong roots in linguistic expression: as seen in the poetry of Archie Shepp and Cecil Taylor, the anti-crooner vocals of Linda Sharrock, Leon Thomas, and Jeanne Lee (discussed earlier in this volume), and Sun Ra's version of the big-band singing star, June Tyson.[25] The words of this music combined with the sounds to express a wide range of philosophical, religious, and political sentiments.

African American rage associated with this sometimes linguistically, vocally, and instrumentally aggressive music was seen by many critics in the 1960s and 1970s with virtually the same amount of shock and scorn that later audiences would react with when the Sex Pistols said "fuck you" figuratively and literally. The black power welling up in jazz before free jazz and then in the avant-garde music that swept through the 1960s was perhaps more disturbing to white American audiences, due to the very real pain it represented. Yet it was partly this specificity of African American experience that was attractive to the rejects and outcast proto-punks of the late 1960s and early 1970s, who would see and hear themselves oddly reflected and echoed back in their darker brothers—Black Panthers teaching them to be white punkers. Punk would even be a potential resource for hip-hop, further complicating the racial dynamics of music history. The rapper Chuck D, for example, has proclaimed his "great respect for Joe Strummer [and how] he used his music—incorporating a lot of black music like hip-hop and reggae . . . he dug musical cats, no matter what type of music they played" (xix).[26]

Musicians of all races during the 1960s and 1970s, at their best, realized that they were fighting a system that oppressed everyone in myriad ways, just as later punk bands would coalesce around evidence of the continuing universal truth of "the Man's" injustice. If there still lingered a significant dose of modernist primitivism in the white attraction to free jazz, there was also a good deal of genuine respect and admiration for the music, and that respect led to, in some cases, direct collaboration, and in other cases indirect homage by way of roiling proto-punk soundscapes that would flare up unexpectedly throughout the 1960s, and blow up permanently in 1975.[27] The outer-space jams at London's UFO club and Detroit's Grande Ballroom were thus connected by an undercurrent of free improvisation spurred on by an interracial cast of interstellar travelers. From John Coltrane to Mike Watt, Ornette Coleman to John Zorn, Miles Davis to John Lurie, Derek Bailey to Vernon Reid and Thurston Moore, Keith Rowe to Syd Barrett, or Sun Ra to Wayne Kramer, the nexus of punk and free jazz continues to kick out the jams.

The Politics of Time

Noticing the music I was playing at the opening of one of my writing classes a few years ago, one of my students said: "It kind of sounds like punk rock." The "it" he was referring to was "One Down, One Up," the title track from a recently issued recording of the John Coltrane Quartet, a recording that circulated for years as a legendary bootleg, holding what many listeners consider to be some of the most revelatory improvising by Coltrane ever to be captured on tape.[28]

My student's comment confirmed the initial inspiration behind this essay, the assertion that jazz, particularly the idiom that still gets referred to as *free jazz*, has something to say—or sing, or sound—to punk, and vice-versa. In the recording of "One Down, One Up," midway through Coltrane's solo, Elvin Jones's bass drum pedal breaks, limiting his sound to punctuations on the snare drum and cymbals as someone else frantically moves the bass drum away from his foot to replace the pedal. But Trane keeps going and Elvin literally never misses a beat. By the time the pedal is fixed and we hear the bass drum and toms come in again, there are still eleven minutes of music left. The length of this performance might not seem punk rock, but the reduction of elements to the most basic, which the musicians then exploit to their fullest potential, makes it a seminal moment in improvisation and reminds us that improvising is always necessarily a DIY project.

If punk is an instance of a mysterious, persistent, cyclical rupturing of the social order, as Greil Marcus's *Lipstick Traces* recounts, then perhaps the typical line that "punk (or jazz) is dead" because it has been com-modified is an inaccurate view of the "true" form of punk and jazz. In the manner of a Coltrane solo, punk and jazz form a potentially available, alternative, possibly utopian soundscape (where accidents like pedals' breaking can nevertheless occur), which can be rediscovered periodically, but which fades or abruptly ends at the end of each performance.

One of the most common Zen-like anecdotes in jazz relates that when Coltrane asked Miles Davis how to stop playing such long improvisations, Miles said, "Take the horn out of your mouth." But what we gain from the rupture of silence in the noise of punk and free jazz is that energy, the ex-citement generated when you put the horn back in your mouth, the guitar back in your hands, the drumsticks to the cymbals, crashing and smashing a new way through an old problem or an old way through new problems. Every time a solo ends, there's the potential for a new solo. As Marcus states in the liner notes of an album by the Swiss punk band Liliput: "To a lot of people, punk, whatever it was, upped and died in the U.K. between 1976 and 1978 . . . Outside of England, where punk purity made no sense, the Death of Punk was meaningless, a tree falling in someone else's forest. Punk—a certain form of the public attempt to discover one's own voice, let's say, a likely embarrassment protected by anonymous noise—was just getting started."

Or, as Sun Ra and June Tyson said, "It's after the end of the world—don't you know that yet?" The music has already created and annihilated the planet, so it's time for the next one. Kick out the jazz jams, the punk jams, the jams with no name, no written histories. The future of jazz was *then*, the future of free jazz and punk rock is *now*. Grab a guitar, or a saxophone, or a trash can lid, and start making a world.

Notes

1. This essay draws on two presentations originally given at the Experience Music Project Pop Conference, in 2006 and 2008. Thanks to my fellow panelists and especially to Kara Attrep, Allen Lowe, Howard Mandel, Elizabeth Freuden-thal, and Dave Novak for their comments at these sessions. Thanks also to the anonymous readers of this volume, whose feedback was incisive and helpful. Phil Dickinson read a version of the piece and I am grateful for his careful atten-tion and useful suggestions. Much of this material was originally inspired by a

discussion group I organized with my colleague in both academia and punk-rock and free-jazz performance, Ralph Lowi. Thanks also to Rami Gabriel for introducing me to the piece by Lester Bangs, and to Allen Lowe, the only person to hire me as a jazz drummer based on my punk credentials. Finally, thanks to Mike Watt. We took your advice and started our own band!

2. The sketch follows Chappelle as he does fake sociological research on the effects of various instruments on different ethnic groups. The electric-guitar portion, with the white rock musician John Mayer providing the live sound-track, includes sections where placid, white restaurant patrons erupt into a punk-style mosh pit triggered by Mayer's frenetic guitar. Afterward, Mayer manages to merely annoy the mostly black clientele of a barbershop with his blues-derived noodlings. The entire sketch is an excellent satire of musical essentialism, highlighted by the culminating moment, where Mayer, Chappelle, and a mixed-race police officer unite in their love of the 1980s hair-metal anthem, "Every Rose Has Its Thorn." While the skit is not explicitly about jazz or punk music, and while Chappelle rarely referenced (and never featured) jazz musicians on the show, the show emphasized an overall ecumenical view of African American music. A clip of Chappelle playing the Thelonious Monk composition "'Round Midnight" on the piano can be found at www.flygunrepublic .com. The uproar over Esperanza Spalding's winning the Grammy for Best New Artist, in 2011, caused when enraged fans of the losing nominee Justin Bieber vandalized Spalding's Wikipedia page, is also perhaps a symptom of this history. Bieber's no punk and Spalding isn't free jazz, but the debate points to the populist controversy over an African American woman who is not a pop or rock artist winning such an award. See Nate Chinen's interesting assessment: "Best-Kept Secret Now Has a Grammy," *New York Times*, February 14, 2011.

3. Bangs discusses the seminal days of the "downtown" New York scene, a period of rich cross-genre collaboration, as discussed elsewhere in this volume, by Marc Ribot. This era (sometimes called "No-Wave") has started to be more well-documented in print, in books such as Tim Lawrence's *Hold On to Your Dreams: Arthur Russell and the Downtown Music Scene, 1973–92* (Durham, NC: Duke University Press, 2009) and Bernard Gendron's *Between Montmarte and the Mudd Club* (Chicago: University of Chicago Press, 2002). The free-jazz side of this era is remarkably captured in Ebba Jahn's film *Rising Tones Cross* (1984), rereleased on DVD in 2007. While I draw inspiration from Bangs's piece for this essay, my focus generally lies elsewhere, chronologically and geographically; nevertheless, I encourage readers to seek out "Free Jazz/Punk Rock," still one of the few pieces to explicitly link these two unstable genres. I should also note that in discussing this music, my definition of "politics" is broader than direct action via parties, governments, etc. Generally speaking, I see the example of interracial, international, and multigenre musical ensembles discussed in this essay as an important example of political agency outside directly democratic institutions or other state-controlled institutions: a politics of alternate spheres

of power relations between races, ethnic groups, genders, and aesthetic pref-
erences.

4. See, for example, Allen Lowe's *That Devilin' Tune: A Jazz History, 1900–1950*.
(Kensington, CA: Music and Arts Programs of America, 2006) and *Lost Sounds:
Blacks and the Birth of the Recording Industry, 1890–1919* (Urbana-Champaign:
University of Illinois Press, 2005).

5. In an article published in 1910, entitled "The Next Step," Luxemburg sketches
out this dialectic: "A party, such as German Social Democracy, which upholds the
principle of organization and party discipline in an unprecedented manner virtually eliminates the initiative of the unorganized masses and their spontaneous
and, as it were, improvised ability to act which until now has been an important
and often decisive factor in all great political struggles" (http://www.marxists
.org/archive/luxemburg/index.htm). Also note that, while terrorist violence
did threaten various nation-states in the 1960s and 1970s (carried out by the
Baader-Meinhof Gang, the Weathermen, and other groups), the specific connection between anarchist political philosophy and violence was arguably more
concentrated in the late nineteenth century and the early twentieth. Luxemburg
herself was technically a socialist, not an anarchist. Like *terrorism*, however,
anarchy became a catch-all for any potential threat to capitalism and imperialism. Matthew Arnold had already set up the Manichean divide between "culture
and anarchy" as far back as 1867. The complete Parsons text, along with links
to other writings by Parsons and biographical details, can be found here: www
.lucyparsonsproject.org.

6. Stewart's essay "Freedom Music: Jazz and Human Rights" is an excellent
primer for those interested in the specifics surrounding the various notions of
"freedom" within jazz. Jesse's scholarship and music-making have been a particularly important signifier of freedom for my work.

7. In an interview conducted in 2006, Rollins was questioned about his punk
hairdo and noted, "I loved it. At the time I did it, it was sort of a statement—
outside of the box behavior. I got different reactions from different people. But I
thought it was a very individualistic thing and I'm happy I did it." The complete
interview can be found at http://lamentforastraightline.wordpress.com. Note
also that Angelo Moore, singer and saxophonist for the band Fishbone (one of
the quintessential African American punk-leaning units) sports a Rollinsesque
Mohawk. These hairstyles also playfully mark the often hidden connections between African American and Native American cultures, and remind us that the
Mohawk people famously helped build the skyscrapers in a primary postwar
space of jazz and punk culture, New York City.

8. See David Ake, *Jazz Cultures* (Berkeley: University of California Press,
2002). Ake's chapter on Coleman traces the race, class, and, especially, the gender dynamics implicit in the debates over the sonic nature of free jazz.

9. George Lewis's *A Power Stronger than Itself: The AACM and American Experimental Music* (Chicago: University of Chicago Press, 2008) and Benjamin

Looker's *Point from Which Creation Begins: The Black Artists' Group of St. Louis* (St. Louis: Missouri Historical Society Press, 2004) are two central examples of this scholarship.

10. In Europe perhaps more than in the United States, these trends were made practical realities by the presence of many expatriate musicians from all over, and groups might include, as in a slightly later (1980s) example of one incarnation of the band Detail, exiled South African blacks (bassist Johnny Dyani), Scandinavians (saxophonist Frode Gjerstad), white Englishmen (drummer John Stevens), and African American musicians (trumpeter Bobby Bradford).

11. "Crow Jim," a ridiculous reversal of "Jim Crow," here refers to one of the more embarrassing moments in the annals of jazz history, wherein white jazz critics excoriated black musicians intent on expressing more overt political themes. See "Crow Jim." *Time*, October 19, 1962, 58–60.

12. Putting a date on the origins of punk is often as difficult as defining what the music is or which musicians are "authentic" punks. Furthermore, I am not arguing that the Sex Pistols were the first authentic punk band; in fact, one could argue that they are the first "inauthentic" punk band. Assembled partly as a Situationist prank by Malcolm McLaren, the Pistols subsequently became a commercial enterprise, ironically being used as one of the markers of British nationalism during the soundtrack to the 2012 Olympics—Queen Elizabeth looked on from the Olympic Stadium as Johnny Rotten's recorded voice wailed about her "Fascist regime" (see Marcus, *Lipstick Traces* and Hebdige, *Subculture*). Crass had even proclaimed that "Punk is Dead" as early as 1978, largely because of the commodification of the music partially brought about by the Sex Pistols. For the purposes of this essay, I'd like to suggest that something like proto-punk started with psychedelic music of the mid-1960s and punk rock proper started roughly around the time of the Ramones, whose tour of England in 1976 galvanized (and in some cases started) the careers of bands like the Sex Pistols, the Clash, and many others. But clearly punk was already an element of music by that point, and had been arguably since the beginnings of rhythm 'n' blues and early rock 'n' roll. As I try to demonstrate in this essay, punk and free jazz are marked by a continually renewable anarchic energy, and tracing a precise origin of those forms may be less important than mapping the various routes and flows such energy has taken. For a revealing lesson in the history of punk, see the etymology of the word in the Oxford English Dictionary. Like *jazz*, the word *punk* has accumulated a rich set of often contradictory or ironic meanings, some of them connected to sex. Yet, unlike *jazz*, the word *punk* existed long before the associated musical style.

13. A trailer for the film, along with other information, can be found at www .afropunk.com. The *White Riot* volume includes essays and interviews spanning a wide cultural and geographical terrain, from New York to Jakarta. Due to its publication date, I was not able to fully incorporate a discussion of the book into this piece, yet I believe its release represents a renewed attention to the kinds of

issues I raise here. I thank Jeremy Wallach, one of the book's contributors, for drawing my attention to *White Riot* (and for hipping me to punk in Indonesia).

14. Carter discusses political anarchism, among other topics, in this fascinating interview: http://www.577records.com/artists/danielcarter/interview.html.

15. For the AMM perspective, which was not as enthusiastic, see Keith Rowe's comments in "Invisible Jukebox," *Wire* (January 2008): 18–21. The relationship between AMM and Pink Floyd is finally recounted in fuller detail in Palacios, *Syd Barrett and Pink Floyd*. Readers may have gathered by now that my deployment of the term *free jazz* is meant to encompass a wide variety of music, even the type of "free improvisation" that is often described by its principal architects (Rowe, Derek Bailey, Tony Oxley, and others) as an explicit turn away from African American jazz and free jazz. I remain committed, however, to grouping free improvisation into the strategically essentialized rubric of "free jazz," since I believe it would have never developed without jazz and free jazz.

16. In 2009, Dammers morphed his "Special AKA" ensemble (most famously known under the moniker the Specials, performing second-wave ska) into the Spatial AKA Orchestra, a direct homage to Sun Ra. The group's first gig included Sun Ra originals. Dammers is one of the most significant characters in the reggae-punk story and so it is fitting that he would now be part of the story of punk and free jazz. For more on Dammers, the Specials, and Two Tone records, see Dick Hebdige, "Dub Version (1982) (The Rise and Fall of Two Tone)," in *Cut 'n' Mix: Culture, Identity, and Caribbean Music* (London: Routledge, 1987), 106–14.

17. The Byron interview is archived at www.seeingblack.com. Despite the potentially negative connotations of his comments here, Byron's work represents one trajectory of the relationship between post-1960s jazz and other forms of music (if not explicitly punk rock). For example, he has collaborated with the guitarist Vernon Reid, the MC Biz Markie, and many others. His music is a prime example of "beyond category" contemporary sound grown from the soil of jazz. It's unclear whether Byron is here referring to Thurston Moore or Lee Ranaldo, who have both collaborated with free-jazz musicians. Moore in particular has been a crucial force in connecting rock 'n' roll audiences with the wide range of post-1960s free jazz. Roe (see works cited) also discusses Moore and Ranaldo in relation to free jazz.

18. Copeland, a highly virtuosic drummer, frequently makes such intentionally hyperbolic and provocative statements, but the underlying attitude regarding the banality of *mere* virtuosity is significant. Copeland himself has occasionally collaborated with jazz musicians, among them the bassist Stanley Clarke. While the perception of the untrained "primitive" in rock music, especially punk, often connotes a positive "authenticity," this same perception of primitive authenticity in jazz has contributed to a lingering racist stereotype of African Americans as lazy, and unskilled, their work not aesthetically on par with

Euroamerican art music. Nevertheless, the case can also be made for an equally misleading stereotyping of punk musicians as unskilled: anyone who has ever watched Mike Watt play bass, for example, has been in the presence of a virtuoso. Copeland's comments, like Milford Graves's below, draw out the underlying fear, however, that years of jazz training might not immediately grant a musician the emotional resonance that is so often valued from even the most technically gifted improvisers like Charlie Parker, John Coltrane, and Art Tatum.

19. Watt frequently acknowledges the influence of a range of jazz music on his own playing, as he does in the full interview, archived at http://the badpennyblog.wordpress.com Charlie Haden once even jammed with Watt's band, the Minutemen, available at www.corndogs.org. Along with Mike Watt, Henry Rollins is another significant punk advocate of Coltrane. See his radio show tribute to Coltrane from 2010 at henryrollins.com.

20. For good examples of classic improvised excursions by Pink Floyd, see Peter Whitehead's film *Tonight Let's All Make Love in London* (1967). As this essay was being completed, new remastered versions of the Pink Floyd discography were released, and future releases will reportedly feature some early live recordings featuring Barrett. Ironically, Nick Mason has assessed these new releases with a less critical tone than is found in his earlier comments on Floyd's improvisational prowess (or lack thereof): "I'm a jazz fan . . . so I think of when they put out, like, the complete sets of Charlie Parker things, John Coltrane . . . with every note ever played, including outtakes that are 16 seconds long. You realize that if I like that, maybe it's perfectly OK to do the same thing for people who are that interested in how we did it" (quoted in Gary Graff, "Pink Floyd Rolling Out the Music Again," *Press and Guide*, September 28, 2011).

21. Information about the connection between Sun Ra, the MC5, and John Sinclair can be found in Szwed, *Space Is the Place* (243–46). Some of the background material of this section has also been compiled in *Sun Ra: Interviews and Essays*, edited by John Sinclair (see works cited). Useful commentary and analysis can also be found in "Kick Out the Jams! The MC5 and the Politics of Noise" by Steve Waksman, in Duncombe and Tremblay. Note also that the album *Kick Out the Jams* was recorded in 1968 but released in 1969. Pink Floyd's debut album, *The Piper at the Gates of Dawn*, was released in 1967. For more on the jazz drummer Tony Williams's love of the MC5, see Kevin Fellezs, *Birds of Fire: Jazz, Rock, Funk, and the Creation of Fusion* (Durham, NC: Duke University Press, 2011).

22. See Bangs, "Free Jazz/Punk Rock." Steve Mackay noted his own connections to free jazz in a "comeback" profile (Edwin Pouncey, "Loving the Alien," *Wire* 274, 28–29). Lester Bangs would, as Ben Edmonds recounts in a piece about the concert bills Sun Ra and the MC5 shared, "later recant and list [*Kick Out the Jams*] among his all-time favorites." See Edmonds, "Their Space Was My Place," in Sinclair, *Sun Ra* (66).

23. It's clear that Sinclair and Kramer, however, as their continued connections with the Arkestra demonstrate, did and do have an earnest appreciation of

and respect for the musical and social ideals that their 1960s-era actions might not have entirely lived up to. Sun Ra, too, is a complex figure, by no means a consistent example of progressive social change. His sexism, for example, as depicted by Valerie Wilmer, is one side of Sun Ra that is not often mentioned in discussions of his social and ethical outlook. For Wilmer on Ra and sexism, see *As Serious as Your Life*, 213–15; for a lengthier discussion of free jazz and gender, see Wilmer, *As Serious as Your Life*, 189–209.

24. For more about Coltrane, Ravi Shankar, and Indian and Western music meetings, see Peter Lavezzoli's *Bhairavi: The Dawn of Indian Music in the West* (London: Continuum, 2006).

25. For more about the linguistic projects in free jazz, see the essays by Aldon Lynn Nielsen and Eric Porter in this volume.

26. Thanks to one of my anonymous reader's comments in regard to hip-hop, suggesting that an equally fruitful relationship could be charted between hip-hop and free jazz. See also Greg Tate's piece in this volume. Hip-hop, like punk, began in the 1970s and was both a continuation and reimagining of many of the currents found in free jazz (among other genres). In some respects, however, the connections between hip-hop and jazz are sometimes also hard to see and hear, due to the still frequent scorn that jazz musicians, black and white, heap on hip-hop in popular discourse.

27. The year 1975 again being a provisional starting point for "mainstream" punk, with the formation of the Sex Pistols.

28. See liner notes and recording, John Coltrane, *One Down, One Up: Live at the Half Note*.

PART II

Crisis in New Music?
*Vanishing Venues and the Future
of Experimentalism*

Marc Ribot

CHAPTER 6

DAYS OF BREAD AND ROSES

Three years ago, I submitted an article to *All about Jazz*, entitled "The Care and Feeding of a Musical Margin." The article examined the trend of club closures, downsizings, moves to Brooklyn, and other forms of marginalization that were, and still are, exerting a downward pressure on my pay and the pay of many of my fellow musicians.

The article examined the collective response of musicians to the threatened closing of downtown venues, musicians' doing increasing numbers of benefits for the venues that remained, and noted the limits of that response. It also suggested a possible alternate action, a political drive for public subsidy, and examined its potential benefits and obstacles, including a history of ideological opposition to subsidy on the part of some musicians.

My involvement with these issues wasn't disinterested: the article was published in the context of a political response to the closing of the nightclub Tonic, a center for new, experimental, jazz, and improvisational music. Tonic had been, for me and many other musicians in experimental and improvisational musics, an important space for presenting music during the previous ten years. Our political response sought to harness musicians' anger at the closing of Tonic, to get the city to donate or fund a new space to serve as a center for new, experimental, jazz, and improvised musics.

Although this was not part of the public position taken at the time, it's true that at least some of the anger and disappointment at the closing of Tonic was felt toward the club's management. Musicians—many booked months in advance, and some of whom had bought tickets for travel from out of town—were given less than three weeks' notice that Tonic would close, too late for most to rebook. More important, the rhetoric used to encourage donations during the years of Tonic's existence had been that of community—"preserving the scene." Those who participated in earlier "save Tonic" benefits had felt they were fighting to preserve a space for creative musics, not simply giving money to nice individuals whose business was in trouble. The abrupt nature of the club's closure underlined a stark contradiction, that this rhetoric and "feeling" of community had been mobilized on behalf of what was, in fact, a privately owned business with no accountability to anyone beyond its investors.

No one can or should fault the club's owners—a likeable young couple then expecting their first child and facing enormous personal debt—for their extremely difficult business decisions. However, the object lesson of Tonic's closure was clear: if musicians want to be informed of, consulted on, or participate in decisions that affect our lives, we had better direct whatever communal energy and resources we have toward organizations that are accountable to us.

On hearing that Tonic was going to close, I contacted Barbara Burch, who, in addition to being part of the collective that runs Neues Kabarett at the Brecht forum, is also a political activist with knowledge of city government. I also contacted Patricia Nicholson Parker (Arts for Art/Vision Festival), who had shown great generosity in trying to organize alternate venues for Tonic musicians whose gigs had been cancelled.

Our response was organized on short notice. An ad hoc group was formed, held several open meetings, and won the support of many key musicians and presenters, and of local 802 of the American Federation of Musicians (AFM).[1] A set of goals was agreed on:

1. That the city council adopt a general principle similar to European cultural policy; that NYC's new music and experimental jazz/indie musical culture is a unique asset, an essential part of the city's history, economy, and identity, and not to be left entirely at the mercy of market forces.

2. That the city recognize the damage done to its cultural heritage and status as a "cultural capitol" [sic] by the displacement of venues central to experimental musics, and act now to protect those venues still left from displacement either by providing funding sufficient to allow them to withstand the explosion of commercial rents, or by legislation forcing landlords to restrict rents of culturally valuable venues, or both.

3. That New York City intervene to preserve 107 Norfolk street as an experimental music venue, or make available a comparably sized and centrally

located space for that purpose. (Tonic press release, April 12, 2007) (see appendix 1)

Both the article and the drive for a space were, at the time, controversial among musicians. Alan Licht, a musician who had also booked Tonic, posted a letter on the *All about Jazz* website claiming that, contrary to "Care and Feeding['s]" representation of downsizing and marginalization, the demise of Tonic and other downtown venues was part of the ordinary ebb and flow of business. In Licht's understanding, downtown was slowly but surely being replaced by "Brooklyn . . . that is where more and more people are going to be headed for nightlife."

Licht's response implied that the changes taking place in the landscape of clubs would ultimately work to musicians' advantage without musicians' collective intervention, as he believed they had in the past. Those of us involved in the Tonic action rejected this understanding: we saw the relocation of many clubs to Brooklyn as a geographic and economic marginalization that would hurt rates of pay. Licht's response sought to preempt questions of whether the market had failed the music by reframing it in more traditional terms (that is, whether these particular musicians had failed in the market): "Where was the audience . . . That's the question we need to be asking."[2]

However, at the open meetings held before Tonic's closure (the first was held in the back of the Pink Pony, on Ludlow), a plurality of NYC creative musicians, while sharing Licht's concern with improving the market for creative musics, were asking questions that went beyond immediate market concerns:

1. If seen from a purely market perspective, the city would be better off selling the Metropolitan Opera to private condo developers. But it won't: it subsidizes opera precisely because it places a value on opera beyond its market value, a position it takes because of continued advocacy by opera lovers.[3]

2. The other question "we need to be asking" is this: why does the city not attach even a fraction of that value to the musics the rest of the world recognizes as New York City's actual artistic heritage? Why do *we* not advocate for it to do so?

3. Cities around the world have given venues free of charge to organizations presenting new/experimental musics in Amsterdam, Ljubljana, Bern, Zurich, Berlin, Rome, and dozens of other European cities. Why not NYC?

4. The city intervenes to protect other industries important to its economic health and cultural identity: using zoning restrictions to preserve Manhattan's west thirties for the garment industry. Why shouldn't it intervene on behalf of our industry?

5. Why have we stood by and watched our cultural assets being destroyed while allowing free market ideologists to tell us what questions we need to ask?

And more importantly,

6. "What can we do about this?"

It was understood at the time that (with two years of the Bush presidency still to go) the answer to the last question, at the national level, was "probably nothing." But it seemed entirely plausible to those at the open meetings that "if the popular support exists to raise over $90,000 to keep one club (Tonic) open, then the possibility exists for a serious political fight at the city or state level" (Ribot, "The Care and Feeding of a Musical Margin").[4]

At the second open meeting, held at Clemente Soto Velez cultural center, on Suffolk St., a motion to squat Tonic in order to dramatize and publicize the fight for a city-subsidized building was adopted by majority vote.

The squat action took place on April 14, 2007, the day after Tonic's official closing, bringing several dozen performers and several hundred fans down to concerts, playing even as movers were dismantling the stage, with two performers (me and the singer-songwriter-violinist-activist Rebecca Moore) refusing to leave even after the arrival of the police, resulting in our arrests.[5]

Following both the publication of the article and the squat action, the ad hoc coalition of artists who had organized around Tonic did begin to gain some political traction around the goal of a city-subsidized space. There was limited support (for the goal of getting a space, not for the squatter action) from city council member Alan Gerson (see appendix 2), with whose help we were able to hold a press conference on the steps of city hall, at which musicians told their stories and spoke about the need for a city space. We received extensive coverage in the NYC press, and began to schedule meetings with other city politicians.

At these meetings, the situation was spelled out for us clearly: access to city-owned buildings, although difficult, was by no means impossible. However, it was first necessary to specify the organization that would be receiving whatever space the city donated. Part of this involved specifying the governance of the organization: how would decisions be made, and who would be responsible for making them?

In the months following the Tonic action, differences over strategy had already begun to appear, with some—including Barbara Burch, of Neues Kabarett—favoring a larger, more inclusive organization that would reach out to more presenters of creative musics and their affiliated musicians, and others—notably Patricia Nicholson Parker, of Arts for Art/Vision Festival (AFA)—favoring a much smaller, more streamlined committee.

Streamlining won out: by the end of the summer of 2007, there were no presenters affiliated with the committee (which had named itself Rise Up Creative Music and Arts, or RUCMA) other than AFA.

The debate over governance further fragmented the committee: proposals by me and Barbara Burch for cooperative or confederated forms of governance were opposed by those representing AFA, who were skeptical of a collective approach and concerned that the committee's drive not compete with their own long-standing attempts to get a city building. The counterproposal by the AFA, that its own board would govern, with some added seats to represent musicians and presenters who had fought for the new space, was not acceptable to other presenters on the committee, who resigned.

When it became clear that AFA was committed to that position, I also withdrew from the committee. I believed that both AFA, whose generous support from the beginning of the project had enabled it to happen in the first place, and the support of the community of musicians in and around the Vision Festival were essential ingredients in any coalition for creative music. However, practically, I believed a much larger community than AFA's would need to be mobilized in order to win a space from the city.

Three years later, the switchover to smaller, unadvertised, and more marginally located venues has, in fact, caused a decline in rates of pay for many of the artists who once played at Tonic.[6] Those venues booking creative musics that do advertise, that have room capacities above eighty, and that are still in Manhattan generally pay 60 to 65 percent of the door (for example, Le Poisson Rouge and Joe's Pub) as opposed to Tonic's 75 percent. These amounts are further reduced by hidden charges.[7] The purely economic effect shouldn't be overstated—most musicians who played at Tonic presented projects there once or twice a month at most, so a 10–15 percent reduction in pay for those nights doesn't mean a 10 to 15 percent drop in overall income.[8] But small differences in funding can, over time, make a big difference in the health of a scene: the historic productivity of NYC's jazz avant-gardes, as opposed to the West Coast counterparts, is partly attributable to the difference of a few hundred dollars' cost and a few hours' difference in flights to Europe.[9]

Coming on top of severe drops in recording budgets, due to the record industry's meltdown, these cuts hurt.[10] Because, combined, recording budgets and local nightclub pay are what musicians live on while developing material—essentially, the research and development department of our industry. Declines in nightclub pay hurt our ability to develop new work and, therefore, to compete on national and global touring networks, the real economy of new, experimental, jazz, and improvisational musics.

Rise Up Creative Music and Arts continues as an advocacy branch of AFA/Vision Festival. Although AFA/Vision Festival has not, to date, succeeded in getting a city building, the Tonic action did introduce the idea of a market failure of creative music in NYC and the need for city intervention into public discourse. This helped create, both ironically and predictably, the political climate in which both Issue Project Room and ABC No Rio received a large-scale city subsidy this year.[11]

Race, Class, and Door Gigs

"Care and Feeding" advocated subsidy as a means to allow a venue to maintain or improve rates of pay for musicians, not as an end in itself or a means of support for those who would make a career out of grant writing and nonprofit management. Among the article's premises is that a link exists between the economic resources available to a musical community and the vitality of its creative output.[12] But resources are helpful only if they can actually be accessed by musicians.

Unfortunately, this has not always been the case. George Lewis recounts the AACM's very mixed experience with an administrator funded by the National Endowment for the Arts, circa 1980: "Curiously, a two year budget projection amounting to nearly $150,000 included funds for various administrative personnel, as well as for rental of concert spaces, but nothing at all for artists' fees and expenses" (*A Power Stronger than Itself* 419). Without means of exerting collective power, pay for musicians will likely continue its downward spiral, even in venues that have been subsidized.

This is unfortunate, because low pay acts as a barrier, excluding working-class people from participation in creative musics. This, in turn, drains the pool of potentially good musicians, impoverishes the breadth of experience reflected in the music, and limits the communities to which the music might appeal. To the great extent to which class and race and gender are still related in the United States, this barrier still disproportionally affects musicians of color and female musicians.

Perhaps Issue Project Room and ABC No Rio, having won significant subsidies from the city, will independently adopt policies guaranteeing all musicians union-scale minimums (against fair market equivalents for more established musicians) and allocating funds to commission composers for new works or projects. If not, musicians would do well to remember that subsidy by itself, although necessary to preserve the possibility of collective economic action in our times, is not necessarily a substitute.[13]

Appendixes

Appendix 1: Avant Jazz, Indie, New Music Cultural Crisis

The following is a press release issued after the closing of Tonic, requesting help in organizing support for a city-funded performance space. It provides context for the issues I've discussed in the preceding essay.

> Responding to community outrage at the eviction of Tonic—a center of New York City's new music cultural life on the Lower East Side for the last 9 years—an ad hoc committee of musicians, cultural activists, and supporters are convening to call for public political intervention.
>
> When: 11:00 am this Saturday, April 14th
> Where: Tonic, 107 Norfolk street between Rivington and Delancey
> Why: To ask for public political intervention to protect new music/indie/ avant/jazz in New York City and to ask the city to provide a minimum 200 capacity, centrally located venue for experimental music.
> What: From 11 am on, musicians and other performers will stage a musical protest against the planned closing of Tonic, a vital NYC new music resource.
>
> Tonic, located at 107 Norfolk Street, has been unable to afford a series of rent increases imposed by landlord William Gottleib Inc, and will be forced to close its doors this April 14th.

Coming on the heels of the closing of CBGB's, Sin-e, Fez, the Continental, and numerous other downtown venues, the closing of Tonic represents the continued shutting down of NYC's hugely important live music experimental jazz, indie, and new music scene.

This wave of club closings constitutes a market failure. If there is not immediate and sufficient public intervention, either in the form of limiting rents or supplying alternate space and funding—or both—New York City will lose an essential part of its heritage, culture, and economy.

Tonic is the last new music/indie/avant jazz venue in Manhattan with a capacity above 90, presenting concerts on a nightly basis. It is also the last such venue in the city with the relatively musician friendly policy of paying 75% of door receipts.

In the words of Steven Bernstein (leader of the band Sex Mob): "My band plays some of the biggest festivals in Europe . . . Meanwhile there's only one club I can play in New York and it's about to close" [qtd. in Sisario, "Manhattan Home"].

According to Patricia Nicholson-Parker, organizer of the Vision Festival:

We have come together to say we deserve a space and in essence, we have already paid for our space. Musicians contribute to the economy of this city every day with world class performances. In the case of Tonic, many musicians came together and invested in the space. Through benefits and organizing they raised significant sums of money (100+ grand) for the venue, "Tonic." The city needs to acknowledge this. It is good for the city and good for the artists and their audiences that the city make available a musician-friendly community club/space which holds up to 200 audience members. It is important that it not be in the outer boroughs but be centrally located in the LES where this serious alternative music has been birthed and where it can be easily accessed by audiences.

This press release is being issued by an ad hoc coalition of musicians and supporters of new/experimental jazz/indie music. We represent a racially and culturally diverse community united in our desire to preserve the cultural legacy and future viability of the progressive jazz, experimental rock, and new music historically based in the LES.

Saturday's action will be the first of an ongoing series of actions towards this goal. Further information and contacts are available at www.takeittothebridge .com

The coalition is asking:

1. That the city council adopt a general principle similar to European cultural policy; that NYC's new music and experimental jazz/indie musical culture is a unique asset, an essential part of the city's history, economy, and identity, and not to be left entirely at the mercy of market forces.

2. That the city recognize the damage done to its cultural heritage and

status as a "cultural capitol" [sic] by the displacement of venues central to experimental music, and act now to protect those venues still left from displacement either by providing funding sufficient to allow them to withstand the explosion of commercial rents, or by legislation forcing landlords to restrict rents of culturally valuable venues, or both.

3. That New York City intervene to preserve 107 Norfolk street as an experimental music venue, or make available a comparably sized and centrally located space for that purpose.

Background

Economic impact:

There has been little discussion of the economic impact of shutting down nightly new music venues in NYC. Beyond its own inherent value as art, new/experimental/indie/jazz music also serves as crucial research and development for a much larger music industry—entertainment products, including music, are a major New York City export, and live entertainment in NYC is a major factor in restaurant, tourism, and hotel industries.

The reason people come here from all over the world to hear music, and hire ensembles from New York to tour all over the world, derives from the unique sound of the city's music. This uniqueness derives in turn from the historic interaction between NYC's mainstream and its avant-garde and other indigenous scenes.

The proximity, the mutual artistic influence, the trading back and forth of players between mainstream and the avant-garde is what has created the competitive advantage of NYC music—its world famous "edge." The avant-garde draws from a pool of excellent professionals also working in NYC pop, classical, and mainstream jazz and rock: these are enriched by the cultural ideas of its avant-garde. This "edge" brings millions in local club and restaurant business, music and film production, and tourism to New York annually, in addition to creating employment for the thousands of NYC-based musicians who tour world markets on a yearly basis.

The Mostly Mozart festival is a wonderful experience for many New Yorkers. However it is neither an export nor the type of music representing New York City's musical culture abroad. Europeans can travel to Salzburg or Vienna to hear Mozart. New York's indigenous forms, however, are being presented every night of the year in cities throughout Europe, Asia and around the world. New music/experimental/indie/jazz has support abroad completely disproportionate with its profile in NYC, as even a brief visit to http://www.europejazz.net/, the European jazz network website will confirm. And tourists from abroad can and do travel to New York to hear this music in its local setting.

But all this depends on its having a local setting: including a viable new indie and experimental music nightly club scene. It is not only culturally barbarous, but also incredibly short-sighted economic policy that the internationally and critically recognized value of this music should be without an adequate, well-advertised, and easily accessible showcase in its place of birth: one funded well enough to be able to both nurture new talent and present established musicians.

Appendix 2

The following is a statement from New York City Council Member Alan Gerson:

The closing of Tonic is a call to action for all of us who have been fighting for the survival of creative New York, and a wake up call to those who have not yet engaged in what now amounts to an existential struggle for New York City's identity in the face of the new global urban competitiveness. I challenge other elected officials to come to the table on the issue of public interventions to save artistic creation in NYC.

The cultural value chain runs on a matrix from production to consumption and from low end to high end with intersecting vectors of non-profit and commercial contracts. Until we deal with this reality and create some market buffers, we will continue to suffer this "market failure" and we will have allowed the total collapse of what used to be a world-class professional circuit of venues for new jazz and alternative and avant garde music.

Notes

1. These supporters included Patricia and William Parker; Barbara Burch; Jim Staley, of Roulette; Janine Nichols, of St. Anne's Warehouse; the musicians Rebecca Moore and Norman Yamada, of the activist organization take-it-to-the-bridge.com; Cooper-Moore; Gina Leishman; Roy Campbell Jr.; Ned Rothenberg; Jason Hwang; James Keepnews; Marco Cappelli; and many others. The 802 supported the musicians with crucial legal and organizing advice. My own emphasis on state subsidy didn't come out of any love for the bureaucratic state. Before the Tonic action, I had been active in fighting against declines in working conditions through groups in and around the musicians local 802. However, with rents going through the roof and venues closing right and left, it was clear that union action against club owners wasn't going to do anything but shut them down faster. State subsidy was thought of as a last resort. This was preferable to the practice of asking musicians to subsidize our own venues, a practice that had already become common by 2006—essentially a tax on our work that was erasing the standards we'd fought for.
2. Alan Licht, letter to the editor of "All about Jazz—New York": "the bene-

fit concerts two years ago were very well attended, and raised a considerable amount of money for the club. So where was the audience before and after those benefits? That's the question we need to be asking."

3. "The status accorded to Euro. classical music in the U.S., and the 19th c./ early 20th c. establishment of major cultural institutions such as the Metropolitan Opera, were not givens. Advocates for the music created the N.Y. Philharmonic and persuaded industrialists like Carnegie to sponsor concert halls. Culture makers, politicians, artists, music lovers, and snobs touted classical music as a vehicle for 'cultural uplift.' Jazz at Lincoln Center also rests on decades of efforts by jazz advocates, always with mixed motives (e.g., John Hammond's 1938–9 Spirituals to Swing concerts at Carnegie Hall)" (Barzel).

4. The first of a series of "Save Tonic" benefits raised $93,000. Benefits were held a year before the club's closing.

5. Protesting performers included Matthew Shipp, Doug Wieselman, Jim Pugliese, Nora Balaban, Dan Kaufman, Pamelia Kurstin, Steve Wishnia, Eric Blitz, Ned Rothenberg, Roy Nathanson, Ras Moshe, Marco Cappelli, Jerome Harris, the poet Steve Dalachinsky, and the dancer Patricia Nicholson. Butch Morris did an inspiring conduction, and Kenny Wolleson was about to perform when the police arrived.

6. A few of the more jazz-oriented former Tonic musicians (e.g., Dave Douglas and Bill Frisell) have found homes at the Village Vanguard or other venues whose rates of pay match or exceed Tonic's. Also, some of the most marketable of the Tonic musicians (John Zorn, for example) have been able to present work under favorable conditions at the Abrams Art Center. However, this isn't an option for musicians unable to risk renting the room.

7. For example, Joe's Pub deducts for tickets paid for by credit cards.

8. There are also other effects: the Stone Room's system of floating curators has provided interesting and diverse bookings, and helped the club avoid the cost of paying a booking person. However, it doesn't provide easy access for artists simply wanting to book a gig. And the club's agreement with other building tenants prohibits the afternoon sound checks and rehearsals that were a very useful feature of Tonic.

9. Ribot, "The Care and Feeding of a Musical Margin."

10. "At the end of last year, the music business was worth half of what it was ten years ago and the decline doesn't look like it will be slowing anytime soon. Total revenue from U.S. music sales and licensing plunged to $6.3 billion in 2009, according to Forrester Research. In 1999, that revenue figure topped $14.6 billion" (David Goldman, CNNmoney.com, Feb. 2, 2010).

11. In 2008, Issue Project Room won a twenty-year rent-free lease for 5,000 square feet on the ground floor of a former Board of Education building in downtown Brooklyn, less than five minutes by car from the exits of the Brooklyn and Manhattan Bridges, and within walking distance of 2, 3, N, R, A, and F trains. Although the space is reportedly being brought up to fire code, Issue Project Room claims it needs to raise $2.5 million for renovations. Marty Marko-

witz, the Brooklyn borough president, has pledged $1.1 million toward the $2.5 million Issue claims it needs for renovations. New York City Council Representative Alan Gerson, who had sided with RUCMA in 2007, was instrumental in supporting ABC No Rio's bid for a space two years later. The group was awarded $1,650,000 in city funding for the planned construction of a new facility at 156 Rivington Street.

12. Hopefully, this premise can be maintained without vulgarity or reductionism—with plenty of room for "symbolic capital" and all of art's ineffable etceteras. However, my writing is intended as a corrective to more common critical practices that focus only on the choices musicians make, while disregarding forces and institutions structuring the choices made available to us.

13. The AACM's first set of rules stated, "Union scale salary will be paid all performing members depending on the locality in which concerts are held. All vocalists must be covered by AGVA and will be paid as performing musicians during concerts" (AACM, "Informational Memorandum of Requirements and Expectations," qtd. in Lewis, *A Power Stronger than Itself* 117).

Whether written out of a desire to avoid conflict with the then-powerful Chicago musicians' union, or out of a sharing of that union's belief in guaranteed minimum rates of pay, the effects of that decision are not to be underestimated. Much of the AACM's subsequent development can be linked to that decision: if the event must pay performing musicians to scale, then the organization has built-in incentives to work to see that the room is full, build an audience and community of listeners and supporters, channel resources to the musicians themselves instead of just growing the organizational budget, and make realistic decisions about how many shows the given audiences and budgets can support in any given week.

The commitment to pay scale minimums is also reflected in the AACM's educational programs and many informal instances—well documented in Lewis's book—of the concern more established members showed for the musical development of younger members, both as tools of community-building, and as means of guaranteeing a high level of musical quality in the work being presented. An opposite set of incentives is produced by the decision to abandon the concept of minimum scale. Pay for nonprofit administrators is pegged only to gross income, without regard for how much of that income actually goes to musicians. This leaves no incentive to pay the musicians themselves, rather than fund other organizational expenses.

CHAPTER 7

SUBSIDY, ADVOCACY, THEORY

Experimental Music in the Academy,

in New York City, and Beyond

"New music," "avant-garde jazz," "indie music," "creative improvisation": In 2007, Marc Ribot, a composer-improviser-guitarist with three decades of experience working in New York City's downtown scene, argued (in an article originally published in *All about Jazz* online) that, by any name, Manhattan's paradigm-pushing music scenes were sputtering, and would die out altogether unless artists pushed for a financial subsidy from the city. The problem was not simply that rents in downtown Manhattan's former creative enclaves had climbed too high, but that profit margins downtown were too thin to sustain the venues that could anchor artists' creative communities. Such venues were increasingly turning to artists for help, asking them to donate equipment and perform at benefit concerts. Ribot's focus was on artists who worked outside the sphere of European concert music, with its division between composers and performers and its emphasis on through-composed scores. Rather, the essay referred to composer-improvisers from the jazz avant-garde, from rock, and noise-based experimentalists, and No Wave groups "influenced by punk rock, John Cage, and Thelonious Monk," who had made up and were descended from New York's vibrant downtown music scene of the 1970s through the 1990s.[1]

Insofar as the downtown scene had a lingua franca, it was jazz, and its musics are often referred to as jazz-with-a-modifier: avant-jazz, experimental jazz, post-jazz. In the bass guitarist Jerome Harris's formulation, the scene's composer-improvisers took a more process-oriented than canon-oriented stance toward the music that fundamentally shaped their performance practices, aesthetic vocabularies, repertoires, and improvisational acumen, even as they brought jazz into the purview of their many creative interests and concerns.[2] These concerns included writing music that tested and expanded upon its own parameters, including those of language, intelligibility, meaning, expressivity, and form. One of Ribot's unstated premises seemed to be that the future of such experimental music (a term I examine further below) lay in creative pluralism and in cross-talk among composer-performer-improvisers with widely varied backgrounds and proclivities. Such cross-talk would likely depend on a creative formation similar to that of the downtown scene in the 1980s and 1990s: a diverse mix of artists who cultivated a personal sound and syntax, an Afrological value they derived from jazz- and blues-based musics in tandem with modernist ideas about individuality. These artists stayed open to influence from any quarter, studied and were attuned to current and historical musical vanguards, wrote and performed original music, and collaborated to develop new compositional and improvisational language out of disparate, not always mutually intelligible, musical idioms and interests. Ribot's focus may be city-specific, but his arguments should be of vital interest to anyone concerned with the "future of jazz," including those of us in academic music studies, where even jazz's past has a tenuous place.

Ribot's essay was provoked by a sense of crisis: even as artists suffered the effects of the shrinking recording industry, rents in the city were rising, and the clubs that had helped to usher in the emergence of punk rock, No Wave, and the downtown scene—including the Knitting Factory, Tonic, and CBGB—were closing. The venues that remained were small, subsidized, not-for-profit organizations such as the Jazz Gallery and Roulette. Indeed, Roulette—as both a venue and an "artist resource center"— has cultivated downtown's experimental music community for the past three decades. Downtown's dimming intensity and the gentrification of its neighborhoods were not news, nor was the idea of arts subsidies in the city, where the New York State Arts Council had spent about $2 million annually over the past decade, in grants to not-for-profit music organizations.[3] Ribot was simply charging artists to set their sights higher, and to fight for a major venue in Manhattan, with substantial funds targeted toward artist fees and commissions. Because of the unique role played by cross-talk and community among contemporary composer-improvisers, this call had a particular urgency.

Historically, along with informal spaces donated or curated by artists—such as Ornette Coleman's Prince Street loft and Sam and Beatrice Rivers's Studio RivBea (commemorated in New York this year, appropriately enough, in a lecture and performance series titled "Lost Jazz Shrines")—commercial clubs have played a key part in jazz's development.[4] Just as Minton's, the Five Spot, and Slug's Saloon served, from the 1940s to the 1960s, as incubators for new, creative ideas in jazz, in the 1980s and 1990s, clubs acted as loci for the new creative formations of the downtown scene. Likewise, because downtown artists were performer-composer-improvisers, and worked in ensembles presenting new music (or new arrangements), to which each artist contributed original ideas, venues served as key gathering places in which to share work and to meet new collaborators. As downtown's venues closed, artists thus lost not only places to perform but also the concrete and conceptual creative commons that had fostered the scene's idiom-bridging ensembles and its interdisciplinary possibilities.

The special character of the scene had hinged on its unique ability to attract and catalyze collaborations among artists of different creative backgrounds. That ability had depended not only on the artistic and social aspects described above, but also on the scene's particular economic and geographic conditions. Rents were low, and Manhattan-based clubs could draw substantial audiences, including visitors from the scene's fan base in Europe and Japan. New York was also a convenient home base for artists who made the bulk of their livelihoods in Europe. Ribot contends, moreover, that the popularity of the music performed downtown in the 1980s had been an anomaly in the annals of experimental music in the United States. In an increasingly hostile economic climate, it was unrealistic for experimentalists to expect anything other than a decline in working conditions. There were fewer opportunities to perform, smaller venues, and lower fees. With Lincoln Center an established presence uptown, artists could push back against such marginalization by lobbying the city to subsidize a major venue in downtown Manhattan, a venue devoted to experimental music. A single venue could not be expected to financially anchor an entire community, but winning civic support for a large, high-profile, and well-subsidized venue would be a crucial victory in the ongoing battle to increase arts funding and improve musicians' working conditions.

It is not surprising that the downtown scene's energy dissipated. Every previous generation of activists and artists based in the Lower East Side has seen its own creative community wax and wane. As the poet hattie gossett wrote of the arts community and Black Arts scene of the 1960s in the Lower East Side:

> we thought it would always be
> whoever woulda dreamed it wouldnt huh? whoever
> woulda thought a pizza/hotdog/souvlaki place
> would usurp our house of dreams & visions on the
> corner of 3rd avenue & 8th street major threshold to
> an exalted state of mind known as the lower east side
> a grand cooker of a scene which during those early
> coldwar days shot out strong steady surges of music
> writing civil disobedience painting anarchy dance free
> sex political organizing that changed the world?
> . . .
> in fact we never thought it would go away (gossett 571)

Over the past several decades, the Lower East Side has served as an incubator for an overlapping succession of new countercultural communities. However, with the passing of downtown's late twentieth-century arts scene and the Lower East Side's nearly wholesale gentrification, it may not be realistic to hope that yet another creative formation will emerge downtown.[5] Manhattan nevertheless offers artists unique levels of exposure, access, and opportunity, and Ribot argues that experimentalists, who in the United States have always operated on the thinnest of economic and cultural margins, should not leave it without a fight.

Since his essay was published, Ribot's call to arms has been partially answered. His argument had been prefigured by the work done by Suzanne Fiol, the founder of Issue Project Room, who in 2009, after six years of building support for her venue, won $1.1 million in civic funds to renovate a new, rent-free space for experimental music, in Brooklyn, leading Brooklyn Borough President Marty Markowitz to proclaim, "I don't understand half the things they do, and when they tell me about them, they lose me. But that's not the point. . . . the arts create jobs."[6] As is evident from his citing Metelkova Mesto, the activist-run Slovenian Autonomous Cultural Center, Ribot is urging his colleagues to fight for a venue that conceives of itself as the nexus of a sociable creative community—a community that is, in turn, dedicated to defending the space as a haven for transgressive art and ideas—and prioritizes its spending and programming accordingly.

This idea is especially timely, given the recent news that the Ford

Foundation has dedicated $100 million to supporting arts venues, with an aim to encourage "the construction of affordable housing for artists in or around some of these spaces and to spur economic development in their surrounding areas" (Strom). Echoing Markowitz's comment above, the foundation asserted that its new initiative "is also intended to help arts organizations improve or develop the management skills needed to maintain their spaces and, ideally, to turn them into revenue generators. Some of the money has been allocated for a series of seminars on marketing, planning, fund-raising and other topics related to sustaining arts centers." Considering the uneven access to professional networks determined by such factors as class, location, background, and immigration status, as well as the increasingly important professional role played by costly programs in higher education, such subsidies for artists' professional development are essential and should be a basic part of any platform for arts advocacy. In New York City, the Bronx Council on the Arts (BCA) espouses a philosophy similar to that of the Ford Foundation, couching its mission for the South Bronx Cultural Corridor in a postmodern mixture of statements about economic development, arts-advocacy ideas, and marketing jargon (Bronx Council on the Arts). Evidently, the new reality for generating healthy arts communities in urban centers entails embracing such concepts as "branding" the community, "creating a job-ready pipeline of creative economy workers," and describing arts spaces as "revenue generators." Although such corporate-speak seems fundamentally hostile to the arts, it is difficult to fault the BCA for marshaling the resources it needs to build support for its progressive social vision, which includes subsidizing arts housing, attracting cultural institutions to the Bronx, expanding current job-training programs, and offering "financial literacy training" to local artists. And yet, even if we fully embrace the arts-development dyad, it is not clear why experimental music should have a place in this schema, in which artists enter into a social compact with communities and civic supporters to enrich them not only culturally but also economically. It's not difficult to see where this transaction is headed: back to the bottom line, and back to the same forces already discouraging artists in New York City from making their riskiest work. Markowitz's largesse toward Issue Project Room and the city's support of ABC No Rio are notable, and perhaps they mark a sea change in local arts funding.[7] However, if the social importance of the arts is framed mainly in terms of how effectively they spur economic development in their surrounding communities, then the most "experimental" arts will be unlikely to find favor in the eyes of arts foundations and civic boosters.[8]

If this is the direction of arts funding, then experimentalists who want to continue working in the city will have to look elsewhere for support. What about the academy, and the grant-giving institutions to which it is connected? The academy, whether private or public, offers a semiprotected space for intellectual production, a kind of buffer zone in which to conduct research without an immediate concern for how the results will fare either politically or on the open market. Academic music departments were once devoted wholly to European concert music, but changes have been underfoot for some decades—not surprisingly, mostly in the arena of ethnomusicology and U.S. music studies, and less so in composition and music theory. Nevertheless, although composer-improvisers in tenure-track, academic, or combined academic-performance positions are still a rarity, there are more now than ever in the past, including recently hired faculty.[9] Likewise, prestigious fellowships and prizes such as the American Academy's Rome Prize in composition, the Guggenheim fellowship, and the Pulitzer Prize, which were once directed solely toward through-composition in the European tradition, have all gone to composer-improvisers in recent years.[10] Even Jazz at Lincoln Center, once a staunch guardian of pre-1960s jazz, has recently presented concerts by Cecil Taylor, Ornette Coleman, Muhal Richard Abrams, and John Zorn's acoustic Masada, and will present in the summer of 2010 a Jazz for Young People Family Concert titled "What Is Free Jazz?" With such precedents in place, now seems to be a fruitful time to advocate for more faculty hires, and new courses, concerts, and ensembles.

The issue of subsidy thus raises concerns that are relevant not only for artists, but for those of us in academic positions who seek to write jazz-based composition and improvisation into the curriculum, while challenging the purview of "experimental music," as it has been conventionally conceived of in academic music studies. This essay is in part a call for a cross-disciplinary conversation—among artists, academics, arts advocates, and those inside and outside the concert music sphere—about the complexities, contradictions, and twists of logic and faith that surround such issues, making it difficult to engage them in practical terms without running up against historically and culturally charged differences of opinion that can seem irreconcilable.

Advocacy and Theory

Without a compelling argument to the contrary, it seems less likely than ever that cities will support music that appeals to a smallish though passionate audience of connoisseurs (unless, of course, the connoisseurs are extremely wealthy). For the most part, such an argument is absent from Ribot's essay, which takes a low-key tack in asserting why some music, by virtue of its ground-breaking nature, is particularly worthy of subsidy. Arts advocates have sometimes framed boundary-pushing as representing the voice of the individual in defiance of totalitarian political and discursive regimes, or as modeling progressive changes in the social or political order. Ribot simply contends that art's populist appeal, and its corresponding ability to generate sales, does not correlate with its quality, and that if a community values good art it should create patronage systems to free artists to make better—and correspondingly more groundbreaking—work. He asserts that in New York City, artists at this particular "musical margin" generate ideas that are taken up by the rest of the music world, which would suffer artistically if there were not a nearby creative margin from which to draw, and he makes a personal case: "That enough Europeans have chosen to value [music's] social benefit, to codify these values into law and fund the laws into being is why about half the music I care about exists." Otherwise, his defense rests more on the generally beleaguered state of risky art than on its artistic or cultural importance.

Given the history of polemics surrounding the musical avant-garde, this straightforward appeal to art is refreshing. But is it sufficient? In a critical sense—as artists throughout jazz's history, and prominently in the AACM, have made a point of addressing—such an appeal to art seems underdeveloped, as received notions about "art" are laden with assumptions that have historically proved problematic for composer-improvisers working outside the sphere of European concert music. Likewise, on a pragmatic level, considering the muscle with which most arts-advocacy organizations rally their rhetorical forces (the primary example in New York City being Jazz at Lincoln Center), it seems likely that advocating for this particular kind of music-at-the-margins will entail a more focused argument.

At the present historical juncture, then, when defending the "music we care about" seems both timely and pressing, on what grounds should the battle be fought? The answer is not self-evident to those of us who aspire

to a pluralistic musical bent, who cultivate an ethnomusicologically informed respect for differences among systems of musical meaning, and
who are aware of the way an art form's "importance" is shaped as strongly
by social function, class origins, and birthright as by merit. Artists whose
creative praxis is fundamentally pluralistic, and whose work depends on
the kind of cross-talk discussed above, tend to be wary of arguing for one
kind of music, or one group of musicians, at the expense of another. They
are well aware that "art" has an Orwellian quality: it may be touted as universal, but some kinds are more universal than others. They also tend to
admire and value vernacular and popular musics—and do not argue, as
modernist composers did, that folk genres become art only when transformed through European compositional techniques. They can also bear
witness to the way jazz was once denigrated, and is still often undervalued, by the bearers of high culture.

  With attention to this dilemma, the current research initiative at the
University of Guelph, "Improvisation, Community, and Social Practice,"
offers myriad avenues from which to engage contemporary composition
and improvisation, envisioning it as site for community-building, concep-
tualizing it a model for intercultural social interactions, and projecting
it as a catalyst for social change. It is interesting to note that the initiative is based on a notion of improvisation as a practice to be cultivated
for the social good, rather than on an argument for its artistic value. In
the context of including composition and improvisation in our collective
conversation about the place of the arts in the public sphere, it is crucial
to consider music's capacity to engage the social, cultural, and political.
Such an approach is also key to developing an ethnomusicological understanding of composition and improvisation, its sociomusical functions, its
"native categories," and its systems of value and meaning. I wonder, however, whether such a full-bore focus on process and community-building
falls short of fully advocating for the music and musicians.

  I would suggest that in order to fully bring composition and improvisation into a scholarly purview—to give it our full attention and scholars,
and to ensure its place in our academic departments—we will have to argue
for it on a formal level, and in so doing engage traditional notions of artistic importance and quality, or, if we reject them, develop new ones. In developing culturally and theoretically nuanced discourse about the music's
formal properties, it will be necessary to draw on jazz and popular-music
studies, ethnomusicology, music theory, studies of musical modernism,

critical theory, and cultural studies. Of course, there is no such thing as a purely formal analysis; all rely on meanings that are culturally determined. However, like the ever-shifting nature of "culture" itself, those meanings are not fixed, and one of the main functions of academic music scholarship is to investigate, and sometimes intervene into, received meanings. To do so we will have to confront certain problems. Given the cultural and discursive boundary-crossing of contemporary composition and improvisation, it will be tricky to judiciously engage the conflicting ideas about art — for want of a better word — that it borrows from its constituent influences, including straight-ahead jazz, European modernist concert music, punk rock, "free" improvisation, and African diasporic genres such as blues and funk. Moreover, formal analyses of improvisational music are always problematic, both because any analysis will engage with an artifact of the event rather than the event itself, and also because the historical record is not impartial, favoring artists who have had access to more recording opportunities and better technology. Finally, in tandem with taking expansive views of contemporary improvisation as a positive model of cross-cultural exchange, we will have to come to terms with our own personal, collective, and inevitably culturally biased judgments about the intrinsic, musical, and artistic value of "the music itself." We are already making such judgments, of course, when we favor certain artists or pieces of music in the listening assignments in our courses, our research, and our personal music collections.

In the process, we will confront the question of whether to retain, expand, or discard received ideas about "experimental music," as such ideas occur both in the scholarly literature and outside the academy. (In New York City, both Roulette and Issue Project Room describe themselves as experimental-music venues, while the music listings in *Time Out New York* include a category called "Jazz and Experimental.") As George Lewis contends, in the 1940s, bebop was written out of the discursive category of "experimentalism" (and denied access to its constituent real and cultural capital as a result), even as artists incorporated improvisational or so-called aleatoric elements into their work. As an unprecedented creative formation developed by brilliant thinkers, bebop serves a good test case to uncover some of "experimental music's" hidden scripts. However, for the same reason, bebop does not put quite as much pressure on the category — and thus on its policing along lines of race, aesthetics, background, access to resources, educational networks, and class — than would another genre.

Assuming that, whatever the other parameters, originality of expression and the pushing of boundaries are folded into our notions of experimentalism, we can consider postwar experimental composition in relation to other genres besides bebop. For example, one of the creative concerns of the experimental composer was to explore sounds that fell outside the traditional purview of the European concert sphere. Many were interested in non-Western instruments, alternate tuning systems, and electronics. We should consider, then, the classed and raced barrier between experimentalism and the palette of electric guitar and harmonica timbres, bent pitches, and overdriven amplifiers that characterized the electric blues music developing in Chicago around the same time as bebop. Experimentalists were concerned with nontraditional instrumental techniques and, sometimes, antivirtuosity. We should consider experimentalists' interest, or lack thereof, in the eccentric phrasing and articulations of early rock's electric guitarists. Following the model of the AACM but tending toward different influences, one of the main projects among artists on New York's downtown scene was to make work that ignored any such categorical distinctions. Coming to terms, on a formal level, with the work of both (overlapping) creative communities will involve teasing out the classed and raced values that led to such lacunae in the first place.

As the musicologist Benjamin Piekut has argued, received notions of experimentalism do not stand up to close scrutiny; rather, they rest on an assumption that "experimentalism" exists, and consist of an edifice of values, aesthetics, and privileged meanings constructed around this assumed entity. Piekut contends that academic music studies has conceptualized "experimentalism" by drawing connections among artists and works related through content, process, or proximity—and thereby positing a putative lineage of boundary-breaking thinkers who fall under the purview of the European compositional tradition. As Piekut notes, "A racial taxonomy of US music . . . associated black music with commodification and entertainment, the discursive opposites of 'serious' high culture" (186). In reference to the examples above of Chicago blues and early rock, I would add that this edifice of experimentalism is predicated on a triangulated relationship among itself, the Euroamerican avant-garde, and commodity culture.

Experimentalist composers of concert music working in the 1940s and 1950s treated popular music tropes—for example, singable melodies and danceable grooves—as anathema to their music. Indeed, the music deemed experimental was construed as being diametrically opposed to popular music and the commercial music culture in which it participated. Experimentalists also developed a narrative about their work that signaled its resistance to the imperatives of the concert-music avant-garde. Although this is a simplification that flattens out a great deal of historical nuance, I believe it is a useful one. Thus, some composers' privileged (though hard-won) position as experimentalists stemmed not only from their ties to a European concert music network, but also from a shared belief that their own musical vanguard *was* a vanguard, in that it functioned as a site of resistance to art's twin anathemas, mandarin high-culture and popular culture of the lowest common denominator, the latter antipathy having been inherited from artists, theorists, and critics who positioned the avant-garde as a site of resistance to mass culture.[11] This is of course part of a much larger discussion. I would suggest that despite the musical and cultural changes of the intervening decades, experimentalism can still be usefully formulated today as a realm (made of music) that discursively contests received traditions (plural) by using musical language in unprecedented, extreme, confounding, unconventional, or illegitimate ways; and as a realm that discursively contests the demands of the mass market. Today, such a contestation derives not from operating at a remove from the "presence and pleasure" of rhythmic grooves, catchy melodic hooks, or the predictable forms of popular song, but by engaging *any* musical material that tends toward a truly sui generis, expressive end.

By virtue of valuing music that has these functions, arguing for its merits, or calling it experimentalist, we participate in certain historically vexed and culturally biased notions about art. We should take the opportunity to thoughtfully consider the music's current and historical relationship to such notions, as well as our own investment in them. Jazz-based composition and improvisation has been charged by its progenitors with simultaneously participating in and contesting the traditions it engages. To engage with it formally, we will have to do the same. Ideally, and in conjunction with artists and advocates working outside the academy, our engagement with the music will add momentum to a paradigm shift already under way, as the academy and its related institutions reconceptualize the notion of vanguard musical creativity and prioritize their resources accordingly.

Notes

1. Marc Ribot, "The Care and Feeding of a Musical Margin." All Web sites cited here were accessed May 6, 2010.

2. Composer-improvisers who are more process-oriented tend "to valorize change, risk, surprise and the development or discovery of fresh varieties of expression and beauty," and rather than being primarily concerned with the "preservation, proper interpretation, and accurate transmission of [past historical] practice," they engage jazz with other U.S. and global idioms, in order to expound upon "jazz's global presence and character" (Harris 120–22).

3. New York State Council for the Arts Web site, http://www.nysca.org. This amount included about $10,000 annually for the AACM; $10,000 for Art for Arts; grants ranging from $22,000 to $109,000 to the Jazz Mobile; $11,000 to $33,000 for Roulette; $49,000 to $162,000 to HarvestWorks; $52,000 to $116,000 for the American Music Center; and about $200,000 to $250,000 each for the Philharmonic Society, New York City Opera, and the Metropolitan Opera.

4. The Lost Jazz Shrines series, which began in 2002, is presented by the Borough of Manhattan Community College's TriBeCa Performing Arts Center.

5. Nor would anyone wish to return to the poverty and neglect that coincided with it. As described by journalist C. Carr of the *Village Voice*, on the Lower East Side blocks of "eyeless and broken buildings," burned out by arson, ominously lined the stinking streets of "a neighborhood built from garbage" ("Money Changes Everything").

6. Fiol died a few months later, in October 2009. See Ben Sisario, "An Avant-Garde Arts Group Bites Off a Lot to Chew." See also http://issueprojectroom .org/. In June 2009, ABC No Rio (a long-standing visual art-punk rock-activist cultural center on Manhattan's Lower East Side) also won $1,650,000 in city funding for the construction of a new facility on its original site. See Kevin Erickson, "Reclaiming New York for Local Arts," and Colin Moynihan, "Punk Institution Receives City Money for New Building."

7. For a consideration of subsidies directed toward free jazz in the 1970s, see Iain Anderson, *This Is Our Music*.

8. For a critique of social arguments that advocates have historically deployed in favor of jazz and improvisational music, see Alan Stanbridge, "From the Margins to the Mainstream."

9. These institutions include Amherst College, Brooklyn College, Columbia University, Mills College, UC-Riverside, UC-San Diego.

10. In recent years, Guggenheims have gone to such composer-improvisers as Geri Allen, Marilyn Crispell, Jane Ira Bloom, and Wadada Leo Smith. Don Byron was the recipient of the Samuel Barber Rome Prize in 2010. After revising its prospectus in 2004, the Pulitzer board awarded its Music Prize to Ornette Coleman in 2007, who had received a Guggenheim fellowship in 1967.

11. From this vantage point, bebop could be received as innovative, but not as participating in the collective project of "experimental music": bebop violated experimentalism's tenets by partaking of traits associated with the commercial—i.e., a pleasurable groove and repetitive song forms based on Tin Pan Alley models. This broadly brushed notion of commercial music could not accommodate the nuances that differentiated rhythmic grooves, individual styles, and genres, and it had no need to incorporate an understanding of (and was perhaps invested in disowning) the role played by African American expressive culture in transforming the "commercial" musical landscape. By drawing a line between their work and bebop, then, experimentalists were perpetuating an inherited discursive regime that uncritically conflated all song- and dance-based, commercially distributed music, and as such had racialized experimental music since the inception of the genre.

John Brackett

CHAPTER 8

SUBSIDIZING THE EXPERIMENTAL MUSE

Rereading Ribot

Clubs, bars, and performance spaces devoted to music close all the time. As any musician will tell you, much of the anxiety that accompanies touring has to do with not knowing if the club or bar that booked you three or four months ago is still in business. This—along with broken-down vans, living on fast food, and searching high and low for laundromats—is one of the many perils of touring. However, when one particular club on New York's Lower East side closed, a group of musicians and artists decided that they had had enough. For many musicians and activists, the closing of Tonic, in April of 2007, became symbolic of New York City's indifference to "experimental music" and the cultural legacies surrounding experimental artistic practices throughout the city's history (such as free jazz, the avantgarde, minimalism, "indie," and so forth). At the same time, the closing of Tonic led many artists to reexamine their own ("marginalized") place within the market, both global and local.

Questions and concerns relating to the place, function, and marketability of marginalized and experimental artistic practices lie behind the calls for a subsidized performance space on New York's Lower East side, calls made by Marc Ribot, Rebecca Moore, and other artist-activists. For Ribot, the closing of Tonic is not just another instance of the continual ebb and flow of a club in a precarious marketplace; it is also a more ominous signal of the "failure of the market as a means of sustaining new and experimental music" ("Crisis in Indie/New Music Clubs"). Ribot goes even further in arguing that experimental musicians' relying on the market as a means of financial support for "new music was always illusory." He describes how many musicians supplemented their small income from live performances by teaching, commissions, and, in the case of Cecil Taylor, washing dishes.

Faced with the realization of the market's indifference toward experimental and marginal musical practices, Ribot urges musicians and artists to fight for a publicly funded performance space in the Lower East Side. Shifting his gaze to Europe, Ribot notes how "cities around the world have given venues free of charge to organizations presenting new/experimental [music] in Amsterdam, Ljubljana, Bern, Zurich, Berlin, Rome, and dozens of other European cities. Why not NYC?" ("Days of Bread and Roses").

Given the rich historical and cultural legacy of experimental artistic practices in New York, so Ribot argues, why is it not possible to create a subsidized space on the Lower East Side? Ribot's arguments are compelling and deserve to be taken seriously; however, certain assumptions in Ribot's article require critical examination. Ribot's appeal for government-subsidized performance spaces dedicated to innovative musical practices raises a host of issues and questions that divert attention away from the fact that a number of musicians (including Ribot) have not taken full advantage of certain aspects of the market. Musicians may wish to pursue, as a way of generating income, strategies that exploit certain facets of the niche market that already exists for experimental music.

A Percentage of the Door, or, "Please Sir, May I Have Some More?"

A primary component of Ribot's argument is that a musician can earn much more by performing in a subsidized space than by performing a club date. Is this true? What data exists to back up this claim? First a bit of Club Proprietorship 101.

Unless they are fortunate enough to own a particular property on New York's trendy Lower East Side, most club owners have to pay rent to someone (directly to a landlord or indirectly to a property management company). Furthermore, expenses associated with running a club are typically very high. In addition to paying utilities such as electricity and water, many clubs pay distributors for food and beverages, linen services, advertising, repairs, and trash collection. All of these expenses add up, and, in such an expensive part of the country as New York City (particularly the borough of Manhattan), these expenses can be astronomical. So where

168 SUBSIDIZING THE EXPERIMENTAL MUSE

does this money come from? If they are lucky, the club owners are independently wealthy and can support a large percentage of the club's operating expenses through their own means. If this is not the case, revenue is
raised through a percentage of the sale of drinks, food, and merchandise,
along with ticket sales. So after the rent, utilities, and vendors are all paid
(not to mention the club owner, booking agents, and others) who gets paid
next? Well, the performers, of course, who are given a percentage of the
money received at the door. Given this scenario, one can easily understand
why touring musicians often complain about remuneration for club gigs
and why Ribot and others advocate so strongly for an alternative, namely
a subsidized performance space.

In contrast to typical practices regarding payment for club performances, forms of reimbursement for musicians performing in subsidized
spaces can vary. It is outside the scope of this essay to detail the many
ways performers can be paid when playing in subsidized spaces, so, to
give some idea as to how these gigs can differ from club dates, I will consider only one space, namely the Issue Project Room. Currently located on
3rd Street and 3rd Avenue, in the Gowanus section of Brooklyn, the Issue
Project Room is the product of the hard work and dedication of a number
of artists living in New York who have fought for a subsidized space in New
York City devoted to experimental artistic practices, most notably the late
photographer Suzanne Fiol. The Issue Project Room originally began life
on East 6th Street in the East Village, before rising rents drove the room
to Brooklyn, where it was forced to make yet another move before settling
in its present location. In 2008, the room was assured some financial (and
geographic) stability by receiving a twenty-year rent-free lease for a 5,000
square-foot space on 110 Livingston Street, in Brooklyn. Furthermore, the
room has since received $1.1 million from Marty Markowitz, the borough
president of Brooklyn, from capital funds that will go toward required
renovations for the space on Livingston Street (renovations totaling about
$2.5 million) (Sisario C2). The Issue Project Room planned to relocate to
the Livingston location sometime in 2011 and will have a capacity of about
250 people, one and a half times larger than its present location. According to the Issue website, they are now located at 22 Boerum Place in downtown Brooklyn.

According to Michelle Amador, the business and development director
at Issue Project Room, performers at the Room are reimbursed much as
they would be if they were to perform at a club.[1] Presently, performers re-

ceive 70 percent of the ticket sales, with the possibility for more money coming from grants. In an attempt to draw as many people as possible to the space, the Issue Project Room charges $15 for tickets purchased at the door and $12 for tickets purchased online. Higher ticket prices may occur for benefit concerts or if artists are traveling great distances to perform in Brooklyn. Ms. Amador explained to me, however, "It is a top priority for [the Issue Project Room] to shift from our 'club model' of providing a percentage of door fees, to providing artists with guaranteed fees." Of course, how high or low these guaranteed fees are depends upon the artist's ability to secure such grants and, if a grant comes through, how much it will be.

If such a "guaranteed fee" model does occur for the Issue Project Room, then it does appear that Ribot's claims regarding the potential of higher pay for performers in subsidized performance spaces than in club gigs can be true. However, a reliance on grants or donations is a precarious way to live, especially given the present economic situation in the United States. Grant money dwindles and grant sources dry up, just as people and organizations have less cash to donate to such worthwhile causes as the Issue Project Room. In the meantime, the club model reigns, and if performers are still relying on a percentage of ticket sales to make money (in both subsidized spaces and clubs) then tickets must still be sold. This means that—other factors being equal—even "marginal" musicians (that is, the creative experimental musicians Ribot is writing about) must possess some degree of marketability that will draw a ticket-buying audience to a particular performance. Even within the niche market that exists for creative and experimental music, certain well-established performers will attract larger audiences than artists who are less well known or are up and coming. Therefore, while the potential for greater earnings may exist for performers in subsidized spaces, it helps if a performer already has a significant audience. This fact would probably hold true, I believe, even for "marquee players" of marginalized music performing in clubs.

Lastly, it must be pointed out that audiences for experimental music exist all across the United States, and not just in New York City. As someone who has spent thousands of dollars flying from various parts of the country to see performances at clubs on the Lower East Side, I am disheartened to read that Ribot laments having to travel for half an hour on the subway to get to Williamsburg, Brooklyn, for a gig (or *even further* to Staten Island or New Jersey) ("Days of Bread and Roses"). If performing live is as important as Ribot claims it is for the group of musicians he is representing, then it would seem that reaching those audiences—no matter how small—is a sacrifice these musicians should be willing to make. With the exorbitant rents now common on the Lower East Side, the days of waking up, walking out of your apartment, rounding the corner, and arriving at the club are long gone. Therefore, perhaps experimental musicians should consider organizing short tours of various clubs across the country. Even for those musicians nervous about leaving the eastern time zone, a number of clubs catering to experimental music exist in Pennsylvania, Washington, D.C., Virginia, North Carolina, and many other states along the East Coast. Along the way, these musicians might potentially build their fan base, and this will in turn lead to an increase in their future earnings through ticket sales in performance venues in and around New York City and elsewhere.

Exploiting the Margins of the Market

There is no doubt that performing live has traditionally been the primary method by which performers, "marginal" or mainstream, earn a living. However, because Ribot appears to equate "the market" with performing live, he ignores a number of other market opportunities available to musicians and performers.

As Ribot notes in his most recent essay on the topic included in this collection, "Days of Bread and Roses," a number of performance spaces hospitable to creative music have opened in Manhattan and Brooklyn, clubs such as Le Poisson Rouge, Joe's Pub, and the aforementioned Issue Project Room. Viewed as evidence of the continual "ebb and flow" of clubs described earlier, the existence of these is a good thing for experimental musicians. At the same time, however, these same musicians should not be overly optimistic about the longevity of any (or all) of these clubs. Therefore, current musicians and performers might consider how they can get the most out of their present live commitments.

One way to get the most out of live performances would be to make recordings of these performances and sell them at shows or over the Internet. In recent years, prices for recording equipment have dropped significantly. For only a few hundred dollars, a musician can purchase a compact mixing board that is compatible with a laptop computer. At the same time, recording software has also become readily available, and, depending upon intentions and budget, a musician can record, mix, and master a high-quality recording of last night's performance in the privacy of her own living room. A musician can decide to burn these recordings to disc and sell them at shows or through a website to fans and interested listeners all over the world. An even cheaper alternative would be to make these recordings available as digital downloads through the artist's site. Fans have been lugging recording equipment to shows for decades, as a way of capturing and reliving a particular performance. While the sale of such "bootleg" recordings still occurs, most fans use the Internet to trade and download these recordings with no money trading hands, no shipping or postage charges, and no cracked CDs or broken tapes arriving in the mail. Uploading a recording to the Internet is an excellent way for a fan of experimental music living in Boise, Idaho, to hear Ikue Mori's performance at the Issue Project Room from the night before.

Presently, many fans download shows through sites such as dimeadozen .org or thetradersden.org—sites that function as "trackers" that direct fans to content shared on computers from all over the world—or through the sites or blogs of the tapers themselves. On the tracking sites just mentioned, a number of artists and bands have requested that their performances and music not be traded. On one of these tracking sites, dimeadozen.org, performances by Ribot are expressly prohibited from trading and download-ing, a decision that comes directly from the artist.[2] Tapers will always tape and these tapes will somehow become available to a larger audience. Real-izing this, why not tape the shows yourself? The musicians themselves may wish to cut out the tapers altogether by taping their own shows and selling them as digital downloads on their sites. For a small fee, fans from around the world can download last night's performance, a performance that may have resulted in modest returns from the door but may poten-tially generate some sort of revenue for some time to come. It has been my experience that fans are much more willing to buy directly from an artist. Not only does the fan imagine that a sort of relationship with the artist has been created, but I have found that fans are eager and willing to support artists directly, especially marginalized experimental musicians who have limited access to the large amounts of capital generally available from large recording contracts and record sales or—and this is Ribot's point— touring and live performances. In addition to live audio recordings, some artists may consider distributing video recordings, demo recordings, or outtakes from commercially available recordings. Artists may also supple-ment such audio and video recordings with short, personal notes on or photos from a recent performance. Materials such as these can serve as a way of connecting an artist to fans who lack the time or resources to travel across the country or around the globe (or all the way from Staten Island) to see a show on the Lower East Side.

Another possible source of income available to experimental musicians is the sale of scores or charts. Many of the musicians described or mentioned by Ribot in his essays also compose their own music. By selling sheet music or charts that musicians around the world can then perform, an artist not only opens up a new source of revenue but also raises his or her visibility to a larger musical and artistic community. Performances of works by an experimental musician can lead to guest performances, residencies, master classes, and a host of other performing or teaching opportunities that may potentially lead to other forms of income. At the same time, the "status" of an upcoming or relatively unknown musician is enhanced by such performances or appearances. For example, an increased familiarity with a composer-performer's music may lead to an increased fan base, which can lead to more (local) performance opportunities where she can perform in larger venues and possibly command higher ticket prices. Such a scenario, of course, brings us back to the idea of the niche-market value of marginalized musicians described earlier. That is, the "unknown" experimental musician has graduated to marquee status with many more performance opportunities and much more income potential.

Although I have been critical of many aspects of Ribot's arguments regarding the perceived failure of the market to support and sustain experimental music and his call for publicly subsidized performance spaces, I can relate to the feelings of frustration and disappointment voiced by many artists who call the Lower East Side their home. However, just as the club industry has experienced an ebb and flow, the Lower East Side has gone through many deaths and rebirths. Indeed, while the Lower East Side is justly famous for the many experimental artists who lived there and the many artistic movements that blossomed there, it is just as famous for the many transformations it has undergone over the years. The specter of gentrification has haunted the Lower East Side for a long time, so long, in fact, that the current situation should not be surprising to anyone who lives there and who has some sense of the area's history. In its most recent transformation, the image of the Lower East side as a dark and dangerous (yet entirely thrilling) section of Manhattan was alluring for many fans of experimental, avant-garde artistic practices. However, it was only a matter of time before real estate companies and investors began to capitalize on the subcultural capital associated with this particular region by transforming what was once an area known for its "bohemianism" into one designed to attract and appeal to "bourgeois bohemians," the "Bobos," as they are described by David Brooks. Furthermore, this trend shows no sign of abatement, as evidenced in figure 8.1, a page from *Brokers Weekly*, April 9, 2008, a weekly residential real estate publication in New York City. Almost a year to the day after Tonic closed, the realtor Adrienne Albert quotes the time-honored real estate maxim: "People go where the artists are" (even despite the "blip" in the nation's economy).

Ribot is right: a subsidized performance space on the Lower East Side would be a welcome addition for many musicians, artists, and fans of experimental music. However, Ribot's claim that the market has somehow failed experimental musicians is, in my opinion, an overstatement. There is more to the market than revenue from performances. There are a number of market opportunities available to experimental musicians, many more than those I have described. At the same time, even if a subsidized

---

18 ■ Wednesday, April 9, 2008   Brokers Weekly

Calling all the shots
Adrienne Albert talks about her latest strategy

By Maggie Hawrylux

While most of the country was buzzing about the Giants ending the Patriots' winning streak at the Superbowl, Adrienne Albert had a more pressing matter to contemplate — how the commercials reflect the residential market.

Albert, a self proclaimed "cross-pollinator of ideas," saw a major change in the pricey ads this year, noting they weren't as extravagant and highly produced as in years past.

For Albert, the founder and national director of the Marketing Directors, this observation confirmed that buyers are going to be tightening up their wallets and buying into residences that center on value rather than the glitz-focused techniques of the past.

"Since late spring, when people began to pull in their horns, buyers became less interested in techniques, and were looking for good value," she said. "The appropriate mechanisms that worked at that time may not be appropriate today."

Residential marketing is a chameleon of an industry, not only having to roll with the punches, but also having to predict the future. "You have to look ahead and try to put into place where the economy will be following trending. How will [buyers] want to live?"

Albert, a 27-year veteran in the business, said that in as little as three years, effective marketing techniques have

changed drastically. Right before the value-conscious techniques of today, marketers were placing properties as glamour pieces — concentrating on the lifestyle and status it could afford the buyer. Before the glam period, Albert said guerrilla marketing was all the rage with building advertisements being pl

We have a very limited inventory now, that's a huge difference."

She added that the current market and the city are overall much healthier than they were 20 years ago — and the strength of foreign currency is only help

> One neighborhood that she sees soaring once the market gets over the "blip" is Alphabet City in the East Village. "People go where the artists are. As the marketplace strengthens again, this neighborhood will grow. The ABCs have everything, transportation, restaurants, shops, and it's really cool.

19...

We're the only ones that survived that recession by just selling one at a time with no auctions or gimmicks."

For this reason, Albert is one of the most qualified to predict what is to come in the market as some analysts warn a recession is looming. "It's different now. In the '80s, supply was out of propor-

taking long... ous ding ... ces. ab- at deal of mic ill

he throes ow time." ll ces. firm represents Setai, a Zamir ... up collaboration; operties; and Liberty

...pment, according to size of Greenwich Village rsey's Gold Coast, is up-have our ups and downs, but k, is mostly up; it flattens and then will go up."

One neighborhood that she sees soaring once the market gets over the

"blip" is Alphabet City in the East Village. "People go where the artists are. As the marketplace strengthens again, this neighborhood will grow. The ABCs have everything, transportation, restaurants, shops, and it's really cool."

But at the end of the day, regardless of marketing techniques, economic conditions or neighborhood, a quality building with a cohesive and educated team behind it will sell.

"The bottom line is getting units sold. In order to get money, you have to give something," Albert said. "It's not all smoke and mirrors."

space did become available, there is no guarantee that any and all self-proclaimed experimental, marginal musicians will benefit equally. Instead of organizing around the rallying cry of the "failure of the market," experimental musicians on the Lower East Side should do what they do best: find ways to exploit the margins. For many years, artists active on the Lower East side have been able to transform and develop a variety of artistic conventions to suit their own particular aesthetic goals. Can't this also be true of how these artists react (and relate) to the current market situation? I am confident that the many resourceful, intelligent artists described by Ribot can find ways to make the market work for them, In turn helping to sustain and maintain the artistic legacy of the Lower East Side. At the same time, the DIY approach I hope to see (although characterized by Ribot as something like a naive impossibility) could go some way in ensuring the sustained longevity of the Lower East Side as a vital center of artistic and entrepreneurial activity. And this is important, because the Lower East Side, as even the realtor Adrienne Albert knows, is "really cool."

Notes

1. The information that follows comes from private e-mail communications with Michelle Amador, from November 18, 2009.

2. Presumably this applies only to Ribot's solo projects or projects led by Ribot. It does not appear to include recordings on which Ribot appears as a sideman (as he does in performances led by Tom Waits, Marianne Faithfull, John Zorn, and many others).

Scott Thomson

CHAPTER 9

ONE MUSICIAN WRITES
ABOUT CREATIVE-MUSIC VENUES
IN TORONTO

In the summer of 2007, I was asked to join a roundtable at the Guelph Jazz Festival, along with Marc Ribot, Tamar Barzel, and John Brackett, to offer some observations about creative music venues in Toronto, and to relate them somehow to the issues raised in Mr. Ribot's article, "Crisis in Indie/ New Music Clubs." Having almost no first-hand experience with the scenes of creative music in New York City, I was (and I am still) ill-equipped to offer any tangible comparison with the situation there. However, as an active musician and organizer in Toronto, I am able to detect some general priorities about creative music venues in Mr. Ribot's article that diverge from my own and, at a guess, from those of many of my colleagues in Toronto. Most of these differences are pragmatic in nature and reflect the histories of the two cities as centers for unconventional music, the discrepant size of the markets for such music, and the public-arts funding structures that exist in Canada and America. The nature of these differences, however, points to more fundamental philosophical differences between the musical culture that Mr. Ribot describes and the one in which I work, which let rise to the surface some basic questions about the role of creative, unconventional, noncommercial music in our society.

Central to Mr. Ribot's thesis is his recognition that market funding is no longer a feasible way to maintain creative music venues in New York. This assertion, far from feeling, as he states in his original article, "shocking and strange," has simply always been the case in Toronto and virtually every other city I have visited. Despite a bee hive of creative-music activity, several record labels, and literally hundreds of (mostly young) composer-performers in Toronto, the idea of a dedicated, commercially motivated venue for creative music never even comes up in discussion, so far-fetched is the notion. In keen recognition of the recent closure of two conventional jazz clubs, the Montreal Bistro and the Top o' the Senator, musicians are aware of the challenges that any live-music venue faces these days, let alone purveyors of such noncommercial music as the stuff we are talking about in this discussion.

So, then, if not the market, who or what will fund our creative endeavors? When traveling in America or in Europe, I have occasionally met artists who assume that all Canadian artists and cultural institutions are funded beautifully by our arts councils. This assumption may be a vestige of a bygone era. For example, during the 1970s, a group of improvising musicians from Toronto (many with connections to the visual arts) banded together to form the Music Gallery, a venue dedicated to new and improvised music that has been steadily funded by arts councils from different levels of government. The Music Gallery exists to this day but, over the years, changes in curatorial direction have meant that, these days, Toronto-based improvising musicians rarely or never perform there. These curatorial changes have coincided uneasily with troubling changes in policy at the various arts councils toward "business model" arts funding in which arts organizations need to prove that they can be sustainable in a marketplace that is subsidized but competitive—bums-in-seats logic wins the day again. And, as Mr. Ribot demonstrates persuasively in his original article, this logic leaves creative musicians out in the cold. Often, in Canada, creative musicians are the exception to the "cultural exception."[1] So this was the musical culture that I entered as a musician in my twenties. There was really no infrastructure for creative music in Toronto. There were virtually no promoters, no festivals, and no venues. However, I discovered that other musicians about my age were working steadily to find back rooms of clubs, loft spaces, bars, wherever they could to put shows and series on.[2] These series would come and go, usually on the whims of fickle bar owners with no sympathy for the musicians who grew dissatisfied by paltry attendance and bar-takes. However, once I was acquainted with the musicians who were programming and playing these events, it was clear that there was plenty of energy and excellent music that was constituting a very healthy, if underrecognized and underpaid, scene.

In 2004, in response to the inconsistent infrastructure for creative music in Toronto, a group of us formed the Association for Improvising Musicians

Toronto (AIM Toronto), a not-for-profit musicians' collective that supports and promotes creative music and musicians in the city.[3] Quite rightly, it has been pointed out that the incorporation of AIM Toronto responds directly to the business-model logic that is prized by the arts-funding bodies of government. As an incorporated organization, AIM Toronto is eligible for project grants and has used them for collaborations by its numerous member-musicians, with artists like Joe McPhee, William Parker, Evan Parker, Michael Moore, Anthony Braxton, and Eddie Prévost. These grants, however, are far too small to subsidize an entire creative-music scene. At best, they give a handful of deserving musicians a rare well-paying gig playing creative music.

More importantly than such administrative structures or "brand name" projects, however, members of AIM Toronto had been renting a loft space in Liberty Village, called the Arraymusic Studio, on a weekly or biweekly basis since 2003, for the Leftover Daylight Series.[4] Countless crucial musical meetings and ensemble premieres have taken place at Leftover Daylight over the years. While people complain about the Arraymusic Studio's unsavory location, musicians from Toronto have recognized its value as a home (some may say "refuge") for original, creative music by local composer-performers. This is despite the fact that gigs at Leftover Daylight almost never pay any money and, if they do, it is rarely enough to cover cab fare home. However, literally hundreds of international-caliber musicians play at Leftover Daylight because, for years, there were so few places for them to play their music in Toronto. These musicians have found and will continue to find their own justification for playing gigs in such venues.

While AIM Toronto, as an organization, strives to put itself in a favorable position to be eligible for long-term, stable government funding, the board is acutely aware that the shifting priorities of neoliberal governments make such a future uncertain at best.[5] In the meanwhile, however, a culture of creative music in Toronto is flourishing. By my estimation, more than one hundred musicians are performing regularly and at a very high level at different series like Leftover Daylight, as well as at the Tranzac Club—a hospitable bar in the Annex with a very liberal booking policy—that makes it possible to hear unconventional music virtually every night of the week in Toronto. None of these gigs pay very well, and virtually all of the musicians have day jobs or sustain themselves apart from their work as creative musicians. And yet, there is a level of creativity and commitment afoot in Toronto's music scene that is as strong as that anywhere I have visited. Apart from the more mundane issues like infrastructure and grant eligibility (and much more important, I might add), AIM Toronto is really the sympathetic residue of all of these activities that take place with very little outside support—commercial, governmental, or otherwise.

Mr. Ribot's original article posits the thesis that creative music, in one way or another, needs to be sustained by an infrastructure that will allow its practitioners to make a living through the creation and performance of music. The undertone of this thesis is that, without such an infrastructure, the music will no longer exist, or at least it will suffer irrevocably. It should go without saying that I applaud those who work toward the goal of having creative musicians make a decent living through performance, and I would be lying if I said that I have not considered this possibility for myself. However, I reiterate that such a goal is flatly unrealistic in a city like Toronto (or virtually anywhere other than, perhaps, New York), a fact that is readily recognized by my colleagues in Toronto, as well. Yet, the fact that the music scene in Toronto thrives without guaranteeing a performance-driven livelihood for its practitioners points to the many reasons other than financial ones that creative music continues to exist. By no means are these artists solely, as Mr. Ribot puts it, "the hunger artists, the already connected, and the independently wealthy."[6]

If making a living from performance were a decisive priority for creative musicians in Toronto, most would have already moved to New York, or indeed to continental Europe, where there is the remote potential for market or government support to sustain them. Some already have. Most others, however, have sought to live in Toronto, a decent city in a decent country, and to help forge a scene that, in its multifaceted existence, offers a bit of hope for continued creativity and unconventional thinking against the tide of the commercial music monoculture. As this scene has developed, ties have been established with artists from similar scenes elsewhere—especially in other Canadian cities like Montréal, Vancouver, and Halifax—which foster just a bit more of the same kind of hope. In my view, this is what creative musicians in Toronto are paying for, and yes, it is we who are really subsidizing the scene, primarily through material sacrifice that may be a necessary trade-off for the intangible but very real virtues that are embodied in strong feelings of community and mutual respect among creative people.

Afterword

The very week that I delivered a version of the essay above as part of the Guelph Jazz Festival roundtable (in September 2007), I presented my first concert at Somewhere There, my small performance studio in Toronto's Parkdale neighborhood, seating fifty, that is dedicated to the presentation of informal creative music.[7] At that time, pervasive threats from condominium developers threatened the Arraymusic Studio, and the Tranzac Club faced police scrutiny, due to a series of noise complaints. Both threats eventually passed, but, for a moment, it looked like the meager venue infrastructure that held the Toronto scene together might dissolve, a scenario that motivated me to implement this long-contemplated idea. In January 2010, Somewhere There was about to host its 650th performance, and activity in the space had increased to seven nights a week of live creative music.[8] It has hosted countless, world-class, local, national, and international creative-music composer-performers to play the music they want to play, and it has allowed audiences in Toronto the opportunity to listen to (and chat casually afterward with) them in a quiet, comfortable environment with an excellent acoustic. It's really a terrific little room.[9]

Practically without exception, the financial arrangement has been that, after a nominal rental fee (currently $30) is put toward the venue's operations, the musicians get all of the door revenue.[10] Nobody has made anything near a living wage for their work at the vast majority of the concerts at Somewhere There. The fact that audiences are small—eleven is the average attendance—is surely little surprise to the players and regular audience members at Somewhere There. Is this a situation of artists' exploiting each other, as Marc Ribot may put it? Nonsense. As I have already said, most artists will voluntarily play such gigs even when they know they will likely not make a living wage doing so. Each player will find her own reasons—primarily artistic ones, but also social, pedagogical, even spiritual—to justify her effective subsidization of Somewhere There through her work. As I see it, these reasons are valid—period—and need no apology in the face of economic scrutiny. I will not speak on behalf of anyone else, but, as the venue's proprietor, I have had to subsidize the space more than anyone, covering small rent shortfalls with money from part-time teaching work. At the end of the day, I do so (resolutely, if not gladly) because I believe that a space like Somewhere There and the artists who work there make Toronto a better place to live. And I am confident that many others feel this way.

While the long-term sustainability of Somewhere There may always remain in question, I would argue that, by functioning outside any real business model beyond the maintenance of its small-scale, persistent operation, it stands a better chance at survival than larger, more ambitiously structured creative-music venues.[11] Do I think that municipal, provincial, and federal arts councils should be paying the rent and operating costs at Somewhere There? Most definitely. I have already started filling out the forms. However, it is absolutely vital, in my view, that Somewhere There not be dependent on such grants (or, for that matter, on audience growth or business-based private support) as larger-scale models inevitably will be. Allowing that dependence would be to let forces with no inherent sympathy for Somewhere There and the values it embodies to determine its fate. And this puts the thing I care about in needless jeopardy. It has been proven that, even without the grants, the place can still stay open and can present more than three hundred shows of creative music a year. If, as Alan Stanbridge states in his essay in this volume, these priorities demonstrate how I have been "bucking the system in a manner that simply ignores the dictates of current cultural-policy imperatives," then I have been doing so because, at this moment, I think it serves the music and musicians best to do it this way.[12]

At this point, I will defer and direct attention to Dr. Stanbridge's essay, which follows in this volume. In it, he responds provocatively to the Guelph roundtable (which he attended) and considers my work at Somewhere There in contrast not only to Mr. Ribot's rather specific New York-centered concerns but also to more general and mainstream arts infrastructure debates in Toronto. He is one of very few academic researchers to take an active and sustained interest in the deliberately small-scale scene afoot at Somewhere There, and I appreciate how, in its principal service to the music and musicians in question, his work shares a clear affinity with my own.

Notes

1. See Alan Stanbridge's chapter in this book for an idea of how creative music and musicians have fared during Toronto's so-called cultural renaissance in recent years.

2. Prime examples from the last decade include the Idler Pub Series (curated by Ronda Rindone); the Ulterior Music Series, most recently at the Victory Café (curated by Mike Gennaro and others); As Is, at the Oasis Bar (curated by Gordon Allen and Joe Sorbara); the Red Guitar (curated by Tim Posgate); the Rat-drifting Series at the Arraymusic Studio; the NOW Series, at the NOW Lounge (curated variously by Paul Newman, Ken Aldcroft, John Wilson, and Michelangelo Iaffaldano); the Panic Density Series, at the Tequila Bookworm (curated by Steve Ward); the Bitchin' Series, at the Gladstone Art Bar (curated by Dougal Bichan); and other, short-lived series at bars like the 360 Club and Graffiti's (both curated by Ken Aldcroft).

3. Along with Ken Aldcroft, Rob Clutton, Nick Fraser, and Joe Sorbara, I was a founding board member of AIMToronto. With the exception of Mr. Sorbara, the entire board has turned over and, as of October 2009, it includes Parmela Attariwala, Nilan Perera, Rob Piilonen, and Nicole Rampersaud. My resignation was the most recent, in December 2008. See Thomson et al., "Roundtable Discussion," for background about the organization.

4. From its inception in late 2003, the curators of the Leftover Daylight Series (originally Ken Aldcroft and Joe Sorbara) rented the Arraymusic Studio from the administration of the contemporary music ensemble of the same name. Arraymusic would use their grant-subsidized space for rehearsals and administration but seldom for performances, and would rent it to Leftover Daylight organizers at a reduced rate. Facing undisclosed financial pressures, Arraymusic effectively doubled their studio-rental rates in late 2008. Partly for this reason, the Leftover Daylight Series moved to Somewhere There Studio in December 2008, where it has remained ever since. Along with Mr. Aldcroft and Mr. Sorbara, the following people have worked as curators and organizers for the Leftover Daylight Series: Nick Fraser, Rob Piilonen, Geordie Haley, Nicole Rampersaud, Colin Fisher, and dozens of guest curators, each with a one-month tenure.

5. What's more, the pressures put on organizations that receive such funding to succeed within stricter business-model structures—maintaining a "large enough" audience and sourcing adequate private revenue—makes me wary of the negative influence such grants may have on AIMToronto, as it has, in my view, on the Music Gallery's programming and venue priorities.

6. Maybe they are in New York, but they certainly are not in Toronto.

7. See www.somewherethere.org. As pertinent as this new development was to the roundtable discussion, it seemed premature to bring up Somewhere There, which was, at that point, an untried experiment—the ink on the lease was still wet. I recall acutely how the grade-school paralogic of "jinxing" the endeavor weighed heavily on my mind.

8. Programming at Somewhere There includes three weekly or biweekly creative-music series, each with separate curatorial teams, that for one reason or another were forced to move from other venues. These "refugee" series include the NOW Series, the Leftover Daylight Series, and the Panic Density Series. See notes 2 and 4 above for more information.

9. For those who are disinclined to take my word for it, consider what Evan Parker wrote to me in an e-mail message following a three-night concert series at Somewhere There in February, 2009: "Somewhere There is just the kind of place where a great music scene is incubated. My first response upon seeing the room was, 'here is a place to focus on essentials.' It's a very friendly, relaxed place with a phenomenal team of people, each anxious to do their best for the collective. More 'professional'— in the best sense—than people salaried to do those jobs often are. Somewhere There is a resource for Toronto that should be valued, supported and nurtured."

10. A sliding-scale clause in which the rent is reduced to match the revenue from very small audiences prevents musicians from paying out of pocket in order to perform at Somewhere There. In May 2009, Somewhere There received its first "project grant" (a stepping stone to more comprehensive and elusive "operating grants") from the Toronto Arts Council (TAC) to subsidize Somewhere There's residencies for the 2009–10 season. Since the space opened, residencies have been at the core of its programming, offering a musician or group two months of weekly performances in one of three slots. The $4,000 grant is subsidizing about 155 concerts, an average of less than $27 a concert. The residents are still playing for the door, but most of the rent for each night is covered by the TAC this year. (From the TAC's point of view, 155 shows for $4,000 must represent by far the best value for money they have ever achieved with the allocation of a single grant.)

11. Somewhere There has moved somewhere else, but it continues to exist and to present music on a regular basis. In February 2008, Ginder Consulting published *Towards a New Music Venue: Report on Quantitative and Qualitative Review*, apparently a very expensive report that was commissioned jointly by the Toronto Arts Council, the Ontario Arts Council, and the Canada Council for the Arts. This report responds to the needs of select stakeholders in Toronto's new music scene, with the goal of finding an optimal solution to meet this community's needs for venues. Oddly, the report acknowledges the manner in which it systematically ignores the constituency of new-music presenters and practitioners who work at Somewhere There, the Tranzac Club, and other venues for creative music that function outside its tacit post-European-classical-music purview. Not surprisingly, given this elision, the report concludes that the "new music community" needs a space comparable to the Ice Breaker, the legendary new-music complex in Amsterdam, featuring at its core a (presumably very slick) 250-seat auditorium. While I would wholeheartedly support such an endeavor, I would argue (if anybody doing such a report would ask) that a space like Somewhere There would still be necessary in order to meet the needs of the

actual new-music community. I virtually guarantee that most of the truly provocative, dynamic, and original Canadian music these days cannot fill a slick
250-seat theater and cover whatever rental its administration's business model
would require, a fact that fundamentally should not exclude this music from the
funding bodies' field of vision.

12. Of course, conditions may change. I can imagine a time to come when,
with age and attendant shifting priorities, many of the artists who are currently
finding reasons to play for little these days refuse to do so within Somewhere
There's current fee structure. Their desires for administrative and fee structures
like those that Mr. Ribot seeks may, with collective pressures, gain more traction then. I believe, however, that a space like Somewhere There will continue
to serve a large constituency of creative musicians, those who feel, as I do (to
quote my colleague, Nilan Perera), that creative music "owes me a life, not a
livelihood."

Alan Stanbridge

CHAPTER 10

SOMEWHERE THERE
Contemporary Music, Performance Spaces,
and Cultural Policy

The world's major cities have always prided themselves on the reputation and quality of their high-profile performing-arts venues, with the Sydney Opera House perhaps only the most iconic example among many. From London's South Bank Centre to New York's Lincoln Center, these venues have played a major role not only in the presentation of large-scale musical productions, but in their contribution to the range of primarily socioeconomic factors that have tended to dominate the rhetoric of arts funding since the 1980s, factors including urban regeneration, image enhancement, city marketing, and the promotion of tourism.[1] But these large-scale venues have a somewhat less successful record in the presentation of smaller-scale contemporary work, whether composed new music or jazz and improvised music, which have frequently had to make their homes in nonspecialized—and often inadequate—venues, such as churches, rehearsal spaces, bars, and cafés. While this has perhaps contributed to the willful bohemianism of some "alternative" musical scenes, there can be little doubt that these performance venues enjoy few of the benefits of the large-scale institutions identified above.

These are issues with which I've been engaged for more than thirty years, as an arts manager and music promoter in the U.K. for fifteen years, from the late 1970s to the early 1990s, and as an academic in Canada since 1994.[2] Since making the move into academia, my research interests have been primarily focused on the discourses that shape and circumscribe contemporary understandings of musical meaning and cultural value— issues that are directly relevant to my current topic. In a previous article, entitled "The Tradition of All the Dead Generations: Music and Cultural Policy," I explored the impact that narrowly prescriptive interpretations of tradition, and equally narrow conceptualizations of "music," have had on contemporary music and cultural policy, as reflected in representative patterns of arts funding, and in the typical musical repertoire of the contemporary symphony orchestra, which, in tandem with opera, represents the most heavily publicly funded aspect of present-day musical activity.

Based on a review of the repertoire of the Toronto Symphony Orchestra and the funding patterns of the Canada Council, I argued that "the tradition of all the dead generations" continues to have a profound—and highly restrictive—impact on the funding and support of contemporary music. In the case of the Toronto Symphony Orchestra, in the 2005–6 and 2006–7 seasons, dead composers accounted for 86 percent of the program. The holy triumvirate of Mozart, Beethoven, and Brahms accounted for fully 25 percent of the program, and only eleven composers, all dead, accounted for almost half of all performances. In the case of the Canada Council's support for music in 2004–5, only five companies—one opera company and four symphony orchestras—accounted for a quarter of the total music budget of $27 million; only twenty organizations, all devoted to Western art music, accounted for half of the total music budget. The rest of the budget, $13.1 million, was distributed between 1,034 organizations and individuals. In light of these statistics, I argued, it is clear that the Canada Council's commitment to "other" musics will only be fully realized if it undertakes a thorough review of its funding priorities, establishing support networks that more accurately reflect the range and diversity of contemporary music-making in Canada, which extends far beyond the narrow confines of the classical canon.

This essay moves beyond questions of revenue, funding, and programming implications for contemporary music to address issues of capital spending and the quality of performance spaces for smaller-scale new music presentation. Furthermore, given the overarching emphasis of the various essays in this volume on the history and development of post-1960s jazz and improvised music, this essay makes a pertinent contribution to these topics, highlighting the manner in which a range of primarily theoretical, philosophical, and ideological issues are directly reflected and represented in the rather more pragmatic and quotidian realm of cultural policy. The persistence of the cultural hierarchies, identified in my previous work on revenue support for contemporary music, is readily apparent

in the area of capital funding, where one finds similar inequities at play—
inequities that continue to have a profound impact on the presentation
and future development of contemporary jazz and improvised music.

In the world of arts funding and cultural policy, revenue support and
capital funding have always had a symbiotic, if somewhat troubled, relationship, and my present home base of Toronto, Canada's largest city,
offers a good opportunity to explore the current situation for the presentation and performance of contemporary music. Toronto is an especially
interesting case study for two reasons: first, many of the city's flagship cul
tural institutions have recently been the recipients of significant amounts
of public and private money to undertake major building and renovation projects, thereby ensuring that Toronto is well served by large-scale
venues; and second, although Toronto has an active new music and improvised music scene, many of these performances—in sadly typical fashion—continue to happen in unsuitable and inadequate venues.

Flagships and Follies

Since 2002, as part of the Canada-Ontario Infrastructure Program, seven
of Toronto's major cultural institutions have been the recipients of $233
million of Canadian federal money (from Industry Canada) and provincial
government money provided by Ontario (under the province's SuperBuild
program). These include: the Royal Ontario Museum ($60 million); the
Canadian Opera Company ($56 million); the Art Gallery of Ontario ($48
million); the National Ballet School ($40 million); the Royal Conservatory
of Music ($20 million); the Gardiner Museum of Ceramic Art ($5 million);
and Roy Thomson Hall ($4 million).[3] The grants range from support for
major capital projects to funding for renovation and refurbishment, and
all involve significant private sector fundraising efforts, with government
money representing only 35 to 40 percent of total project costs (B. Jenkins
175–76).

Underpinning many of these initiatives, and thoroughly implicated in
the City of Toronto's *Culture Plan for the Creative City* (2003), is the work of
Richard Florida and his pronouncements on the "creative class," its impact
on cities, and the importance of "the three T's: Technology, Talent and Tolerance" (Florida, *The Rise of the Creative Class* 6). It is worthwhile noting
that Florida is a recent addition to the faculty at the University of Toronto,

as director of the aptly named Martin Prosperity Institute of the Rotman School of Management, highlighting the extent to which Florida's concerns revolve around cash, not culture.[4] Jim McGuigan has addressed some of the serious problems inherent in "doing a Florida thing," arguing that it is "not surprising that some are inclined to view Florida as a busy, globetrotting trader in a good old American product, snake oil, instead of a serious scholar with some genuine wisdom to impart for cultural policy" (292).[5]

Notwithstanding such criticisms, however, Florida's work—in a manner distressingly similar to repeatedly exaggerated claims (often in the face of hard evidence) for the socioeconomic role that culture plays in urban regeneration strategies—continues to influence the cultural planning of many of the world's major cities (and some of its more modest municipalities) in an apparently unshakeable fashion.[6] As McGuigan suggests, however, confirming the implications of Florida's appointment to the Martin Prosperity Institute, "Florida's principal concerns are not to do with cultural policy as such but instead are about the articulation of neoliberal economics with cool culture" (298).

Commenting on the rash of major capital projects in the city, and echoing McGuigan's critique, Barbara Jenkins adopts a highly skeptical perspective on "Toronto's Cultural Renaissance," noting the extent to which many of these projects represent somewhat dubious contributions to the city's cultural life. Jenkins contends, "These buildings are better understood as both participants in, and reflections of, contemporary patterns of global economic competition and the changing role of culture in capitalist production. In the Canadian case, they are particularly remarkable in that the $257 million the federal and provincial governments will pour into the Toronto projects follows years of devastating cuts to arts funding" (170).[7] She continues: "Notably absent in any discussion on the part of the federal and provincial governments is any mention of the increased operating costs necessary to run these shiny new buildings" (182). Jenkins's comments here bring to mind similar issues from the early years of National Lottery funding in Britain in the late 1990s, which was initially restricted to capital projects, often for organizations that had little prospect of supporting these so-called lottery follies in the longer term.

Jenkins concludes: "Architecturally, Toronto will surely benefit from some very attractive buildings. Ironically, however, in the final analysis this building extravaganza appears to have very little to do with art or architecture" (183). Laura Levin and Kim Solga offer a similar criticism when they observe that events such as Nuit Blanche, the Luminato Festival, and the Live with Culture campaign generate "the façade of a Toronto alive with culture rather than investing seriously and for the long term in the cultivation of local artistic labor," arguing that Luminato "is perhaps the best example of a culturefest originally mapped on to Toronto's existing arts scene with an eye more to tourist promotion than to the support of local culture workers" (40–41).[8] In a telling early critique of the employment of culture-led initiatives in urban-regeneration strategies and city-marketing schemes, Ron Griffiths not only addressed the question of whether such strategies actually achieve their stated goals, but also raised significant concerns with regard to "whether the support given to the arts and culture has been beneficial in creating conditions for their production, as distinct from their consumption" (43), and he went on to note the ambiguity over the beneficiaries and purposes of these cultural initiatives.

Toronto's two most heavily funded, "starchitect" designed museum projects—the addition to the Art Gallery of Ontario (AGO), designed by Frank Gehry, and the Michael Lee-Chin Crystal at the Royal Ontario Museum (ROM), designed by Daniel Libeskind—both appear to conform readily to such critical analysis.[9] To this observer, at least, the Libeskind Crystal, completed in June 2007, already has the convincing feel of a folly. Famously scribbled on a napkin at a family wedding reception—a story now firmly ensconced in architectural folklore—it soon transpired that a napkin was perhaps not the best design medium, and plans for a primarily glass structure were soon scaled back, with a greater emphasis on what looks like a cross between aluminum siding and warehouse cladding.[10] The success of the interior exhibition spaces of the Crystal remains to be seen, as does the new space created by Gehry's addition to the AGO, although, in line with many of these architects' previous high-profile projects, both seem considerably more focused on form than on content. A recent paper by Matt Patterson indicates that emerging opinion on these projects suggests that the AGO's "transformation" has been considerably more successful than the ROM's "renaissance," with the AGO taking the opportunity of a major capital renovation to reassess its curatorial and exhibition practices, adopting a more contextualized, visitor-friendly approach.[11] In sharp contrast, the ROM project has been criticized for its aggressive architecture, its arrogant approach to its stakeholders in the community (most notably in its abortive plans for a luxury condominium of forty-six stories as part of the overall proposal), and its failure to adopt contemporary modes of museum display.[12]

In terms of the performing arts, the most heavily funded infrastructure project is the Four Seasons Centre for the Performing Arts, costing $186 million dollars, designed by the Toronto-based firm Diamond and Schmitt Architects and providing a new home for the Canadian Opera Company (COC) and the National Ballet of Canada.[13] Having heard several performances in the main auditorium, which seats 2,163, I can hardly fault the design and acoustics of the space for large-scale opera and dance performances, although my experience of smaller-scale music presentations in the COC's new building has been somewhat mixed.[14] In November 2007, I was invited by the concert accordionist Joseph Petric to join him on stage as part of the COC's lunchtime concert series, to introduce a program of contemporary electroacoustic and solo works for accordion, entitled "The Accordion Now: From Street Corner to Concert Hall." Having known Joseph for a number of years, and being a great admirer of his music, I was happy to oblige.

The concert took place in the Richard Bradshaw Amphitheatre, which is located at the top of the building's main atrium stairwell—an airy, attractive space, but one far from ideally suited to live performance, and accommodating a maximum of only 150 people on hard, wooden bench-style seating. The audience's response indicated that the concert was undeniably a success, although in common with many spaces designed with acoustic classical music as their priority, the amphitheatre—with its hardwood floors and glass surfaces—has an extremely difficult acoustic, especially for amplified music, and the amplified elements of the electroacoustic pieces were compromised as a result. Moreover, the inability to blackout the space meant that the video element accompanying one of the electroacoustic pieces could not be projected suitably, and was reduced to being shown on a large-screen television at the side of the stage.

Aside from these specific problems, however, perhaps the most striking aspect of this amphitheatre space is that, apart from the main auditorium, seating 2,163, it is the only other public performance space in the COC's new building. And although the programming team deserves kudos for mounting an interesting program of free lunchtime concerts and dance events, encompassing some contemporary work alongside more standard classical fare, the nature of the amphitheatre space presents some severe programming restrictions. This seems sadly typical of a major city well served by large-scale venues, but with few suitable facilities for the presentation of smaller-scale contemporary music performances. Given the new building's multimillion-dollar budget, this represents a significant missed opportunity, and the lack of any alternative medium-to-small-scale spaces as part of the capital project seems like a remarkable omission, simply highlighting the extent to which the focus of the infrastructure program has been on major flagship developments, with the emphasis firmly, as Ron Griffiths has suggested, on cultural consumption rather than cultural production.

Exclusion and Reterritorialization

This mainstream emphasis on flagship capital projects is all the more troubling when one considers the current state of venues for new music performance in Toronto. In addition to the city's major music organizations (for example, the Toronto Symphony Orchestra and the Canadian Opera Company), Toronto has both a well-established new-music scene (the Music Gallery, one of the city's key new music promoters, was founded in 1976), and a burgeoning improvised-music scene, courtesy of the Association of Improvising Musicians (AIM) Toronto, which has been active in the city since 2004. It virtually goes without saying, of course, that neither of these organizations, nor any of the city's other new music presenters—Arraymusic and the Tranzac, for example—saw any of the cultural capital from Toronto's recent windfall, and the majority of Toronto's new-music and improvised-music performances continue to happen in unsuitable and inadequate venues.

Since 2001, the Music Gallery, Toronto's "centre for promoting and presenting innovation and experimentation in all forms of music," has made its home in St. George the Martyr Anglican Church, an interesting venue, but one with limited facilities, a problematic acoustic, poor sight-lines, and wooden pews for seats—a secular form of martyrdom, perhaps.[15] Venues such as the Arraymusic Studio or the Tranzac Club offer little more by way of comfort and salubriousness, and simply tend to confirm the cultural hierarchies at play in terms of support—whether capital or revenue—for contemporary music-making. In this sense, then, much composed new music, more challenging forms of contemporary jazz, and virtually all im-

provised music continue to fall between the cracks in the current structures of cultural policy, forms neither traditional enough to enjoy the
benefits of established arts funding patterns, which remain focused on the
Western art music of dead generations, nor cool enough (or, indeed, lucra-
tive enough) to partake in Richard Florida-inspired visions of cultural and
creative industries initiatives.

These problems are hardly unique to Toronto, however, and even in New
York City—which still tends to be regarded as a Mecca for experimentalists and avant-gardists—opportunities for the presentation of free jazz,
improvised music, and new music have become increasingly scarce in recent years. These issues were highlighted in a discussion panel at Ontario's
2007 Guelph Jazz Festival Colloquium, and the closure of several alternative venues in New York was addressed by the improvising guitarist and
composer Marc Ribot, a regular collaborator with figures such as John
Zorn, Laurie Anderson, and Tom Waits.[16] Ribot spoke about his involvement in protests against the closure of Tonic, a club that had been central
to the downtown music scene for over six years. In April 2007, the club
was finally closed, to make way for a condo development, and, in an interesting example of small-scale urban revolt, Ribot was arrested for his part
in these protests. In an article posted on the *All about Jazz* website shortly
after the closing of Tonic, Ribot bemoaned the lack of funding for new
music, noting that, even at the smallest-scale level of financial expectations, the market now appears unable to support such ventures. Noting the
unsustainability of an endless round of benefit concerts to shore up ailing
and poorly funded venues, Ribot argued: "Without capital, venues either
eventually fall back on the old strategies of musician exploitation, abandon
new music priorities, fail, or all three. If those venues are 'artist run,' the
only difference is that we get to exploit ourselves. Hooray for progress."[17]

Against this somewhat polarized cultural backdrop, the opening in September 2007 of a new, small-scale performance space in Toronto by Scott
Thomson, a musician and composer on the local improvised-music scene
and an active member of AIMToronto, was a fascinating addition to the
city's contemporary music scene.[18] Thomson named his venue Somewhere
There, drawing his inspiration from a line in the song, "Imagination," by
the African American jazz composer, keyboard player, bandleader, black
activist, and all-round mystic, Sun Ra: "If we came from nowhere here, why
can't we go somewhere there?" In fuller context, the lyric reads: "Imagination is a magic carpet / Upon which we may soar / To distant lands and

climes / And even go beyond the moon / To any planet in the sky / If we came from nowhere here / Why can't we go somewhere there?" (quoted in Szwed, *Space Is the Place* 141). Commenting on the discourse of space that dominates Sun Ra's rhetoric, his biographer John Szwed has argued that, for Sun Ra, "space was both a metaphor of exclusion and reterritorialization, of claiming the 'outside' as one's own, of tying a revised and corrected past to a claimed future" (140).

Adapting to his own purposes the Afro-Futurist critique inherent in the original line, Thomson's choice of name is both an accurate, if perhaps somewhat ironic, commentary on the current state of new-music performance in Toronto, and a positive, oppositional response to the challenge of going from "nowhere" to "somewhere." Somewhere There is an especially bold and enterprising project, bucking the system in a manner that simply ignores the dictates of current cultural policy imperatives. In fact, in its unblinking focus on the development and presentation of creative improvised music as a culturally specific artistic form, Thomson's project seems almost quaintly anachronistic, harkening back to a time when many of those laboring at the art and culture coal-face attempted, as Jim McGuigan has suggested, "to facilitate something differently pleasurable and meaningfully better for most people than the usual produce of cool capitalism" (299). And, I would add, something differently pleasurable and meaningfully better than the usual products of a narrowly traditionalist understanding of "music," with all its attendant policy implications.

Somewhere There is located in a former storage room at the rear of a large, independent furniture store in the Parkdale area of Toronto, and offers a comfortable, intimate, 800-square-foot performance space with an excellent, dry acoustic (described as "perfect" by two highly regarded Dutch improvisers who performed there in 2008). The venue also has a small gallery space, showing the work of visiting and local artists. Through the aid of donations and gifts from friends and supporters, the space houses an upright piano, a drum kit, and a small PA system, and Thomson has furnished the room with an assortment of chairs and one especially comfy sofa. A comment commonly heard from visitors is that the space "feels like someone's living room," an observation that pleases Thomson to no end. Although the space may be rather short on the facilities one might associate with subsidized venues, Thomson keeps his refrigerator well stocked with beer and wine, offers splendid coffee to visitors, and the toilets are adequate.

Somewhere There receives no direct funding, and the rent for the space is covered primarily by operating income and subsidized by some rehearsal rentals, although Thomson also personally subsidizes any additional shortfall. Aside from the venue's website, and primarily due to budgetary constraints, Thomson does little advertising or promotion, encouraging artists to promote their own work. The admission charge is currently $8.00, and musicians play for the door takings. Attendances are generally modest, ranging from single figures to around forty or fifty for special events, the maximum that the space can accommodate.[19] Somewhere There has gone from initially presenting four to five shows per week, to offering a week-long program of events, including regular two-month residencies for performers and groups, allowing them to develop their music over an extended period. Since opening in September 2007, and as of March 2010, Somewhere There has presented over 650 events, 60 percent of which have been recorded for archival purposes. In the longer term, Thomson plans to share the coordination of the venue with a team of volunteers, ultimately aiming to secure funding for, at the very least, rent and running costs.

In many ways, Thomson's initiative is a typical example of artists' taking matters into their own hands, opening alternative, loft-style performance spaces for the presentation of contemporary music—the celebrated New York Loft Jazz scene of the 1970s and 1980s being a salient case in point.[20] It is interesting to note, however, that the Guelph Jazz Festival Colloquium panel discussion of 2007—in which Thomson was also involved—revealed a significant gap in philosophy between Marc Ribot's hard-bitten New York realism and Thomson's somewhat more idealistic approach. Indeed, it is relatively easy to view Thomson's project as simply another instance, in Ribot's terms, of contemporary musicians exploiting themselves. Having witnessed and been involved in several similar initiatives in London in the 1980s, I reacted to Thomson's project with considerable skepticism, raising significant doubts not only about the lack of an appropriate fee structure for musicians, but also about the longer-term sustainability of the venue itself. But observing the success of Somewhere There over the last two and a half years has done much to change my mind. The new music community in Toronto has been highly supportive, and the venue is clearly satisfying a previously unfulfilled need, contributing to a transformation of the Toronto music scene.[21] In presenting more than 650 shows in the space of thirty months, Thomson has become one of the most active promoters of creative improvised music, not only in Toronto, but also in Ontario, and, indeed, across Canada.

Moreover, Thomson's project is firmly grounded in a clearly articulated musical philosophy, which he outlined in an article in the online journal *Critical Studies in Improvisation*. Entitled "The Pedagogical Imperative of Musical Improvisation," the article highlights Thomson's commitment to improvisation as musical process rather than cultural product, and he argues that "instead of signifying a set of sounds or methods that are empirically identifiable away from their moment of execution, 'improvisation' refers to the deployment of a range of sociomusical skills *as they are being learned* within collaborative performance" (7). Hence the emphasis, in Thomson's programming of Somewhere There, on longer-term residencies, which effectively serve a research and development function, allowing musicians to workshop their ideas over a two-month period. In this sense, Thomson has always envisaged Somewhere There's fulfilling as much of an educational and pedagogical role as one devoted strictly to the presentation of neatly packaged performances.

Why Can't We Go Somewhere There?

Of course, such high-flown philosophizing about the ephemeral and ineffable nature of musical improvisation has little to do with urban regeneration, cultural tourism, prosperity growth, or "cool culture," and, in consequence, an initiative such as Somewhere There flies far under the Richard Florida radar. But, in its idealistic—although far from utopian—aims and objectives, whether musical, aesthetic, or social, Somewhere There has a great deal to do with creativity, with tolerance, with talent (and, yes, with technology), which—in a manner similar to my previous argument with regard to revenue funding—simply highlights the need for a radical reappraisal of the often misguided priorities inherent in much capital funding for cultural projects. This would involve a shift away from an overarching emphasis on the consumption of traditional cultural products in large-scale showcase venues to a modified perspective that also accommodates a focus on the often smaller-scale processes of creation and production in new and innovative musical forms, and an acknowledgment of their particular venue-based needs. Given Thomson's enterprising nature, it is not hard to imagine what might be achieved with a modest revenue grant and only a tiny percentage of Toronto's recent infrastructure capital funding. As Sun Ra asked, if we came from nowhere here, why can't we go somewhere there?

Notes

1. See Garcia, "Cultural Policy and Urban Regeneration in Western European Cities," for a useful review of these issues in the Western European context. See also Stanbridge, "Detour or Dead-End?"

2. My period in the U.K. included positions with several arts center projects, including the Almeida Theatre, in London, the Midland Group, in Nottingham, and Midlands Arts Centre, in Birmingham. I also served as director of jazz services, a national touring organization, and as director of the Glasgow International Jazz Festival, which involved everything from major stars in major venues (e.g., Stan Getz in the Theatre Royal), through a series of medium to small-scale events in a wide range of performance spaces (e.g., Derek Bailey in the former Third Eye Centre), to a host of local musicians playing in bars and pubs throughout the region. Hence, the nature and quality of venues for live performance—for the presentation of both mainstream and "alternative" musics—have been significant issues for me throughout my career.

3. The figure of $56 million includes $25 million from the federal government, and the donation of the land for the project, valued at $31 million, by the provincial government.

4. See: http://martinprosperity.org.

5. For a thoroughgoing critique of Florida's concept of the "Creative Class," see Peck, "Struggling with the Creative Class." See also Murray Whyte's article in the *Toronto Star*, which suggests that "Richard Florida's honeymoon is over."

6. For an early critique of such strategies, see Griffiths, "The Politics of Cultural Policy in Urban Regeneration Strategies." See also Evans, "Measure for Measure," and Miles, "Interruptions." See Hartley, *Creative Industries*, for an alarmingly uncritical reading of Florida's thesis. For a more critical perspective on the cultural and creative industries, see Hesmondhalgh and Pratt, "Cultural Industries and Cultural Policy," and Garnham, "From Cultural to Creative Industries."

7. The figure of $257 million, quoted by Jenkins in "Toronto's Cultural Renaissance," includes $24 million in provincial funding to the Ontario College of Art and Design for a major new building.

8. It is interesting to note that Levin's and Solga's criticisms address not only large-scale, "official" Toronto culture, but also those "alternative," "culture jamming" projects that set out to challenge such dominant discourses. See Levin and Solga, "Building Utopia." For a more optimistic reading of alternative cultural strategies in the urban context, see Miles, "Interruptions."

9. The Michael Lee-Chin Crystal is named after the primary private donor, who contributed $30 million to the project. See www.rom.on.ca/crystal/name.php.

10. See also Kingwell, "The $195-million Scribble," for a polemical critique of Libeskind's controversial design.

11. Given my own views on these issues, the AGO's transformation is to be warmly welcomed—see Stanbridge, "Display Options: Discourses of Art and Context in the Contemporary Museum."

12. Mark Kingwell has argued: "We're not necessarily getting buildings that are interesting or serviceable or inspiring to the community. We're getting somebody's ego on paper and then stuck up into the air for who knows how many decades" (qtd. in Roberts, "The Torontonians"). See Stuffco, "ROM Condo Project Takes Heat from Critics." As Gail Lord has argued: "The Royal Ontario Museum is the only major museum in the world that has taken the view that the vast majority of exhibits should consist of artifacts in cases . . . There is no other institution I know of that has so consistently returned to the Victorian notion of the museum" (Nuttall-Smith, "Who Can Save the ROM This Time?").

13. See "About the Four Seasons Centre," Canadian Opera Company, accessed August 20, 2012, www.coc.ca.

14. The design and acoustic of the recently opened Koerner Hall, seating 1,135, part of the Royal Conservatory of Music's capital project, is similarly unimpeachable.

15. See www.musicgallery.org/about.

16. See Tamar Barzel's contribution to this volume.

17. See also Ribot's contribution to this volume.

18. See www.somewherethere.org, and Thomson's weblog: www.sowehear.blogspot.com. See also Infantry, "A jazz niche below the radar, but on the map: New Parkdale venue for the non-mainstream migrates to the Tranzac Club for improv festival," and Thomson's contribution to this volume.

19. The Interface series, put on by AIMToronto, which involves local musicians performing with visiting artists, has its base at Somewhere There, and has been an especially successful event. See my review of the Evan Parker Interface series in *Signal to Noise* magazine, "Live Reviews: AimToronto Interface series with Evan Parker."

20. See, for example, Litweiler, "Free Jazz Today."

21. To rain lightly on this happy parade for just a moment, I must note that an occasional personal frustration with regard to Somewhere There has been the sometimes surprising lack of support from members of the new-music community, especially for some of Thomson's milestone events, or for shows that one would have anticipated—and which deserved—a larger audience. These issues seem crucial to the longer-term sustainability of the venue.

PART III

Sound Check
The Jazz Photography of Thomas King

AMIRI BARAKA

HAMID DRAKE AND WILLIAM PARKER

SUN RA ARKESTRA

DJ SPOOKY

MARILYN CRISPELL, GEORGE LEWIS, MIYA MASAOKA,
AND HAMID DRAKE (LEFT TO RIGHT)

FRED ANDERSON

ARCHIE SHEPP

VIJAY IYER AND RUDRESH MAHANTHAPPA

ART ENSEMBLE OF CHICAGO (ROSCOE MITCHELL, JOSEPH JARMAN, FAMOUDOU DON MOYE, COREY WILKES, JARIBU SHAHID)

JANE BUNNETT

FAMOUDOU DON MOYE

CHARLIE HADEN

ANTHONY BRAXTON

NICOLE MITCHELL AND ROB MAZUREK

SATOKO FUJII

DOUGLAS EWART AND WADADA LEO SMITH

PART IV

Get Ready

Jazz Futures

Greg Tate

BLACK JAZZ IN THE DIGITAL AGE

"If you love black people, could you raise your hands?" That's a rhetorical question I sometimes ask audience members, but it's not a trick question. I'm often glad to see we get a few responses. I'm not trying to haul anyone in on charges of exoticism or paternalism.

I recently asked my friend Vernon Reid if he thought we'd ever see jazz resurrected as a creative force in modern black life and he said, only when we got back to doing it for the love and not for legitimacy and lifestyle. My late friend Billy Quinn once said he had no problem with the term *jazz* having once been a euphemism for sex, since the music had always sounded like love to him. My own love for jazz didn't begin in the bedroom, in the streets, or even with records. It actually began with the love I discovered in a book: LeRoi Jones's *Black Music*. I was guided to an act of love for the black avant-garde after deciding to create a comic book about a trumpeter who blew over a postapocalyptic city from high above, on the stratospheric lip of a crystal skyscraper. I must have been thinking about Miles Davis already. Little did I know I'd soon be thinking about Dewey, also known as Inky, also known as the Prince of Darkness, as often as I thought about myself, for the next thirty years.

There are as many jazz initiations as there are jazz listeners, but since mine came about at the hands of black cultural nationalists, I've always thought of jazz as first and foremost a liberating and even postliberated enterprise—a tachyon-beamed, future-sent black cultural revolution in sound. Being raised in a black cultural Mecca, namely the Washington, D.C., of the 1970s, certainly didn't hurt in fortifying this point of view. Here was a time and a place where the people promoting and advocating for the music were also advocates and organizers of social change at universities, media organizations, and businesses that employed the black working class. Some were poets, painters, sculptors, and filmmakers whose work conveyed and amplified the Struggle; some were even card-carrying communists and socialists. All tacitly followed the belief espoused by Paul Robeson in 1937: "The ARTIST must take sides. He must elect to fight for freedom or slavery. I have made my choice. I had no alternative" (119). Later figures would take up Robeson's charge and follow suit: Max Roach, Archie Shepp, Jackie McLean, Stevie Wonder, Bob Marley, Fela Kuti, Steel Pulse, Public Enemy, and Rage against the Machine.

My jazz educators were all big-time vinyl junkies who already owned complete Miles, Trane, Blue Note, ESP, and Actuel collections when I met them. It was in Washington that I got to interview Dexter Gordon, Sonny Rollins, and Betty Carter while barely out of high school and where I routinely witnessed, among predominantly black audiences, performances by the likes of Muhal Richard Abrams, Henry Threadgill, George Lewis, the George Coleman-Frank Foster big band, Miles Davis, David Murray, Julius Hemphill, Oliver Lake, and the Sun Ra Arkestra. My parents weren't big jazz fans in the sense of buying records or being concertgoers. But both had grown up in Memphis, where their courtship was played out on Beale Street, listening to Mingus, Rahsaan Roland Kirk, and others. In addition, my Mom had gone to high school with Frank Strozier, George Coleman, and Phineas Newborn Jr. So even though my folks made sure I knew who Malcolm X, Martin Luther King, and Nina Simone were; checking for Trane, Miles, and the rest became my own kind of adolescent vision quest.

To be sixteen years old and be a jazz lover back then was to be something of a generational anomaly. It meant many of my friends were about ten years older than I was and tolerated my trying to be erudite about the music they loved and had pointed me toward. Most of my younger buddies were heavy into rock and funk, as was I, and wanted to be Carlos Santana or Jimmy Page when they grew up, as did I. To my ears, the rhythm 'n' blues of that era wasn't so far from jazz anyway—it just had more amazingly graceful vocalists, and if you listened to Stevie Wonder, Marvin Gaye, Chaka Khan, and Curtis Mayfield, you heard voices that could match any horn this side of Jeanne Lee for plaintiveness and improvisational pliancy.

By that time, rhythm 'n' blues was usually played by session musicians who had as much jazz information at their fingertips as blues and gospel. This is certainly true of the cats who created the sounds of Motown, P-Funk, Earth, Wind and Fire, Ohio Players, Kool and the Gang, the Isley Brothers, Mandrill, and others. What's equally interesting to note is that the rhythmic and sonic language of electronic keyboards in modern pop was as much developed by certifiable jazz players—Hancock, Corea, Joe Zawinul, Lonnie Liston Smith, and George Duke—as by Stevie Wonder and Bernie Worrell.

Equally peculiar to this era was a sense of a unified black community that didn't require the worlds of black jazz and black pop to play by the rules of intracultural segregation that prevail today. In the fusion moment, you could go to venues like Howard University's Cramton Auditorium and see Weather Report open for the afro-funk band Osibisa, or witness Billy Cobham's Stratus unit on tour with P-Funk, or, strangely enough, Bob Marley and the Wailers warming up the stage for Chick Corea's band Return to Forever while future members of D.C.'s Rasta-punk pioneers Bad Brains sat taking notes on both. Of course, D.C. had its own brand of live funk and hip-hop called go-go: freewheeling bands of twelve members or more who weekly put on marathon, funkathon shows generally six to eight hours in length. Outside New Orleans it remains the only black music that demands that young black musicians become instrumentalists.

This state of affairs, this kind of adventurous programming, this kind of polyglot music community, was pretty normal back then in urban America but is almost unheard of in the states today, where it is seemingly forbidden for fans of one kind of music to occupy a concert hall with fans of another, except at a Björk show.

So exactly what did happen to the black music scene I grew up with? Well, the simple answer to that is commercial disco happened—commercial as opposed to the underground variety, which had started in D.C.'s gay clubs in the early 1970s. Most hip-hop producers will tell you they don't sample records that were made after 1977, because that's when the soul left the wax, when black pop stopped being made by bands and instead started being made nearly exclusively by producers and programmable machines. Steve Coleman will tell you one reason he started playing jazz was that there was nowhere left to play funk in Chicago after bands got replaced by turntables in the late 1970s. Miles Davis went into semi-retirement for about five years, beginning in 1976. The dialogue Miles had prophetically already been having in his 1970s music, between jazz culture and the emergent electronically enhanced forms of reggae, dub punk, No Wave, hip-hop, Detroit techno, Chicago house, drum and bass, electronica, and other forms, got retired with him like a Blade Runner replicant. Keith Jarrett summed up Miles's passing, in 1991, by saying that for all musicians a certain resonance had left the room. Miles's presence in jazz from the moment he hired Coltrane all the way through *Bitches Brew* did two very significant things for jazz musicians: it made risk-taking and experimentation commercially viable, and it made a forced hybridity of free jazz, soul, and funk ideas seem not only hip, but inevitable and inexorable to his harmonic camp, which is another way of saying almost everyone on Blue Note at the time.

The early 1980s were also when the performance and cheap housing possibilities for free-jazz musicians pretty much dried up in lower Manhattan. So, whereas in 1977 you could go out on any given evening to hear Julius Hemphill, Henry Threadgill, Anthony Davis, and Arthur Blythe in one loft, and Lester Bowie, Cecil Taylor, and Jimmy Lyons in another, Oliver Lake and Michael Gregory Jackson dueting in a third, all for the cost of a couple beers, by 1982, when I actually moved to the city, that deal was pretty much done. The strain of music those players represented didn't die out, of course, but became the foundation for the range of things being done by people like John Zorn and Bill Laswell in the 1980s. Yet the demise of that musical scene was also the last time relentless, progressive, black jazz musicians had a street presence on the ground, as it were, in NYC bohemia. That generation was also hit by the slashing of government funding for the arts by Reagan, a slashing that also trickled down to inner-city high school band programs.

The upshot of this has been what we've experienced as jazz culture in the states for the past twenty-five years—where the musicians rewarded recording contracts by American labels largely play a somewhat regressive and well-mannered form of postbop, where the musicians of the avant-garde in the 1970s appear in NYC about once a year, and where the dialogue between all generations of black musicians has become about as random. In this time, all the major jazz languages, from Dixieland to M-Base, have become universal. Big band jazz programs for teenagers have become about as popular as soccer in lily-white American suburbs, while even lite pop jazz has all but disappeared from the menu for young black pop listeners.

Now all this leaves a few questions on the table:

- Does it matter whether progressive black musicians play jazz now or in the future?
- Does it matter whether black people ever listen to another lick of real jazz from now until the end?

- Has jazz more than fulfilled its sociocultural, aesthetic, and political mandates for black people, given the advances well-educated black folk have
made in American society over the past twenty-five years?
- Have jazz's possibilities as a black art form been exhausted, or does the virtual absence of a coherent community of black jazz listeners explain the
creative stagnation of the art form at present?

Another way of asking these same questions is to explore the notion of
exactly what information the African American genius, living under American apartheid, brought to the formation of jazz that jazz is losing or has
lost access to today. Even more pointedly, what will jazz lose if it loses contact, loses the call-and-response conversation it used to enjoy with black
working-class humanity and that group's racialized self-consciousness and
ritualized cultural practices? There is, of course, the further question of
whether we err on the side of novelty by thinking of jazz in teleological,
futurological terms, of thinking of jazz as in need of a newer postmodern
postblack destination point.

Why does jazz have to be going anywhere, since where it has been already staggers the imagination with its telltale monuments? Staggering are
its *Kind of Blue*s and *Love Supreme*s and *Speak No Evil*s and *Nefertiti*s and
Spiritual Unities, Percussion Bittersweet and *The Shape of Jazz to Come* and
*Unit Structure*s and *Spring for Two Blue Jays* and *Fanfare for the Warriors*,
its *Vade Mecum*s, *Thembi*s, *Dark Magus, Destination Out, The Heliocentric
Worlds of Sun Ra* and *Let My Children Hear Music* and *Inside Betty Carter*
and *Creative Orchestra Music* and *Just the Facts* and *Pass the Bucket*s and so
on and so on.

There's also to be considered in this the transcultural, interdisciplinary
impact of what we can call the jazz effect, the jazz tinge, jazz transmissions, jazz sensibility, jazz residue, so clearly present all over the twentieth-
century artistic map, from Mondrian to Matisse to Pollock to de Kooning
to John Cage to Allan Kaprow to Julio Cortázar to the Black Mountain
group (about which the founding poet Charles Olson once remarked there
was no Black Mountain school, there was just Charlie Parker). We see the
impact of jazz aerodynamics in the way buildings by Frank Gehry and
Zaha Hadid are designed, and echoes of jazz's concrete expressionism in
paintings by Rauschenberg, Basquiat, and Richter, in the way dances are
choreographed since Martha Graham, by the likes of Merce Cunningham,
Alvin Ailey, Garth Fagan, Pina Bausch, and William Forsythe, and in the

way films are edited from Godard on (who himself once said there was more narrative in a John Coltrane solo than in most movies).

What jazz clearly made manifest in the postwar world of art and letters was the privileging of individual will and the grand opportunities that lie in seizing or freezing the improvisational moment. With that came the necessity of complicating the folk vernacular utterance without compromising the folk vernacular voice and vounce, and the folks' way of violating, of doing violence even to the rules of engagement. This, of course, was something Picasso had picked up from the source, namely the unity of multiple perspectives on space, time, quantum forces, and collective memory found in African sculpture.

Vernon Reid also once remarked that he thought the black rage we once heard in free jazz had migrated to hip-hop. As I survey the stage of the black intellectual conversation going on today, I find that the self-conscious engagement with philosophy I once heard in 70s jazz, politics, religion, and literature has migrated to contemporary African American visual art, where one is expected, after Basquiat's example, to wrestle with race, politics, history, identity, and knotty conceptual questions as a matter of course. Why this is no longer the case in jazz has something to do with the class aspirations and subject position of most younger musicians, who are not, at the end of the day, social rebels, but middle-class arts professionals whose art has no significance even among a black middle class—American consumers oriented to mass media, who prefer soul and hip-hop to postbop. This leads us to the question of why there has been no viable rapprochement of jazz and hip-hop comparable to Miles's *Bitches Brew*.

Once, during an interview, Wynton Marsalis asked me what quantifiable musical relationship I could conceivably hear between jazz and hip-hop. My first answer, besides the obvious rhythmic one, was the timbre and tonality of the voices, the male voices in particular. Even Wynton didn't find anything to argue with in that. Developing that idea even further, I'd say the great MCs of hip-hop and the great players in jazz share the characteristic of having unmistakable tones, tones one can identify in sometimes one or two notes, and certainly within eight bars. The sonic, rhythmic, lyrical organization of the ideas of Trane, Wayne, and Joe Henderson are immediately distinguishable to the serious listener from those of Ornette, Eric Dolphy, and David Murray—as those of Biggie, Rakim, and Chuck D are distinguishable from the flows of Q Tip, Ghostface Killa, and Trick Daddy.

The problem with most hybrids of jazz and hip-hop to date is that they proceed as if that riddle can be resolved by beats and technology, when really the most remarkable, memorable, dramatic musical events in hip-hop are the ones that derive from the form's most human elements, its mighty-mouthed MCs dropping "pearls and gems of wisdom" and its super-human beatboxers, like the one and only Rahzel, who can somehow make the back of his Afro-Tuvan throat sound like two squabbling turntables and a light saber battle between Darth Vader and Luke Skywalker at the same time. What would happen, I've wondered, if Rahzel was given, say, Trane's *Meditations* to extrapolate upon or Sun Ra's *Atlantis*: sounds like we'd never heard in our life, no doubt, at least not from the body of one human being. But in what context today would such an experimental collaborative foray between black avant-gardes take place—on whose watch and under whose willpower?

Jazz in the 1960s and 1970s pushed hard on the question of how free music, and especially a black music, could be, and could still be, musical. Improvisational sound artists "utopically" asked what role music might play in transforming society. Another question we might ask today is What is the future of radical black consciousness, and even the black male voice in jazz, and does anybody here even care? In posing this, I'm reminded of a comment made in the 1970s by the saxophonist Billy Harper, questioning whether the assumption that jazz was "on the way out" wasn't tantamount to asking whether the black man was on the way out. Given the current rates of incarceration, unemployment, and homelessness for black men in the United States, Harper's rhetorical and slightly testosterone-fueled lambaste may be more relevant than ever. There is also to be considered what we'll call the Coltrane conundrum: Where does any art form go after it's found god? Or at least as it realizes a means of evoking the source of all life, as some feel Coltrane did—some even to the point of starting an actual church in his name? Where could it go, but to search for the devil, perhaps? Perhaps Miles Davis and hip-hop present a rhythmic, symphonic inquisition on the origins of evil, human fate, and the problem of free will. But I digress.

The episteme we know as "race" in America is useful in political discussion, but is not so surgical a tool to use when holding forth on creativity. Focusing on ethnic, tribal, and regional sensibilities takes us closer to the action in an America that remains a very clannish, tribalized nation, one where crock-pot more than melting pot may be the defining anthropological paradigm. One of the most illuminating aspects of living in Harlem for a quarter century is that you are constantly reminded how every decade of Harlem's existence is visible for inspection on a daily basis. And this isn't just in the faces of elders, but in the architecture, in the fact that you can now go to hear jazz in Minton's again, and in the fact that outside of the Apollo you are more able and more likely to hear live jazz in "H-town" than live hip-hop or rhythm 'n' blues. Jazz resides in Harlem, a community of people who are all about owning the moment in ways that have left much contemporary black-music practice. Much of this can be attributed to the fact that modern hip-hop and rhythm 'n' blues have become virtual black musics, increasingly designed more for downloading than public dancing or displays of affection, more readily made to be enjoyed as ringtones and iPod Shuffle snippets than as album cuts, as disposable, beat-driven musical Ritalin for the Attention Deficit Disorder set.

As all that was once solid about even black popular culture melts into air, black culture becomes more digitized and disembodied. The paradox is that what happens on the ground to real black bodies in Harlem's non-virtual streets becomes more striking and apparent as rappers and their entourages, having to shoot and be shot at to maintain the profit margin and the public-interest margins, becomes even more suicidally pronounced. Yet even as black culture becomes more defined by commerce than by creativity, I am reminded of Ornette Coleman's statement that the most sacred thing on earth is human feeling, and Vernon Reid's notion that the music will get more soulful again when it becomes the product of a profound love of music for music's sake.

As someone who years ago formed Burnt Sugar, the Arkestra Chamber, an improvising ensemble of twenty to thirty members, I clearly don't think live music, jazz, or huge, unprofitable orchestras are exhausted, antiquated means of pursuing personal and communal human truths and feelings. I do sometimes wonder if I'm guided more by quixotic nostalgia than by a mission from god, though who's to say these are opposing ideas? But just because the cultural landscape has changed so drastically, so digitally, around black improvisational music, that doesn't mean I've lost all human feeling in my heart, lungs, nuts, fingers, limbs, or my vivid memories of remarkable jazz things past.

Paul D. Miller (DJ Spooky) and Vijay Iyer

CHAPTER 12

IMPROVISING DIGITAL CULTURE

The transcript of this discussion (from the Guelph Jazz Festival Colloquium, 2008) between musician-authors Vijay Iyer and Paul D. Miller continues a virtual discussion carried out in the pages of a collection of essays that Miller edited, entitled Sound Unbound: Sampling Digital Music and Culture *(2008). Both Iyer and Miller contributed essays to that volume, and here they turn up the volume on their respective notions of improvisation, sometimes converging and sometimes diverging in interesting ways. In that earlier text, Miller presents a kaleidoscopic verbal collage of anecdotes and theoretical snippets to invoke the nature of his anthology-cum-mixtape: "Sound Unbound is about volume—of content as sound bite, of attention with no definite deficit, of memory as a vast playhouse where any sound can be you. Press 'play' and this anthology says 'here goes'" (Miller 9). Miller employs a similarly play-ful mode of presentation in his dialogue with Iyer, and like their ostensible subject matter (improvising digital culture), Iyer and Miller remix and sample ideas and arguments from a broad collage of cultural and political traditions from the twentieth century. The conversation, complete with its "vexations" (to cite a composition by Satie that Miller brings up in the following pages), trans-formed into a compelling musical dialogue later in the evening, when the duo performed in a concert setting at the festival.*

One feature of the discussion that particularly interests us is the distinc-tion drawn by Iyer and Spooky between what it means to improvise, in broad social terms, and the meaning of improvisation that is understood primarily in musical or artistic terms. Iyer and Miller explore the difficulty in separating those categories when dealing with the kinds of improvised-music traditions we highlight in this book, specifically the legacies of African American musical practice taken up by musicians in the 1960s and 1970s (many of whom are still active performers). As Iyer states in the beginning of the dialogue, many musi-cians from this "Great Black Music" tradition (as the members of the Art En-

226 IMPROVISING DIGITAL CULTURE

semble of Chicago call it) have noted that improvisation is a necessary survival tool, and their music functions as a sonic and artistic version of daily improvisational practice. "In other words," Iyer asserts, "you might say that there are degrees, layers or levels to what we call 'improvisation.' There's a primal level at which we learn how to just be in the world, and then there's another level at which we're responding to conditions that are thrust upon us." Based on this provisional definition of what it might mean to improvise, Iyer's comments set a slightly cautionary tone to the conversation, which Miller proceeds to remix into a tricksterish set of variations on a theme. As Miller puts it, "I think the dialogue between me and Vijay here is not only between different systems of production of music, but how improvisation itself is the bridge between radically different compositional strategies."

Moderated by Carl Wilson, music critic for the Globe and Mail, the discussion traversed about an hour's worth of give and take, listening and collaborating, between two of today's most important musical voices (both of whom are also, it bears repeating, devoted to actively constructing their own definitions of what they do as musicians, with a wide range of published writings). The collaboration also featured a few responses to the audience members' questions, demonstrating the kind of call and response at the heart of both analogue and digital improvisations.

VIJAY IYER: First of all, I'm honored to be here and to be back here, and happy to be speaking to you all. I was sitting in on the previous panel, and I'd like to pick up from what Natasha Pravaz was speaking about.[1] She referred to Richard Schechner, and he emphasizes the idea of performance and the performative moment capturing the subjunctive mood. Schechner is referring to the aspect of ritual or play that comes to be in performance. The subjunctive mood means that somehow there's a degree of fantasy involved [in the performance]. Schechner is specifically referring to Laurence Olivier's performance in the play *Hamlet*: Olivier both is and is not Hamlet at that moment.

I want to contrast that idea [about performance] with something that Muhal Richard Abrams said recently on a panel that was convened by George Lewis in New York City, which was specifically about theorizing improvisation. [Abrams] encapsulated improvisation as "a human response to necessity." It seems to me that there is such a gulf between Schechner's subjunctive, fantasy mode of performance and what Abrams is referring to in that specific context. He kept circling back to that definition, as if those four or five words somehow encapsulated everything we needed to know. And I want to try to unpack it a little bit. I think one of the key aspects of [Abrams' definition] is that improvisation is embedded in reality. It's embedded in real time, in an actual historical circumstance, and contextualized in a way that is, in some degree, inseparable from reality.

This resonates with an idea about improvisation that I've been working with recently, which is that improvisation should actually be regarded as identical with what we call experience. This means that there is, in fact, no difference between human experience and the act of improvisation, which means that we're actually always improvising. It means that improvisation is central to consciousness and to everything that we know. In a way, this insight about improvisation makes it so primal, as a concept, that it becomes almost impossible to place value on it. It is something that structures who we are and how we move about in the world. This means that there is improvisation that you could call "bad" or "evil." That is, for every Roscoe Mitchell or Charlie Parker or John Coltrane or Alice Coltrane or Mary Lou Williams, you also have a Dick Cheney or a contractor with Halliburton with an itchy trigger finger. They're improvising, too.

So, when we talk about improvisation, we can't always view it, I'd say, as a model for social change, unless you look at a definition like Abrams' as a kind of interventionist definition. That is, Abrams is trying to put a certain tilt on what we're calling improvisation, in a way that is, in a certain sense, empowering or activist: a human response to necessity. The history of the AACM [Association for the Advancement of Creative Musicians] encapsulates this idea, which is elaborated in George Lewis's book [*A Power Stronger than Itself: The AACM and American Experimental Music*] in astounding detail.

So, when we start kicking around this term, "improvisation," I want to see how neutral we can be with it. Or else, when we choose to use these kinds of activist or empowering kinds of definitions that we're very aware that that's what we're doing. Because that means that we're theorizing positively of what improvisation can do. In other words, you might say that there are degrees, layers or levels to what we call "improvisation." There's a primal level at which we learn how to just be in the world, and then there's another level at which we're responding to conditions that are thrust upon us.

Of course, for aggrieved communities, these levels become indistinguishable; survival under such conditions becomes inseparable from the basic fact of one's existence. Does this then collapse the distinction I'm making between apparently neutral and activist definitions? The question is how and where we situate power in acts of improvisation. We need to be able to analyze and critique the improvisations of absolute power—portrayed, for example, in the casual torture and murder enacted by decadent fascist elites in Pasolini's *Salo*—just as much as we examine the revolutionary improvisations that we associate with collective actions of the dispossessed.

Now, this conversation is about improvising digital culture, or actually the phrase that we used was "improvising digital community," which is perhaps something different. I think that means that we're talking about what we can do together as improvisers and as people whose realities are interpenetrated with technology. In other words, it's again a sort of slant on things: it's not just culture-at-large, it's community, which is a certain possibility that we have in culture. So, all I want to say up front here is to set forth these kinds of parameters so that we know what we're talking about as we continue the conversation.

PAUL MILLER: First and foremost, I want just to say, "thanks for having me," and it's a real pleasure to see Ajay in good health and good spirits.

One of my favorite mottos is from the science fiction writer William Gibson, who says, "The future is already here, it's just unevenly distributed." I think this is a great way of thinking about the notion of nonlinear pattern recognition. Right now, we're looking at a lot of issues around how cultural production is proceeding in the twenty-first century's era of dematerialization and repurposing, or the economic structures that we have come to think of as globalization. So, as above, so below; that is, we have the macro versus the micro.

To me, DJ culture and electronic music have been an urban youth culture response to what's been going on with the macro structure of global digital society. Music is kind of a mirror you hold up to society to see how things evolve. For example, the saxophone's been around for a little bit over a century, and there's a very specific mechanics that had to go into the production of the saxophone. There had to be a social process to [imagine] how orchestras would use it as a played instrument. The same thing happened with almost every instrument in the evolution of what we think of as the composer's tools. So, if a saxophone hadn't been invented before then, would a composer have been able to write music for it? Or, would someone have been able to think about it as a part of the music that they were composing for? If the tool wasn't there, was the composer someone who was at the edge of that particular future? Or, were they someone who was dreaming about instruments that could play what was already in their mind?

The problem with the twenty-first century is related to how much information we have out there and how we navigate through it. The density of the mound of information that we're creating at this time is around about seven to nine petabytes per year, which is the Berkeley Computing Center and Google's way of measuring the volume of information. If you think about the sheer volume of petabytes, it's almost every human word ever spoken since we as a species have ever existed. In terms of scale, you can think of it like this—imagine naming and giving a detailed, precise label for every star in the universe, or being able to literally label almost every molecule of oxygen on the planet, if you so desire. That's the kind of density I'm talking about. How do we navigate it? How does music help us understand how we are organizing human experience? Rhythm structure, cadence—polyrhythm, polytonality—these are some of the key issues I'm highlighting. So, there is an uneasy tension between context and content. How we look at navigating between those two frames is, I think, improvisation.

For me, as an artist, digital media is not necessarily about the process per se. It's about never saying that there's something that's finished. Once something's digital, essentially, you're looking at versions. Anything can be edited, transformed, and completely made into a new thing. For example, if you want to make architecture look like [Edgard] Varèse, I'm sure you can download a Varèse font, and then go for it. Or, for that matter, if you want to make Varèse remixed with the Philips Pavilion, for example, which is a great piece of work between Le Corbusier and the composer Varèse, then you could probably scan photographs. Photoshop it, and turn it into music too.

There are lots of ways that software is a kind of unstable interface between context and content. I think the dialogue between me and Vijay here is not only between different systems of production of music, but it's about how improvisation itself is the bridge between radically different compositional strategies. As an artist, much of my work is based on found materials: records. If we look at the root of the "record," the phonograph, we can play with the rupture or the break in the term: phono-graph, or the phonetics of graphology, or writing with sound.

My new book, *Sound Unbound*, just came out, and Vijay has an essay in it. Pierre Boulez also wrote an essay. Steve Reich wrote the introduction, and many other composers whose work I really value and respect [contributed to the book]. Some of the most fun parts of putting the book together were the research. I ended up finding all sorts of new, fun, quirky pieces.

The idea [that I want to talk about] is "material memory," or how the phonograph is literally about "documents put into play." A record is essentially a document and so is a file. If you're recording a voice, once that voice leaves the body, it essentially becomes a file someplace on somebody else's hard drive. [What I want to examine here is] improvisation, and its relationship to materiality. Think of it as digital mnemonics, or how we use different kinds of recall to make raw data into useful information. So, again, like the metaphor of the saxophone: If it didn't exist, would someone be able to write music for it? At the point that an instrument comes into play, what makes it popular? What makes it become part of everyone's vocabulary? And, at that point, how does the instrument transform the compositional act? So, for me, music is much more about questions than about answers. It's a continuous sense of [asking] questions.

[I want to] interrogate the communal response to collective consciousness. [That is, I want to examine what happens if, say,] I share this record with you, and we share this memory: Does each of us have an interpretation of that memory? How does that memory influence [our interpretation of] the sample, or the data set?

A sample is essentially a chunk of data. It is something that has gone into a computer and has been made into a quantitized fragment that can work in a system of sequences of rhythms. To me, improvisation is part of this notion of pattern recognition. This notion also has a psychological facet, which involves [thinking about] the self as a part of the whole structure. What this means is that you are not separate from the scene that you are viewing.

There's the notion of Schrödinger's cat in physics, which is that by looking at something, you change it. In 1939, John Cage came up with the idea that turntables are essentially a kind of frequency playback system. So, in 1939, the audience walked in and there were two variable speed turntables on stage playing crazy frequencies. People were really pissed off and they wanted their money back. You have to imagine a mellow Buddhist like John Cage making everybody angry; you can imagine that must have been a controversial moment. Let's call it "classical music as the punk rock of the time." [In response to the audience,] John Cage said, "You know, frequencies *are* the piece." [But the audience's view was that] there was nobody on stage, just a lot of records playing random fragments.

In the twenty-first century, the "imaginary landscape" becomes the wireless network. It becomes something as simple as being able to download or upload ringtones to a cell phone. The wireless imagination is [a] good metaphor for thinking about improvisation.

One of my favorite photographers is Étienne-Jules Marey, because, put simply, he was a pioneer of early stop-motion photography. Stop-motion photography allows you to break any kind of motion into its component elements. So, if you see someone running, [for example,] you can actually see his or her legs in every separate frame. They were able to break motion into small fragments. So, that's visual sampling. What ends up happening at the beginning of the twentieth century is that the machinic process of looking at motion or images as components actually becomes part of composition, in general. Erik Satie's *Vexations* [is a good example of this because] you're meant to play motifs over and over. [Something similar] ended up happening with [the music of] other composers like [Olivier] Messiaen. In this sense, there's a convergence happening within the classical scene [at this time].

I want to show you one of the first films to deal with sampling. Georges Méliès was a magician in 1900 who wanted to apply magic technique to cinema. In 1900, films were edited by hand. What he would do is project himself back into the scene, record that, and then play with the projection. What you're going to see [in the film clip] is someone making seven copies of themselves and improvising. This is a very famous film in film studies, but I want you guys to think of it as a jazz motif. In French, this film is called *L'Homme Orchestre* (or, in English, *One-Man Band*).

[Plays Film Clip]

PM: [In the film,] you saw someone literally improvising with recordings of themselves. It was put in a sequence, and you have to remember that this was done by hand. Film was actually physical celluloid. So, they'd have to project it, record that version, and then play with it, that is, literally improvise as the film was playing. You can look at the film for the sense of its choreography.

VI: I just wanted to ask: what about what we just saw suggests to you that there was improvisation involved? I'm asking because I'm interested in how you read it.

PM: Well, you've got to remember that Méliès started out as a magician, and magic is about being able to play with perception. What he ended up doing was trying to figure out how the audience would respond to film. That's the improvisation. He was never quite sure exactly how people would respond to the symbolism. For example, he would do film tricks where he would show up as a little black imp or demon being edited or erased out of the scene. Because of the newness of film, the audience wasn't quite sure how to respond to the projected image. So [I'm interested in] the idea of magic being [incorporated] into a film sequence.

There is a sense of play involved [that relates to improvisation]. So, Méliès knew exactly what he was doing. In fact, he's one of my all-time favorite filmmakers, precisely because he's looking at applying magic technique to film. [Similarly,] Orson Welles (who is also one of my favorite filmmakers) was also into theater. Orson Welles was actually a magician, as well. One of my favorite films is *F Is for Fake*. [Welles depicts] this guy who is Europe's most famous counterfeiter. So, the guy is improvising constantly, by making up identities. This guy was able to [make counterfeit copies of] Modigliani, Picasso, and all these major painters. And, all these museums bought copies of his work, but later couldn't reveal that they owned copies because it would destroy the value of the art objects they thought were "real"—so after a certain point, they became real after enough people said they were. So, again, copies is the core theme, here. What ended up happening was that the guy was so good that the museums didn't want to admit that they had fakes in their collection, since, by saying that it was a fake, they would lose money because it's a value issue.

I'm going to draw a connection between Méliès and Orson Welles because they both play with recorded media. I'm sure most of you know Welles's *War of the Worlds*. *War of the Worlds*, for me, is one of the first mass media "delusions." Since radio was very new, people actually thought the U.S. was being invaded by Martians, simply because they heard a really good storyteller on the radio. They had to call up the army. They had to call in the National Guard. There were riots. So, re-corded media can really trigger quite a few responses. Although the jazz context might be different, I'm interested in examining how improvisa-tion works in a multimedia context.

VI: I guess I'm trying to see if we can, in the course of this conversation, ar-rive at a productive idea about, definition of, or agreement on what we mean when we talk about improvisation, so that we can just be more specific about what it means to improvise digital community.

PM: To me, digital community is about this sense of networks: it's people who you relate to, send files to, and exchange information with. If we were to draw a diagram of everyone in this room and the relationships they have—between you, the moderator, the audience, and me—there's lots of layers of connectivity going on. That's a social process of how human beings create meaning. Improvisation, for me, is much more about looking at music not as music, but as information.

VI: Yeah, and I agree with that. And I think that's where musical impro-visation becomes somewhat indistinguishable from improvisation at large, because [improvisation is] about navigating an informational landscape, whether it's music or not. And perhaps improvised music is something that magnifies [that idea of navigation], in a sense that it seems to be about that process.

I would also again argue that everyday life is improvised to such an extent that it becomes invisible. We, in fact, forget that improvisation is the order of things. So, what I want to get at is this: What is it about new digital notions of community that emerge from that same process? Or, how can we read or theorize about digital community, and our new kind of networked selves? [How can we do this] in a way that makes use of that awareness of what improvisation is, and its fundamental role in everyday life?

PM: Well, you have to remember that jazz in the twentieth century was very region-specific up until the [advent of] recording media. People's relationships to recorded documents, records, changed the relationship to how they viewed the live experience. For the twenty-first century, it's the opposite; in fact, most of us probably respond to recordings of a band before we even go see them live.

VI: So, there's a sense of place that gets kind of diffuse . . .

PM: Yes. Would most of the audience agree that most of us are listening to recordings? If you hear a recording of a band, and you like them, you might go see them, you might go to their website, or you might hear them on a playlist recommendation. [There are] all kinds of social networks for recommendations or what is called "collaborative filtering."

VI: But that refers to consumers, and that's not all that we are.

PM: I'm not . . .

VI: I'm not trying to shoot you down. I just want to see how else this comes into play. In other words, to me improvised music has never been about selling records. It's not about commerce. It's about, once again, a human response to necessity. It's music that emerges at the crossroads of different forces that make it the only recourse for those who find themselves in those conditions. It's a refusal to be silenced; it's a desire to be heard.

We have improvised as listeners; we have improvised as players, and perhaps that overlaps because a player is also a listener, at some level. We're also always improvising. I want [to see if we can make any general statements] about improvising digital community today without falling into the trap of commerce, because digital communities now tend to be interpenetrated by the vectors of commerce.

PM: Yeah, I mean economics is probably the most, I'd say, deep-structured human endeavor. When you think about economics, you can think of— my next album's called *The Invisible Hand*, for example. I'm a huge fan of this notion that we look at organizing principles and patterns and how people interact with one another. Now, economics and commerce obviously are linked, but the idea of the gift economy, for example, or what I just give away, is not necessarily about commerce; but, there is a notion that there's an exchange going on. So, economics is not necessarily always about what they call "capital gains." [Cross-culturally, there are differing perspectives on what constitutes ownership and commerce. The gift economy is one example of a different kind of model.] I mean, I'm not saying . . . there's also an ironic term that Marx and Engels came up with, this notion of "everything that's solid melts into air" once you have this notion of the hyperaccelerated economy. So, if you're an Indian and a Dutch guy shows up on your island—like Manhattan—and says, "Hey I have these red beads. All this land is my land now. I'll give you these red beads." I mean, that's a very unequal exchange, if you know what the value is. But if the Indian's like, "Hey, nobody owns the land, everyone owns the land." Is that commercial for them? Or, are they just inviting these new weird white guys who smell weird from Europe to make a fire and cook a meal, hang out on our island?

That's what is so funny whenever you have these strange European models of ownership applied to other cultures. Other cultures, like those of Japan, India, and China, have highly refined tuning systems and artistic production practice. However, one of the common denominators between many of these cultures is that the artists would never sign their names.

I think that Europe was one of the first cultures to actually come up with this notion of copyrightable and patentable playback systems for ownership. So, if you look at the Renaissance, for example, and the book by Vasari, *Lives of the Artists*, that's one of the first moments in history when the artist is now brought to the foreground. The artist becomes rock star for them. The same thing was going on in music. The composer was no longer some guy in the background playing some cool music for the king. So, that's one system. In West Africa there's a lot of music that comes out of a [different] history, where people were [working with the] collective sense of the gift economy. So, exchange is not always about commerce.

CARL WILSON [MODERATOR]: So Paul, to sort of tie that back in to the idea of digital community, I think one of the possible shifts that happens with the digitization of information is that the notion of community in improvisation that sustained itself through most of the twentieth century was that the group, the ensemble, was the sort of community among which the improvisation happened. And, I think part of what you're getting at a little bit, with talking about other cultural models and the role of the artist, is that maybe that idea is dispersing in some way through these sort of networks of information.

PM: Yes, there's an infamous Brian Eno statement in *Wired* magazine a couple of years ago where he said, "The problem with computers is that there's not enough Africa in them." I think it's the opposite; there's actually a lot of Africa in them. Everyone's beginning to exchange and trade freeware. [You can] rip, mix and burn. That's a different kind of improvisation. What I think Vijay is intimating is that we're in an unbalanced moment in which so much of the stuff is made by commercial [companies]. My laptop is not my culture. The software that I use—whether it's Protools, Sonar, or Audiologic—[is not my culture per se]. But, it *is* part of the culture because it's a production tool.

VI: Well, the thing I was just sort of cautioning against was the idea that "we are our playlists." I just didn't want [our discussion] to become like "because we listen to these things, this is who we are," especially at a moment when the privileged can listen to anything, which means that listening starts to . . . well, it starts to sound like noise or it starts to decrease in value. Or, [there's a sense that it's possible to be] listening without place. Listening in cyberspace or listening in a place that has no, I don't want to say that cyberspace has no community, because as we know it does. But, what I find to be somewhat of a mistake is the eliding of live performance. It's those moments of live performance that, in fact, feel more alive than they ever did. They feel more animated.

PM: But, is it after you've played in the memory stage of a live performance? Because what I'm saying is that a recording is essentially a distillation of a live moment.

VI: It is, and yet the liveness of it gets diffused, or it gets lost, when you can stockpile at a terrifying rate, which means you can have a year's worth of music [on a device that can fit] in my shirt pocket. So then, what does music mean anymore? The live moment ends up bringing you back to that primal recognition that music is human action. It comes out of people using their bodies to take action, and using devices of whatever kinds to create events, audio events. But of course, then there's the fact that you can sit and make electronic music just by moving your knuckles around on a laptop for a while, and then that can be played on a dance floor or sold to thousands of people.

In a way I find that live performance brings people back to the fact that music is an embodied thing. [It is something] that people do with other people and with their own bodies. And, there's something that feels more urgent about that reality than I can remember in thirty-three years of music-making.

PM: Well, it's like we've come full circle. In the twentieth century, the idea of the recording actually displaced the live experience altogether. And that's the idea of mass culture, mass production, the mass scale of what we call "pop culture." This was literally about [creating] mass consumers of music. [The] Rolling Stones could not have existed, if there was not a music industry behind them pushing a certain very limited, narrow product. Essentially, you have a sense of artificial scarcity.

In economics, what ends up happening is that you have physical objects being defined by scarcity, and that's what creates value. If you go to a rich person's house and they have a Picasso on the wall they want to make sure that they know that they have *that* Picasso, and the scarcity [is what makes it valuable]. But value, in the twentieth century, went through a whole tumultuous cycle as the "culture of the copy" kicked in. If everyone has a [copy of a] Picasso painting, does that mean it still has value? (I'm sure most of us have heard of Walter Benjamin's "The Work of Art in the Age of Mechanical Reproduction.") So, [there's a connection between the notion of] the live experience and the notion of having a unique object. What ends up happening with music in the age of cybernetic replication is that [these ideas of authenticity are challenged]. You need to think about how the root word of *replication* is based on the term *reply*. It's a response. It's not about a passive situation. I think what ends up happening with a lot of hip-hop, techno, drum and bass, all those styles of music that I call home, is that—essentially, they're about saying that the recorded medium is your archives. It's something that's a living, breathing archive. Your memory of a song might be subjective, but once it's made objectively available, anyone can remix, remake, and reedit [it]. It's that sense of reply to a thing that made kids in the 1970s go wild.

So, if you're Afrika Bambaataa playing in a park in 1975, and you're having a DJ battle with Grand Master Flash, they wanted to know who had the most amount of bass because that would make people move. And that's a whole Jamaican sound system thing. You have to remember that in New York we had this huge urban renewal project by Robert Moses and it ended up destroying a lot of the city parks for the cross-Bronx expressway; so, the social patterns [changed]. Kids would gather in the park during the summer. They'd turn on the fire hydrant. If you were in the south Bronx, you didn't have too much else going on. It was a very heavy economic situation.

So, after the riots of the 1960s, people were trying to figure out urban decay. Detroit was dying. L.A. had gone through a whole bunch of turmoil. [As did] Washington, D.C., Philadelphia, most of the main U.S. cities. In Canada, you guys didn't riot so much. I think half the war veterans were up here maybe chilling out. You guys just sent back an American, and I was like, "What?" . . . Stephen Harper. So, the war and turbulence of the 1960s, the crazy riots and assassinations, that's the birth-cry of certain kinds of social structures, and [gave rise to] hip-hop. I really don't think people would just go and hear a record play someplace; they would want to have a social environment for their kind of community. It's shared experience.

CARL WILSON: But is there a shift now? [What Paul has outlined is] twenty-five years of hip-hop history. But, I think part of what Vijay's talking about in relationship to the live experience is [that there's a difference between] the live experience and your experience with a file full of MP3s in isolation. Perhaps, you're in community, in the sense that you're exchanging files. But, I think [Vijay's] trying to point out that there's an important contrast between that kind of exchange and the kind of exchange that happens at a live session.

PM: Let me play you a response. The whole notion of hip-hop as "not live" is very problematic. In fact, when I was coming up on the scene, there was a lot of beef between the older jazz musicians and younger hip-hop kids. In fact, I was one of the first DJs to work with Amiri Baraka, and he [would say things like,] "You know, Paul, this hip-hop's OK, but why's it always repeatin'?" It's a valid question.

The funny thing [about] repetition is that it's a very real thing. There must be some psychoanalytic thing about why people think repetition, on one hand, is not musical, while on the other hand it's about deep immersion. So, [while there's] live poetry, live playing, live theatre and concerts, I'd say [that] right now your average kid's relationships to video games, to their cell-phone ring tones, to their text-message communities, and to their instant messaging [are stronger]. Trust me, they are a community.

[Miller says to Iyer] "How's your kid?"

VI: Three and a half. She's sending text messages.

PM: So, [these new technologies and hip-hop are] a translation of certain impulses. I want to play a quick example of one of the earliest hip-hop MC battles, and I think you will chuckle over the kind of historical issues going on. It is actually very old school. It's Run DMC versus Kool Moe Dee.

[plays clip]

VI: I agree that this music is improvised, in the sense that the entire history of the music that we're talking about was improvised, not just on the note-to-note level, but on the level of its very existence. In the same way that, if you were in the woods and you had a stick and a blanket, you would improvise a tent out of those things. This [musical example] is something that arose out of what was at hand and what was necessary. And, especially in the case of hip-hop's origins, which you've just described, [it drew upon] the energy of that moment: the human impulse to create, in response to conditions that are imposed on us. So what you've just portrayed for us resonates with that notion of improvisation I described earlier.

What I also think is interesting about all of these musics is that they also radically revise the idea of composition. It dehierarchizes the idea of composition. If you think of the root words of *composition*, it's just about placing things with other things, which is what you do as a DJ. This is what hip-hop culture was: it's about taking these found objects and found sounds, and placing them alongside each other in a way that's about building with these raw materials, with these constitutive elements. So, reframing these guys as composers, essentially, is crucial too. I also want to be able to name things as both [composition and improvisation], so that we don't fall prey to that binary. That is, the binary between composition and improvisation is false. In other words, these cultural phenomena should be able to be read, in terms of their improvised *and* composed elements, because everything has those elements.

PM: This [roundtable] is about a dialogue, where each artist here has radically different approaches to compositional strategy. I'm going to keep riffing on that term *compositional strategy* because essentially collage [uses] everything on the table. You can take lots and lots of different [materials]. Anything goes.

In my book *Sound Unbound*, we tracked down the estate of the composer Raymond Scott. He made a lot of early computer music. He was one of the first composers to make music for TV commercials like jingles, but he called the jingles "audio logos." What I love about that is that the idea of a recognizable motif has a whole psychoanalytic relationship to memory. So, you can hear certain sequences of sounds, you can hear ring tones, you can hear a whole sense of how a sequence works in electronic music, but it's still playing with memory. As we move further into the twenty-first century, this idea of the "database aesthetics" [is] a kind of basic root of how people look at digital life or living in a digital information economy.

I was walking down the street in Luanda, Angola, and they had just ended a twenty-five-year tribal war, care of U.S. tax dollars at work. They had a lot of gold, oil, and diamonds. Now, there's about 30,000 plus Chinese walking around downtown Luanda because of the relationship of the Chinese petroleum corporations to the Marxist regime of President Dos Santos. So, I'm walking down, [and I see that] all the buildings have crazy high-caliber-bullet pock marks; it has a serious ex-war zone look. But, in the midst of it all, every single kid on the corner had bootlegged DVDs, and every possible ripped, mixed, burned copy of Tupac, or Puff Daddy, you name it. They also had a style of music called Kuduro, which is like techno mixed with certain Angolan and Brazilian motifs because Angola was a Portuguese empire.

So, all the kids are raging about Kuduro, and if you go to Rio, which is across the black Atlantic, as Paul Gilroy likes to call it, you can hear this style called baile funk. *Baile* sort of means the ghetto area; it's a kind of very underground style of music. So, the people of these two different cultures across the Atlantic share a common history of colonialism, a common history of responding against colonialism. [Both styles have] a very interesting common denominator.

I found the PDF of the score of "Imaginary Landscapes," so I guess I can stop asking you to visualize it. The instructions for the complete composition says, "Begin at 33 1/3 RPM. Thereafter, shift clutch with each X appearing in score." The actual score for this piece becomes about shifting speeds, playback systems, and duration. In physics, the sustained release of a note or a tone actually has a sound envelope, and that can be added in and transformed simply with playback speeds. So, if you hear something very slow, it has a radically different sound than if you play it very fast. So, [Cage] was playing with variable speeds. And I like thinking about that as a new form of polyphony, where the composer is trying to figure out this quirky object called the phonograph in 1939. You have to remember that it was probably [considered] high tech for that time period.

If you think about the way that we listen to encoded music these days, the format you encode something in is MP3, AAC, FLAC, or OGG. Each of these encrypted ways of playing something can be interrupted. And, I think that there's some tricksterism, whether it's playing with words, with fragments of a recorded medium, or with how people will respond to something that's a perceived sequence. That's that magic that I think Méliès was going for back in the beginning of the twentieth century. Magic is a kind of improvisation, and maybe we're looking at the twenty-first century as an [appearance] of magic realism. [We are] playing with the materials around us, and seeing that playfulness as irreverent to this notion that every found record or every found picture. . . . anything can be changed. That's kind of what I hope we have as a common ground.

Questions from the Audience

AUDIENCE MEMBER 1: Doesn't improvisation sort of imply a sense of community? If you just go online and look at digital files that everybody looks at from a different context what does all that mean? That's ignorance, to me. You have all this information and you don't know what it is? You mentioned Raymond Scott. If you go out in the real world, almost nobody knows about him.

PM: But a lot of people have heard the Loony Tunes theme.

AUDIENCE MEMBER 1: Do they know it's by Raymond Scott?

PM: It doesn't matter. You can say that the memory of that sound has influenced millions of people. You're not going to know every song you hear, all the time.

AUDIENCE MEMBER 1: But, if you have all this data, in general . . . and you have no context for understanding . . .

VI: Well, you always have context. It's more about how active you are in seeking out that context. I guess the question is how active does one become in fleshing out one's context, or in responding to it, or being really engaged with it, and does that then make you more fully realized?

PM: And, by the way, I don't think that everyone looking online is making community. It's a way of saying, "We share something." And that sense of sharing goes beyond nation-states. It goes beyond geography. It goes beyond class and race. One of the fun things about this strange, entropic early twenty-first century file-exchange culture is that it's actually eerily post-geographic. Some kid in Brazil will download a mix from Finland. Sigur Rós gets bootlegged and remixed in baile funk. That kind of social sculpture is very beautiful, but also it's so huge and so bizarrely . . . I don't think about the kid down the block. I'm thinking much more about what kids are going to be doing in the next ten years or so, as geography, as the twentieth century defined it, and you're saying the notion of community in the physical space that's . . . I think a lot of kids who are playing massive multiplayer [games], they don't know where their partners are, unless somebody tells you. Or, if you're in Second Life . . . The country Sweden was the first country to open an embassy in Second Life. If you want to bypass all the lines, there you go. But, I think there's a lot to be said: this is new, and we're still feeling our way out. I would say that this isn't the end all and be all. I definitely hope that not everybody leaves here saying, "Oh, DJ Spooky's saying that everything's great online." Yeah, there are lots of issues.

AUDIENCE MEMBER 2: You talked about improvisation between the artists in a live venue, but in that event of improvisation the audience also plays a role in the improvisation. So, in that case, in a situation like that, and let's say it's recorded, is there really any ownership to that? I mean, is it part of a community at that point, and then it's just out there, is there really any ownership to that?

VI: Well this has been one of the great issues in twentieth-century copyright laws, and it continues to be an issue. If you look at the history of what's called "jazz," you'll see a history of responses to that issue. For example, in "Bird of Paradise," Charlie Parker plays over "All the Things You Are." There's a preexisting song, but it's named "Bird of Paradise." The melody is never played, and so it becomes this composition. But, he improvised it. Why did it become a composition? Because the record companies said, "OK, what are we going to call this?" And then he could have, for that moment, [claimed] ownership of that version or that rendition of that song. This is why they then said, "Well, why don't we just write our own tunes over these harmonic progressions that we already have." That was a way of circumventing the ownership issue. So they composed and they'd improvise and who owned that? The record company.

AUDIENCE MEMBER 2: Improvisation is a moment in time; we've crystallized it. How can you own that moment in time?

VI: There are multiple issues interpenetrating here. One is the issue of who owns music. Period. Then, there's the issue of the relationship between artists and those who wish to own their content, which is another dynamic that creates imbalances. People have responded [to this dynamic] in different ways. [Some have said,] "Well, we're composers, too," so let's write our own tunes and only play over our own tunes and create our own harmonic progressions. Then it got even wilder because it was like, "We're going to create this improvised situation that's ours. And no one owns it but us." But then there are these people who sample things and are also improvising, using a technique that [DJ Spooky] pioneered. And that became another issue. This has been a dynamic that [has shaped] the history of music as we know it.

[The session concludes with a sampling of various compositions and improvisations.]

Notes

This conversation was first published in *Critical Studies in Improvisation / Études critiques en improvisation* 5, no. 1 (2009). It has been transcribed by Elizabeth Groeneveld.

  1. Natasha Pravaz, "Brazilian Music and Community Building in Toronto," (presented at Diaspora, Dispersal, Improvisation, and Imagination, the Guelph Jazz Festival Colloquium, September 3, 2008, Guelph, Ontario, Canada).

Douglas Ewart, Nicole Mitchell, Roscoe Mitchell,
Famoudou Don Moye, Matana Roberts,
Jaribu Shahid, Wadada Leo Smith,
and Corey Wilkes

CHAPTER 13

ANCIENT TO THE FUTURE
Celebrating Forty Years of the AACM

Like the conversation between Vijay Iyer and Paul Miller, featured elsewhere in this volume, this roundtable discussion between members of the Association for the Advancement of Creative Musicians (AACM) was convened as part of the Guelph Jazz Festival Colloquium (2005). And like the discussion between Iyer and Miller, the AACM panel features myriad perspectives on improvised music and the implications that the music has for social relations. Featuring a range of new and founding members of the organization, the panel marked the occasion of the AACM's 40th anniversary. This is particularly significant given the high-profile "damned with faint praise" moment for the AACM in Ken Burns's television miniseries documentary Jazz: A Film by Ken Burns *(2000). In the series, the prominent ensemble made up of AACM members, the Art Ensemble of Chicago, becomes an example of the supposed "death of jazz" during the 1970s. Despite on-screen interviews with the late trumpeter Lester Bowie, a member of the ensemble, Burns's documentary uses the group as one of the foils for later jazz saviors (other culprits in jazz's death include Cecil Taylor and the electrified Miles Davis). Doomed, states the narrator of* Jazz, *"to playing small audiences of college students, in France," the Art Ensemble is the film's ultimate scapegoat for jazz music's downfall in terms of public and commercial relevance and success. Seen from a different perspective, however, the Art Ensemble and the larger framework of the AACM is precisely the kind of organization that has sustained improvised music. As the comments in the panel discussion suggest, the AACM and its various ensembles have always carried out the twin missions of paying respect to tradition while making new traditions, and people are listening. The presence of the surviving members of the Art Ensemble—Roscoe Mitchell, Famoudou Don Moye, and, via a phone call during the conversation, Joseph Jarman—in this* discussion gives the lie to the institutionalized version of jazz history promulgated by Burns's documentary. Not only are these musicians still playing for a variety of audiences (and audiences, large and small, young and old, are discussed at length in the course of the roundtable); they are still educating younger musicians who, in turn, represent the best of traditions of innovation, social justice, and community-building fostered by the AACM. Rather than a supposed decline and fall, the AACM's story tells of a pivotal moment in the history of twentieth-century jazz, when musicians decided to take their destiny into their own hands. The roundtable offers readers an intimate glimpse into this history and its implications for the future.

One of the many notable features of this panel discussion is that it was the source of a phrase now familiar to many in the improvised-music community: the drummer Famoudou Don Moye says of the AACM, "I don't have a lot to add . . . except that it has been and it remains to be a power stronger than itself." A Power Stronger than Itself subsequently became the title of the AACM member George Lewis's history of the organization, published in 2008 to great acclaim—and, again, helping to rectify notions of obsolescence or just plain slander about this seminal group of African American innovators.

The conversation includes diverse perspectives, reflecting the different members assembled: Douglas Ewart, Nicole Mitchell, Roscoe Mitchell, Famoudou Don Moye, Matana Roberts, Jaribu Shahid, Wadada Leo Smith, and Corey Wilkes. Also present in the audience and adding an interesting context to some of the discussion is musician Eugene Chadbourne (again demonstrating the wide range of influence that the AACM has had).

Echoing a phrase by the historian Vincent Harding, which historian and music scholar George Lipsitz in turn often uses to describe the potential effects of supposedly "small" events, Jaribu Shahid notes that the cumulative efforts of the AACM have been "like a pebble dropped into a lake and the ripple effect is still being felt." Shahid observes, "There are a number of people who come after this who . . . want to act like this didn't happen. I think it is important for us to realize the importance that these individuals here and a lot who are not here anymore have made in the world of music." Matana Roberts, a more recent member of the AACM, confirmed this legacy and summed up the protective, familial bonds of the organization. Speaking of her time away from Chicago, during which she faced new challenges, Roberts states, "It's meant a sense of knowing who I am . . . and I was thinking about a good way to describe it [the AACM]. It is like being dangled from a skyscraper but I have a bunch of cords . . . so, I am not going to fall too far even if I fall." The cords and *chords woven and played by the AACM are too tightly connected to the fabric of American—and global—musical life to be easily ignored or forgotten. This panel gives testimony to the enduring legacy, current challenges, and ongoing dedication of the AACM, "ancient to future."*

The following has been excerpted, with permission, from "Power Greater than Itself: Celebrating the AACM in Guelph," first published in the online music journal *Point of Departure* 3, found at http://pointofdeparture.org.

Friday, September 9, 2005: Macdonald Stewart Art Centre, Guelph Jazz Festival Colloquium

Transcription by Marianne Trudel and Bill Shoemaker

TECHNICAL NOTE: Audience members asked questions off-mic. Sometimes, their questions were prefaced with lengthy statements that were not fully audible. These statements have been summarized. Their questions have been transcribed as accurately as possible.

AJAY HEBLE: Good morning, everyone, and welcome to day three of the Guelph Jazz Festival and Colloquium. We've had a fantastic opening two days, and this morning we have a very special panel called, "Ancient to the Future: Celebrating 40 Years of the AACM." I'm going to turn things right over to Douglas Ewart, who will introduce the panelists and moderate the discussion.

DOUGLAS EWART: Good morning, everyone. On the behalf of the Association for the Advancement of Creative Musicians, we would like to extend the warmest greetings to each and every one of you. For those of you who may not know, the Association is celebrating its 40th year of existence this year, and what we thought we would do this morning is have each one of the panelists speak a little bit about the relevance and the importance of the association to them in their lives. So, I would like to start this morning by maybe having Roscoe Mitchell speak. We will have each panelist make a statement for approximately three to five minutes, and then we will field some questions from you.

ROSCOE MITCHELL: Thank you, Douglas. Well, I would say that the AACM is very important in my life. It has been an important vehicle for many people that I have met through the years, and I would consider myself to be lucky to have been in Chicago at the time the AACM started, and I would look back to the experimental band of Muhal Richard Abrams, as where these ideas started to formulate. Back in the 60s, Muhal had an experimental band. We met every Monday night and there we were all encouraged to write our own original compositions, bring them in to the band, and get them heard and so on. Those were the early seeds for the AACM: people started to talk, musicians had taken a look to what had happened to some of the great musicians that came before us, who really didn't have real connections with each other and then people started to think, We want to have an organization where we can be more in control of our own destinies. We wanted to have a place where we could sponsor each other in concerts of our original compositions, provide a training program for young, aspiring musicians in the community, reach out to other people and other cities and have exchange programs. It was around that time, after the AACM was formed, that I met Lester Bowie. who had come from St. Louis, and there was many musicians that we met through Lester Bowie and we started exchange programs. Later on, I moved to Michigan and I formed the CAC, the Creative Arts Collective. We maintained the same basic fundamental principles of sponsoring the members in concerts and having exchange programs with musicians from other cities in [an] effort to be in control of our own destinies and provide employment for musicians. Even the schools on some levels became involved with that. Back there you had Richard Teitelbaum, who was teaching here in Toronto, at York University. There were concerts in Toronto, many concerts in Toronto at that time. Many of the student groups formed groups inside of the university so that they could have a say in the different musicians that they were bringing in to the campuses, other than just a status quo. So, to me, the AACM is more than an organization. It is a lifestyle. And I am constantly reminded [of] what the AACM has meant to so many people when I go out to do concerts and people come up to me and they express to me their experiences upon hearing the musicians from the AACM for the first time and how it affected their lives and the lives of their children.

DE: Wadada Leo Smith.

WADADA LEO SMITH: OK. What can I say? All of you are here to hear us talk about the AACM. That is probably important. I guess the most important thing that I would like to relate to you about the AACM is the notion of community. The whole idea that the structure of community is based around not just existence but an ongoing revolution, new ideas, a new way of thinking and an idea that is based on the actuality that once you come up with a beautiful idea, you have to put it into effect. And, from that, the community grows and expands, you know, and the idea of that, which is really great and benefits to the whole community in every way, also expands. And you can see that by the kind of artistic communities that have been formed around the world. That's the most important part. Thank you.

DE: Donald Moye.

FAMOUDOU DON MOYE: Good morning. Bonjour tout le monde. Guten tag. Buon giorno. Hola. Roscoe Mitchell and Leo stated it pretty well. I don't have a lot to add to that except that it [the AACM] has been and it remains to be a power stronger than itself.

DE: Jaribu Shahid.

JARIBU SHAHID: Good morning. Coming from Detroit, I guess I can speak on more of a cursory relationship with the AACM, how important it was for us when we were trying to develop our music to know that such an institution existed, that it was possible for an institution like this to exist. And that people that could involve themselves in a community that would allow for different kinds of thinking musically. I was involved with the Creative Arts Collective, in Detroit, and it allowed us to do concerts. It's where I met Roscoe and we had Anthony Braxton and Muhal and Douglas, and a number of people came in to work with us, and I can speak about how it influenced a lot of musicians in Detroit, and I am sure in a lot of other cities, as well. It's like a pebble dropped into a lake and the ripple effect is still being felt. There are a number of people who come after this who kind of want to act like this didn't happen. I think it is important for us to realize the importance that these individuals here, and a lot who are not here anymore, have made in the world of music.

DE: I would like to introduce our vice-chairman, or chairwoman, Nicole Mitchell. Chairperson? Chairwoman!

NICOLE MITCHELL: Chairwoman! 'Cause that means evidence.

DE: Yes.

NM: I have been in the AACM since 1995, so a lot happened before I came and it is important for me just to state that the AACM is like a family; it is a mentorship and the beauty of it is, as Roscoe says, the community but also because now we have such a great sharing between generations and at the same time there is this legacy. So we have this great history and legacy and yet we keep to the philosophy of striving for your own voice and to complete that goal of creating original music. That is what I always tried to do and it is very important to me, because I am kind of in between; like, I have been around for ten years and at the same time there is a lot of younger members coming in, and I feel like a bridge, that I have to bridge the gap between those that came before me and have brought so much and have taken so much responsibility to bring us to where we are today, and those who are coming in that are still new to the ideas and to coming into these relationships with people. That is what it is about: it is about relationships with people; it is an association. And that has brought so much wealth to me to be able to connect with all these different perspectives on music, on life, and, at the same time, have that diversity celebrated. And that is what I think is a real strength of the organization. And the ideas and the possibilities have not even come close to being realized. It is just up to us to realize the power of the vehicle and be able to bring it forward into the next future that we are into now.

DE: I would like to introduce our next speaker, Matana Roberts.

MATANA ROBERTS: Good morning. What the AACM has meant to me . . . I grew up on the music of the AACM, through my father, who would take me to concerts, play me record after record after record. And, it has created in me, since becoming a member of the association I think in 2001 or 2000 . . . It's meant a sense of knowing who I am. It has given me a better sense because for the moment I don't live in Chicago. I live in New York City, and I was thinking about a good way to describe it. It is like being dangled from a skyscraper, but I have a bunch of cords [laughs], so I am not going to fall too far even if I fall. The AACM has and is still giving me such a sense of community and being involved as it did when I was in Chicago at the AACM School and teaching children. The ability of the AACM to go back to community to give—I really don't think that there are enough musicians and artists that are doing that in such a way that the AACM has continued to do so over a number of years. And the other thing about the AACM, for me, is it has taught me that I can be as free, as open, and as creative as I want to be. Because of the myriad of generations and organizations, I have so many people to look up to, to see that I can fly like that, too. I can go in that direction if I want to do that, and the standard of musicianship and the standard of music-making is at such a level that it is inspiring. So, that is what [it] is for me.

DE: Corey Wilkes.

COREY WILKES: Good morning. I think I am one of the most recent members of the AACM, about a whole week now [laughs]. But I have been performing with musicians of the AACM over the last two to five years, roughly. Being a part of the AACM now, or I should say from the outside looking in, it meant creativity, freedom, and unity, which is the most important, and the understanding that you have to go all the way out in order to explore yourself. You can never understand everything if you don't go out of the box. You have to go out of the box to go in, you know. So, exploring that freedom in your music and lifestyle is going to help you a lot and make you go a long way.

DE: I am caught chewing a grape [laughs]. I wanted to say that the panel reflects the resilience of the Association for the Advancement of Creative Musicians. We have several generations of AACM membership here and one of the things people often ask me is Why is it that the AACM has existed for as long as it has? Because the era in which the organization was formed, many organizations were formed, not just musical but political [groups] and from the visual arts, from the writers' areas, and so forth. And I said to them that I think it is the flexibility that we have within the organization. It is not that we are friction-free, but we always advocate for each other. No matter what is going on, there is always someone there to say This is the way this person is and we should accept them in this way. That does not mean that they should transform themselves in some way, but that acceptance of who we are right now; now is the time, now is always the time. So, you have to accept in order to have transformation. In order to have a development, you have to accept where you are as a person and where other people are as individuals. I think that is one of the strongest aspects of the organization, for me, having gone through the stage of being a student, one of the earliest students at the Association School of Music, which was formulated in October, formally, in October 1967. And I am sitting a couple of chairs from one of my first teachers, Roscoe Mitchell. So, we can see the development of the organization, where the idea is to always foster new spirits, new souls, and that is evidenced right here, today. I think at this point we can get some questions or comments from the audience and since we only have a few minutes, we would like everybody to speak at once [laughs].

AUDIENCE MEMBER 1: Good morning. I am a musician from Mexico. In 1980–1981, somebody from the organization asked me to suggest people to come to Mexico. I suggested the Art Ensemble, from Chicago. The presence of the Art Ensemble of Chicago in Mexico was very important—this work with musicians, and this work with young musicians then, that understood that something has happened, and that something would happen different. I see here that the AACM has different generations, but I think a problem that we have everywhere, in Canada as well as in the U.S.A. and Mexico, is how to deal with young persons, how to make our audiences younger, and how to make people understand and love what we do. What can you do? What has the AACM done, and what would you suggest for us to do?

RM: I have always felt that we owe a responsibility to our younger people, that is, to pass on the tradition. In fact, when I was growing up, this is the way it used to be. During those times, if someone was doing something that you wanted to learn how to do, the only thing you had to show them was that you were really interested and wanted to know that, and they would show you that. And, certainly, I have lived in a time when this was happening, but it is a thing that you have to nurture. I mean, you can't expect young people to know anything about anything if you don't expose them to any of these things. It was different when I was growing up, because you could almost talk to anybody and they knew something about everything, but now it is not like that anymore. So, it is probably time to re-nurture the young. They have to be exposed to these things in order to know them, and what I felt about this music is that, from my own point of view, it takes a long time to get to be what I would like to be. And then, I have also found out, maybe some people thought that this music stopped, but it doesn't stop. In my case, I could say that maybe some things that I thought about in the 60s, I start to come close to now. So, it is a question of involvement. Back then, you would not only have a festival, you would have concerts that go on throughout the year, I mean, on a smaller scale. I mean, you don't bring everybody for one concert. It's back to the old thing of exposure.

I will give you another example: listening to the radio as a young person, on one particular station you might hear a variety of different things throughout the whole day and everybody knew, no matter if it was a song from jazz or a popular song or a religious song or the blues or whatever, everybody was always exposed to all of these things. Now we have radio that plays the same songs over and over and over, so there you don't have any exposure. I think it is good that jazz went to colleges, but maybe it is not that great, because there is no focus put on any music that is creative. It used to be, if I go back to the 60s, you might go to a concert at a college and there you could see a wide variety of programming at a college. It might be the Art Ensemble there, it might be John Cage. I am just giving these two examples, because that is a far-stretched example; but what we noticed is that people could make up their own minds about the things they want to listen to. People should be exposed to things, and then they can have some choices, but if they are not given the choice, then that starts to cut off the different avenues that they might choose to think about.

DE: Nicole?

NM: I was going to say for your community, I am sure that there's lots of musicians that play this creative music that you are interested in and there's ways of creating programs for the youth. For example, when I was on my way here, I went through Ann Arbor, and my band performed at an elementary school, and I brought one of the pieces that I wrote with graphic notation called "Symboloces Series," and I showed them what we were playing and explained different shapes, and then we played it. And this school happened to have a music program where they had recorders, so then I gave the music teacher a copy of the music so that they could try to play it later. And there's lot of ways to do that, to expose the youth to this music, especially those that are learning instruments already, because they come up and they don't just get the chance to find out about it until they are worn out, in a lot of cases. And the younger they can be exposed to it, the more, you know. I mean, they are so open. I had a little five-year-old scat to an atonal piece. She was like: Can I play your flute? Can I play your flute? And I said: You need to go home and tell your parents you want to play the flute, and I know when she went home that day that she went home to ask for a flute. So, I think that is really just about finding creative ways and then it is good for the artists, too, because we really enjoy sharing—so finding ways for your local musicians to do more programs in the schools and educational situations.

AUDIENCE MEMBER 2: I wanted to ask if the AACM came out in a very turbulent time, socially and culturally. How has that influenced the creation of the AACM and how has that maintained or sustained itself as
you move into different generations and extend out to younger people?

DE: Well, the 60s—we say it is a turbulent time but I think it is always a
turbulent time, particularly for our experiences, black people on the
planet and coming out of Chicago, were the most segregated and still
to this day. There have been changes made, but if you ride public transportation, it is very visceral, what occurs. As soon as you get to a certain place, the train makes a transformation. I happened to teach at a
institution in Chicago, the school of the Art Institute of Chicago, and it
is very interesting that I have to make my students go into the South
Side by planning field trips that forced them into that community, because there is still that fear of black people that they had grown up with
and that is enhanced in a sense by many institutions, whether directly
or indirectly, because they don't plan anything that occurs in the community. They will bring black people to the school, but they won't go
where black people are; so, I think, for us, we have always had to adapt.

Self-determination is what the organization was founded on. When
the organization developed, one of the reasons that it was so crucial
was some of the sources of outlet for us were drying up. Places that
the music was once able to be heard were being systematically closed
down. I don't want to go too far afield but politics is an important part
of everyday life—daily—and the climate was very difficult for black
musicians, particularly to survive in Chicago, so we had to devise a
method in which to survive and the Association for the Advancement
of Creative Musicians provided that platform because we were self-
producing, we did our own posters, our own distribution, and started
our own recording companies, and so on. And it is still as important
today as it was in the 60s, and one of the things Roscoe mentioned was,
you know, we are in such a hurry now, you know; if an idea is more
than a day old it is no longer relevant. I think one of the things, when
we think about creativity, is not just music but even the first toys that
kids play with: we have kids that play with things that they don't make
themselves, that they can't fix, things of that nature. I think creativity
is on a lot of levels and we have to think about that. So, when we are
thinking about creativity, we can start by improvising with our children, with pots and pans, pencils, just giving them a wider imagination

and more control over what is it you do, what the kids eat, where they eat—all of these things are related to creativity. Kids don't know how to cook now because everybody eats out, and they don't even know what good food is, so those are some of the things that we need to think about when we think about creativity, and not just in terms of music and painting, but creativity in every aspect of survival, and thriving rather than just surviving. Any other questions?

AUDIENCE MEMBER 3: I was wondering, in the early stages, what ensembles, what groups there were. I know Leroy Jenkins and Muhal Richard Abrams were important in the early stages. What were they playing?

RM: The AACM has always been an organization of small groups and large bands. Out of the AACM, you mentioned a couple of groups but there were several others: Joseph Jarman's quartet, with Christopher Gaddy and Charles Clark. Both of those musicians have passed on. Wadada Leo Smith groups, groups with Anthony and Wadada and Leroy Jenkins and so on. We have always made a practice of having large ensembles and smaller ensembles. In fact, the AACM is a group of people that has instruments that people don't even have. I mean, in order to really see the AACM full-blown, opportunities would have to be presented so that it would be possible to present some of these situations. Speaking from my own point of view, I have a percussion set-up that I have been developing since the 60s, which is 10' by 10' floor space, and I have all these instruments that I have been collecting from all over the world and so on. But, I go back to when jazz went to college. See the thing about going to college—it's a good thing if you reflect things that have already happened, but you also have to keep yourself in tune with what is going on now, you see. He [Douglas Ewart] was talking about the political situation. Back in my times, you had a lot of individual thinkers, which you don't have now, and then people functioned in certain roles for a certain amount of time, and then it might be time for them to move on to other parts of their lives. The problem that I see that happened is that no one came to fill in these spaces with these great, great people who were doing all these things. So, somewhere in there, there was a breakdown, but it stills goes back to [the idea that] we have to stand for something. We have to stand for something. We have to be individuals with visions, and we can't just, like, change our vision just because it is something that is in style today that wasn't in style yesterday and what

I see with a lot of younger musicians today . . . [RM's phone rings.] Excuse me. [to caller] I'm going to pass you over to Douglas.

DE [taking phone]: This is crucial, everybody.

RM: So, what I see from a lot of younger musicians today is that they come to me and they are disillusioned. They said OK, I went to college and now I can do this and now what? You know, whereas the AACM has always been an organization that encouraged people to look inside and find individuality, because once you do that, then you have an endless source of energy to draw from. If you are not doing that, then you are always placed in the position of waiting to see what everybody else does and then trying to do that, and it is difficult to be someone else, but it is really easy to be yourself. So the main thing that you have to do is to try to find out what your individual calling is and, once you have that, you go on endlessly.

AUDIENCE MEMBER 4: The students in the courses I teach—their model of political engagement right now is based on hip-hop. It seems to me that one of the biggest contrasts between the 60s ideals and the hip-hop ideals has to do with the socialist vision of economic organization, and to me the AACM represents a less entrepreneurial idea than that which comes out of hip-hop—and I'm just wondering what kind of dialogue the AACM might be having with perhaps a younger generation of musicians who are coming out of hip-hop.

RM: Well, you bring up a good point there. Now, what I would like to do is go back to what I said earlier about people knowing about stuff. Hip-hop is popular because it is an accepted art form that makes a lot of money, so this is what people like hearing all the time, you know. So now there has to be more situations created where people are interacting more like they used to. I remember concerts in Chicago that were only musical concert . . .

[AM 4 interrupts to make a distinction about "underground hip-hop."]

DE: I think that every form has its heights. There are hip-hop artists that are doing strong work. I think any form has weak stuff in it, and because of the commerciality of hip-hop, it has a lot more weaker forces, and because you can captivate people with . . . Music is a really potent force and what I have done with my classes as an experiment where we look at—I don't want to call an artist name per se—we looked at a piece that was really denigrating women with the music. It was seductive. When you turn the music down, people clamored for it to be turned off immediately, and so we have to realize the magic of music—that it can bring good things, and it can bring bad things. We have to watch that. Wadada?

WLS: You know, life is very hard when there is a disconnect. And there is a disconnect, essentially worldwide. I recommend that we need a consultation for what it is [that is] coming. I think that the biggest problem with AACM and every other kind of artistic community is that they are not privileged with having a consultation among themselves about what they're doing. This consultation will not include how to make more money or how to get more personal power and stuff like that. But it would be about how we engage the artistic element to improve and strengthen our communities. In reconstruction time, after Johnson and those guys that we call presidents, education [policy] didn't make provisions for education for African Americans, and so, African Americans got together in each community and made those schools and those churches. And, to do that, one individual doesn't come up with the idea how to do it. For example, teaching and learning is a very important process of socialization, where you learn something and then you go immediately and teach it, you see. And the problem that I have learned [of] is that there's a disconnect based on the fact that there is no consultation, that is, no constant and urgent gathering, where you explore the dynamic range of what one particular artistic community is doing, historically or otherwise, to see what is possible. You know George Bush and all those clowns that run the United States government, they have allowed thousands of people to die and starve in this Katrina disaster. And people were waiting for them to do something, and I don't think they're going to do anything. The best thing to do is that, from a social point, is that African Americans should go back to that model after Reconstruction and not ask the government, and not ask institutions to help them. Because until the clear idea of preservation occurs, you are gonna have these issues, because the level of love and commitment worldwide regarding African people on the whole planet is not only at its lowest but it probably cannot go lower, you know?

MR: I just wanted to address your question because I thought it was interesting, being a person of African American descent with a college degree. I have sat in music classrooms and listened to teachers speak to African American students about music, and it kind of goes along with what Wadada Leo Smith was saying, that there is this disconnect, and I think there is also a disconnect in terms of education, in regards to hip-hop and improvisation in music. There are all these links there and what I feel like from being a student and also from teaching—I have been teaching, time to time—there is a disconnect between educators and African American students. I went to a predominantly white college in Chicago, but the one thing that saved me creatively was members of the AACM, because my particular college program did not care about creative music, but that is a whole other story. I was a classically trained person for a while and I had left that behind because I didn't see enough people that looked like me amongst my peers and the history. As beautiful as was Beethoven, Bach, Wagner, all of them, as beautiful as those musicians and composers, I still didn't see anybody that looked like me, so I gravitated more toward jazz music for that reason, and I think that is why you see African American students gravitate more toward hip-hop. But what I think a lot of people understand about hip-hop: the word *hip-hop* is the same as *jazz*. The word *jazz* covers a wide range of music. It is ridiculous! The amounts of different types of musicians and music that you put under that one word, for the purpose of name or genre so that you can sell music. I mean that is what labels are for. So, hip-hop, to me, is the same sort of thing. Underground hip-hop—it just describes a wide, wide range of music, and I saw a lot of educators that I dealt with at that time that kind of threw it off as a commercial thing, but they weren't really paying attention to people that weren't commercial and a lot of college-educated African Americans are not [commercial]. It is not about 50 Cent, it is not about Puff Daddy, any of that. They are not really listening for that. They are looking for something with more substance, and there are a lot of hip-hop artists out there that are like that. I think one thing that I do with small children, which I don't know if it is helpful. I mean, there are so many great jazz records that have sampled over the last ten-to-twenty-year period, and you can say what you want to say about sampling, but at least they are bringing—with the exception of that awful situation with the Beastie Boys and James Newton that was completely disgusting—but there are other people that are doing it in a correct way in terms of giving people credit. You take that music to these kids that are listening to that and you play it for them and then you play them the record that the music came off of. That is how you have to start making those connections with, you know, high school students, and I don't really know if that is being done at the college level, but you have to find that connection, because young African American college students are looking for pieces of themselves that you cannot find in white academia. I could not find myself. The only reason why I found it was having a strong family foundation and also Fred Anderson, people like that, giving me opportunities and showing me by example that there are black people playing creative music. Just open your eyes and open your ears, and here it is. So I think that that gap can be closed, but I think on the part of educators—and I only speak of this because I've had bad educators—that they have to work harder at closing that gap.

AUDIENCE MEMBER 5: I am interested to hear what the process is for you inviting musicians into the collective and if that has changed over time?

DE: It hasn't changed, really. As Roscoe said, one of the things that you have to do is show an interest in the music, you have to come around the music, you have to be recommended by a couple of people in good standing, and then the process goes through the body of the AACM, where they deliberate as to whether you would serve in a trial period of a year. During that year you are expected to be an active member, to do all the things that is necessary to help the organization go forward. Part of that is being active in the schools, being active in the concerts, being active in keeping the organization current, real, now, and learning about the legacy of AACM, so that is pretty much in a nut shell what the process is. You know, people often want to become a part of something, but it is only for convenience's sake. They really don't want to invest themselves in it. I know the process, for me, was a seamless kind of transition, just being around. I remember sitting in the trumpet section next to Wadada, learning from him, going to the AACM school, and then I suddenly found myself as a member. We have a more formal kind of induction now than it was in the past, but pretty much the process is your commitment to the music. We did get a phone call saying that Joseph Jarman is suffering from food poisoning and, so, he wasn't able to make it here. We had to have somebody go over to his house. He had a doctor there and so forth, so I just wanted to relay that to you. That was the interruption.

AUDIENCE MEMBER 6: In talking about some of the political and social implications of the Art Ensemble, and self-determination, and make-mistakes for musicians who might not otherwise have a platform, I'm wondering [beeper goes off] . . .

DE: Uh-oh, time is up [laughter].

AM 6: How did that translate into the music itself, or did it? Did you see that, or did you feel that, or did that somewhat make it into the music? Did the music itself have political or social meaning? Maybe musical freedom representing some sort of political freedom? Did the music somehow embody . . .

WLS: How are you gonna separate that? You cannot separate it. First of all, you said the "Art Ensemble," and actually meant the AACM, because everybody in the AACM is political. And everybody that is sitting out here in chairs or standing, breathing, and pumping hot blood throughout their body is also political. You can't really ask a question like How did you become political? Maybe you have other intentions about what you want to find out with that but won't get much. So you want to rephrase it? How did you become political? Are you political?

AM 6: That is not really what I was asking. What I was asking is How did the music itself embody some of the political ideas of the AACM, if at all. Maybe they don't. I don't know.

WLS: Do you consider Louis Armstrong political?

AM 6: Yes.

WLS: OK. How about Otis Redding?

AM 6: I don't know. I haven't thought about it.

WLS: Well, it is just like this. Everybody drinks the same water, OK, and being political is something like getting up in the morning, brushing your teeth, gargling, and then, afterwards, drinking a glass of water. It is part of your normal life. You don't have to make your music something, you know. Your music is. Whatever you do is already what you are and you don't have to make yourself something, you are already that. Every piece of music that a person produces, whether it is understood or not, says exactly what it means to live in a society and be a part of that society. Was that society some place that they feel that they need to change everything in order to get everything to be right and equal, was that status quo and that change basically the same thing? Sorry.

RM: It should reflect life. I would like to back up just a little bit because I should have recognized a person that is here today: Eugene Chadbourne. Eugene Chadbourne, back in the early days, was very instrumental in helping to see that different things happen. He ran the Parachute Center out there in Calgary. But I also mention that people move on in their life: Eugene is also a great musician. He has got things that he needs to express in his life. I mean, when we are sitting and listening to the music that doesn't say anything to us, something is wrong there. And this is the problem with the young people: they don't have any music that they can relate to. So, when history looks back at this period, they are gonna see a dark period. Nothing happened. We have such a great, great legacy of music and art that we are privileged to look back upon and I have always found that the things that I often go back to are the things that were happening that, you know, related to the life at that time. I mean, I would go out to hear John Coltrane in a club and the bandstand was behind the bar. Now, how these people were serving drinks and doing all that and it was that quiet, I will never know. Now, you can go out and hear music now and everybody's talking. They are not even listening to it. It is not related to their lives. Certainly, we are not in that period now in our lives. Eugene?

EUGENE CHADBOURNE: Well, since you mentioned me, I think you underestimate the younger generation. All the comments that you make, not to pick an argument or anything, but raising teenagers and having one of these houses where all the teenagers come because I look the other way to some of the stuff they do. But they are really listening to an incredible range of music. I mean, I know twelve- and thirteen-year-olds that are stoked with what is on the radio, but it is amazing the stuff they listen to. A lot of it is coming from the Internet. They are listening to stuff that I wish I could say: I know that because I played it for you, but they didn't pay any attention when I played it. But they are really listening to a lot of different music.

RM: Well, Eugene, I am gonna ask you a question: Where are they? I mean, those people I see are the people I have seen twenty years ago. I mean, it is great to see everybody and everything, but I don't really see that many young people. I was at the concert last night. I didn't see that many young people at the concert.

DE: Look in here. There are a few young people here, but everybody is over ninety! [Laughs]

JS: I think that it reflects a great deal on what is available to them because they are looking, like you are saying, but what is available to them is a much smaller palette. I think that has to do with the globalization of all the world's resources and ideas in the hands of fewer and fewer people and we got to take that back! [clapping, cheers] What the AACM is an example of is just that, of the community deciding that they need to do something, and doing it themselves. We keep looking for a handful of people to do these things for us, and he is absolutely right about that. The reason why hip-hop is so big is because of how much money it makes. Because celebrating the lower aspects of our people makes money for a few people in suits. It used to be even major record companies had a strong jazz department, but not if these suits are in control. You have to understand that the whole jazz catalogue makes less money than one of their pop groups, and, as long as this is the only important point for them, then that is all that is gonna be happening. So, I think it is a world-community problem, and as long as these few people are trying to make all these decisions for other people, running the world by force, then we are all gonna be in trouble. This is a world-community problem.

DE: I don't want it to seem dismal. We know there are young people listening, there are always a few people, but we are looking at the whole situation. One of the problems that we are facing, for example, is the fact that, in a country like the United States, you can have somebody who can't make a sentence in charge, I mean, seriously. I mean, it is a problem. We know we are in dire straits when you are in a situation like that. Some of the people that voted—one of the states that voted primarily for Bush—is experiencing it now: Louisiana. So, let's not lose sight of what we are talking about. It is not just listening to music; it is what happens to you after you listened to the music. That is just like eating, just like breathing; if you are not doing it correctly, you are gonna get hurt. We can see about the air, about the food, and we have people talking about how we don't have a problem, [saying that] there is no global warming. All these things are related. We are not talking about music in some kind of isolated chamber: we are talking about reality of existence. And so, when we talk about notes and form, we talk about the universe that we live in and so we have to be concerned. And yes, we are involved in teaching young people to this day and we say this panel reflects quite an array in terms of age and in terms of when people came to the association. So we haven't given up on the idea that young people are our future: it is reflected here, but we are talking about the strength of the planet. Where we are right now and where we are going.

Where resources have been squandered. If the people of the world were really fired up, if the youth were really fired up, we would not be in Iraq. Not that way. We would be thinking creatively. You know, 200 billion, maybe 500 billion, has been spent over there. And we are talking that they have allocated 62 billion dollars to rebuild New Orleans, really, Louisiana and Mississippi. People haven't talked about Mississippi. Mississippi got a hit that was worse than New Orleans. New Orleans is a man-made kind of devastation because of neglect. Plus, we got to be talking about young people reading, not just listening to music. We talk about the whole spectrum. Any other questions, because we are at that time. Yes?

AUDIENCE MEMBER 7: Briefly, could you maybe, as a panel, speak a little bit about some of the conflicts which might emerge in the AACM or its divisions. I ask this because sometimes mainstream media—I'm not talking about things like community radio stations or community newspapers—but mainstream media often times will talk about the AACM as if it's this one block of musicians who all review the same thing, who all have the same history. But, as a strategy, how do musicians, amongst themselves, on-stage or off, deal with things like divisions, dissent, or conflict in a way which might help us as students of music and appreciators of music?

RM: Well, you bring out a good point there. I mean, community radio stations, that is on you guys. People that have the knowledge and so on, make sure that the information gets passed around and so on. What is very odd about where I live [is that] there is really a good community radio station there, WORT, that's been there for twenty years, and it is representative of the type of radio that I listened to when I was growing up. I have always believed you're supposed to give people choices and they can make up their own mind. When you go out in Madison, it is the total opposite. And, in fact, Madison used to be one of the radical universities. When I first got back from Europe and went there in the 60s, the whole of State Street was full of teargas from student revolutions and so on. People don't have to do anything but it will go down. I mean, we don't need all to be puppets, just doing whatever anybody says. People have to have a clear vision in their head of what they would like to do and stick to their own vision and not be swayed. If you believe strong enough that you're thinking valid thoughts, if anything it's going to be salvaged. In the situation we're in now, it's going to take more people actually getting out there and doing things. By the way, my kids listen to music too; they are influenced by me but if there is a situation that is gonna exist where you are gonna bring a pool [of] young people back in again . . . If I look at Madison, some of the greats in this music have taught at Madison. Cecil Taylor taught there, Bill Dixon, you see, so it is not a situation that never did exist, but you have to reach out for these people. You got to have things that go on in the universities, and I have taught in universities. But the thing I don't like about it is that it is too much arguing going on, people defending their own political views and so on, and for a serious artist, it is not a good situation. Some people can handle it better than others; I don't handle it very well. In some cases, what I have done is I've withdrawn, because the work that I am doing in this period, I feel, [is] important, because maybe I am starting to really learn how to get to things that I am thinking about.

NM: I want to address that part of your question about how we address the challenges and frictions in the organization and how that can help others to learn how to work more as a community, or more unified. We have a lot of deep personalities in our organization. I think that's clear to everyone. I found that when we have differences and we have clashes in terms of ideas, all we have to do is go back to that love of the organization, because that's something that everyone has in common, even if everyone has a different perspective about the organization and what we want to do through the organization. Pretty much everyone involved has a deep love and respect and determination for the organization to continue. When you focus on that prosperity, and everybody's on board, that's how you get things done without getting stuck in personalities.

DE: I would like to add something about the radio stations. There are some communities' stations that, when you get out there on the road, like we are, and you have nothing but a CD player, the people who have the power in terms of transmission power, of wattage power, in the Bible Belt, the narrow conservative stuff, you hear people talking about assassinating Hugo Chávez. I mean, we're in trouble. The other thing about this organization that's crucial is that you need bridges. You need people who can mediate and people who have connections. It's these personal relationships that can provide the bridge. Not everyone can be a bridge. And sometimes no one is particularly chosen, but they can provide the connections that establish those bridges. And these things are necessary for this or any other organization, because everyone cannot necessarily relate to everyone else. When you're a family, there's going to be some stuff. If there's no stuff, it's most likely not a family. So we're almost at the beginning of the road, so maybe we'll field one or two more questions to wrap it up. Not everybody at once. So we'd like to thank you on behalf of the Association for the Advancement of Creative Musicians.

Tracy McMullen

CHAPTER 14

PEOPLE, DON'T GET READY

Improvisation, Democracy, and Hope

I have taken the intriguing title of this volume, *People Get Ready: The Future of Jazz Is Now*, as an opportunity to bring together some ideas on improvisation, democracy, and hope. The Impressions's hit from 1965, "People Get Ready," written by Curtis Mayfield, was a Gospel-inspired song of hope that lifted the spirits of civil rights and antiwar activists working for a better future. But our volume's title does not stop there; it immediately follows with an alternate take on the future, one for which we do not need to get ready, because, paradoxically, the future is *now*. There are a variety of ways to conceive of this idea of "the future is now": for example, it could suggest that past hopes should now be realized, or that this time, change *is* happening. The title may unintentionally underscore the postmodern compression of time with its capitalist and technological demand for constantly new products and consumers who greet each passing moment as outdated upon arrival. I take the antinomy of "getting ready" for "now" as a way into discussing improvisation and its relationship to time and the self and what this means for our ideas about hope and democracy.

In addressing these questions I will bring some diverse philosophies and practices into conversation—Jacques Derrida's notion of "democracy-to-come," Buddhist understandings of the "self," and specific approaches developed in the tradition of jazz improvisation. I will suggest that the African American tradition of improvisation offers different perspectives on the self, hope, and the future than one informed exclusively by a liberal-humanist, post-Enlightenment tradition that privileges subject-object divisions, the coherence and defense of identity, and the related objectification of time into the past, present, and future.[1] But the "African-American tradition" is not equivalent to the Buddhist tradition, nor is it completely separate and set against a "European tradition." Nonetheless, similarities and differences between traditions can be elucidated without falling into the "extreme views" warned against by Buddhism.[2] Scholars such as Nathaniel Mackey have already made connections between long-held practices in the African American tradition and the more recent insights of poststructuralism regarding the subject, suggesting that "the dismantling of the unified subject found in recent critical theory is old news when it comes to black music" (522).[3] Jazz has challenged and offered needed alternatives to Enlightenment traditions of thought by virtue of its connection to alternate values and practices.[4] In addition to the African-derived or more traditional African American practices that scholars like Samuel Floyd, Ingrid Monson, and Guthrie Ramsay investigate (such as the ring shout, call and response, and communal traditions) some ways of practicing improvisation within the African American tradition of jazz can also be productively viewed through the lens of Buddhist philosophy.

That Buddhism, poststructuralism, and African American musical practices all share the perspective of a nonunified subject might serve to highlight the anomalous perspective of the Western Enlightenment tradition and not a lumpen desire on the writer's part to wrangle a variety of "others" into a single category. It is the naturalized and ideological ground of the Western tradition, which informs our concepts of hope, the future, and the self. Improvisation can offer a way of being in the world that does not erect fictitious boundaries around a self that cannot, in fact, be located. Encountering the world with a sense of improvisation, rather than a frantic concern with discerning, enacting, and performing rules or fulfilling expected responses, could open up new possibilities, placing the emphasis on awareness and the "new" rather than on safety and the known.

Because both *hope* and *democracy* have been shadow terms in the discussion of improvisation, a closer look is needed at ideas of hope and democracy and their relationship to the self.[5] Rather than understanding democracy as the interaction of various diverse individuals, Jacques Derrida, in my view, places the emphasis on the continual "how" of each person's interacting, their individual responsibility that nonetheless does not emanate from a unified subjectivity. Derrida's concepts of the "here and now," "undecidability," and "infinite responsibility" are linked to possibilities found in jazz improvisation.[6]

"Democracy-to-Come"

When is democracy? In *Deconstruction and Pragmatism*, Derrida's idea of democracy-to-come is brought into dialogue with Richard Rorty's concept of "social hope." Although there is not space here to closely detail Rorty's ideas, the crucial difference between Rorty's conception of social hope and Derrida's to-come is that Rorty relies on an American pragmatist's hope in the future, while Derrida's to-come is actually something, paradoxically, that is in the here and now.[7] Derrida writes,

> When I speak of democracy to come (*la démocratie à venir*) this does not mean that tomorrow democracy will be realized, and it does not refer to a future democracy, rather it means that there is an engagement with regard to when, in the messianic moment, "it can come" (*ça peut venir*). There is the future (*il y a de l'avenir*). There is something to come (*il y a à venir*). That can happen . . . that can happen, and I promise in opening the future or in leaving the future open. This is not utopian, it is what takes place here and now, in a here and now that I regularly try to dissociate from the present. . . . I try to dissociate the theme of singularity happening here and now from the theme of presence and, for me, there can be a here and now without presence. (82–83)

Rather than a thought of the future or a hope for the future, the future is cited here as a simple fact, a brute fact, to which we open: "There is the future. There is something to come. That can happen . . . that can happen." Derrida is saying *this* can happen, or this, or that. A variety of things can and will happen. This is the brute fact of the future. Imagining the future as containing any particularities (or reifying the particularities of the past) is a way of stabilizing the unstable here and now into a "present." The present is a designation that is manufactured in relation to an "absent" (and therefore "other") past and future. Vincent Descombes writes, "The present is present only on condition that it allude to the absent in order to be distinguishable from it (an absent which is the past or the future)" (148). The present is a construction based on related constructions of past or future.

If we stay open to Derrida's to-come we are in a place of "undecidability." Derrida writes, via Ernesto Laclau, "When I decide I invent the subject" (84). In undecidability the sovereign subject cannot take form. Therefore, undecidability "is not simply a moment to be traversed and overcome . . .

by the occurrence of the decision" (86–87). It is here and now where "the singular event of engagement" can occur (82). In what can be viewed as a counter to Rorty's "innovation" and "hope for the future," which relinquishes responsibility for its outcome, Derrida writes that within the here and now we have "infinite responsibility."[8] The responsibility is infinite because the to-come is always coming, it never begins, or ends. Now it is infinitely coming and if we are with it, we are infinitely responsible in that here and now; the subject has not taken shape through the decision, and thus the responsibility (to the "singular other") is complete, total, infinite. In this sense, there is no need for "hope," there is only and always the perpetual engagement with the singularity of the here and now. Hope would be a fall back into the decision that envisions a separate future and thereby creates a separate present, or "presence."

While I find Derrida's elucidation of the here and now, undecidability, and infinite responsibility extremely useful, I believe his argument must be extended if we want to understand and, in fact, practice the genuine radicalism inherent in these ideas. In my view, Derrida is hobbled by the primacy he gives to language in his philosophical inquiry. Although Derrida attempted to evade the binaristic and dualistic nature of language, I concur with Vincent Leitch that "binaries and dualities . . . haunt one another, [in Derrida's] quasi-transcendental concepts" (20). Significantly, Derrida never applied his analyses directly to music, for fear of treading into an area that existed so far outside his known domain.[9] Here is where Buddhism can take us further, regarding both Derrida's concepts and the ways they are practiced and manifested in music. If we remain within the realm of language and the symbolic, we remain within the realm of polarity. However, if we recognize a type of knowing that is "non-conceptual," we can explore the here and now, the space of undecidability and infinite responsibility, further.

Buddhism's *Prapañca* and *Shunyata*

All schools of Buddhist thought describe the "ordinary mind" as a mind that functions via dualisms. This ordinary, dualistic, conceptual form of knowing is called *prapañca* in Sanskrit. The dualisms of prapañca are not only specific privileged binaries, such as the Western preoccupations with essence and appearance or mind and body, but all dualities, including existence and nonexistence, self and nonself, past and future. The point is the same as that outlined in Western structuralist philosophy, that in language and thought we will always understand in terms of binaries: red is understood against not-red, tree against not-tree, and so on.[10] These limits set the terms of our knowing when we unquestioningly rely on the power of conceptual thought as the final arbiter of knowing, leaving the mind to "oscillate ceaselessly between one limiting view and its opposite" (Tarthang Tulku 25).

All schools of Buddhism teach that there is another way of knowing that is not based on conceptual thought. This way of knowing is often described as "direct experience." Buddhism teaches that we can have direct experience, but that this is not easy. The ordinary mind mediates experience. The Tibetan Buddhist lama Tarthang Tulku writes, "It may seem we could leave concepts behind and investigate mind through direct experience, but this is far from easy. Experience arises as feelings, thoughts, and impressions interact with consciousness to label and identify appearance. Meanings arise from dialogues that depend on mental imagery and sense perception. All this is the activity of mind. Since it is mind that narrates experience, experience as such cannot lead us to understand mind" (13). This description is similar to Joan Scott's argument in her essay "The Evidence of Experience," wherein she asserts that descriptions of our "experience" tend to be narrations of ourselves as subjects. However, Buddhism does not stop at the conceptual ordinary mind; it suggests that we can access another type of knowing. Because we cannot trust our experience with ordinary mind, Buddhism lays down a path that leads to the eventual realization of what is called *sems-nyid* in Tibetan, *shunyata* in Sanskrit, and often translated into English as emptiness-mind, or emptiness.

It is through *shunyata* that one can break through binaries. The mind of sems-nyid understands "not arising; not ceasing; not arising and ceasing together." Tarthang Tulku writes, "Ordinary mind falsely perceives arising and ceasing, and thus reifies every instant of experience." Through shunyata one recognizes that "when no phenomena and no single instant have ever arisen, there can equally be no ceasing or vanishing" (43). This type of knowing can be productively compared to Derrida's idea of "here and now" as opposed to "presence" (a reification of the present through its implicit relationship to a past and future). Tarthang Tulku writes that "in terms of the three times [past, present, and future], since the mode of arising that ordinary mind takes to be the infinite 'nowness' of experience has never actually occurred, the vanishing of any phenomena or instant, perceived as the past, can also not take place. And when nothing has ever come into being or vanished, there is also no possibility for a future arising" (43). Tarthang Tulku here stresses that "ordinary mind" will grasp onto an idea of "infinite 'nowness'" as a type of object. This can be related to Derrida's discussion of the decision as the moment of stabilizing the unstable. Tarthang Tulku makes clear that while we may imagine we understand something conceptually, the experience is not something that can be grasped conceptually. He writes that "our conceptual understanding of the words used to describe the experience is categorically different from the ineffability of the experience itself, which remains beyond the reach of the intellect" (44). This is not the "experience" of the ordinary mind described above. It is a more direct form of experience that will come through training in recognizing shunyata.

Shunyata may be the most "direct" form of experience, yet as we train in uncovering this awareness we become comfortable with nonconceptual knowing in a more everyday way. In Buddhism, the foundational practice for developing this type of awareness is meditation and "mindfulness practice." Meditation is a way to calm afflicting thoughts and emotions, bring clarity, and eventually see the innermost workings of human awareness. Mindfulness is a practice of bringing full attention to one's daily activities in the here and now, rather than letting the body do its work while the mind is thinking of events in the past or future. As the well-known Buddhist exhortation puts it, when you're chopping wood or carrying water, simply "chop wood; carry water."

This emphasis on tranquility, clarity, mindfulness, and awareness has attracted many artists and athletes who seek a higher level of concentration in their performance. Unlike those who can revise their work before it takes its final form (writers, visual artists, composers), athletes and improvisers perform their "final product" in real time. Therefore, the ability to remain focused during the performance is paramount. Artists who have incorporated meditation and mindfulness into their practices cite its ability to help them develop this focus in the moment of performance. But for many, the practice goes further and affects their views on life much more broadly.

The practices of mindfulness and meditation lead to an understanding of shunyata, a type of understanding that does not rely on conceptual binaries that cohere into decisions and stereotypes, subjects and objects. Mindfulness and meditation are essentially practices of "paying attention" and not wandering off into thoughts of the past and future (or solidifying into "decisions"). To the extent that jazz performance can hone these practices, it can be a way to work with "undecidability," that is, to engage with a "singular event" with "infinite responsibility."

Herbie Hancock, Improvisation, and the
Here and Now

Herbie Hancock is probably the most prominent jazz Buddhist, but jazz musicians' interest in Eastern traditions can be traced back at least to the 1940s. While not always specifically Buddhist, a significant number of African American musicians have explored Eastern philosophical traditions to support their musical, personal, and spiritual lives. Gerald Early writes that it was "not unusual for a black jazz musician, particularly a jazz musician who was a young adult during the forties and fifties [to look] toward the East for inspiration and many, as a result, became Muslim. Others, such as Mingus, free-lanced superficially with the terms of Hinduism and Buddhism" (Early 28).[11] And although Early describes Mingus's interaction as "superficial," he also notes how Mingus was put to rest in a Hindu ceremony, writing, "His ashes were scattered along the Ganges River in a Hindu ceremony. Presumably all of this was done on instructions Mingus left behind" (29). Early notes that Charlie Parker also studied Eastern religions, and the study and practice of Eastern philosophies by Alice and John Coltrane are well known (Berkman, "Appropriating Universality" and "Divine Songs"; Nisenson; Cole). In Hancock's circle alone, Buster Williams, Bennie Maupin, and Wayne Shorter are all practicing Buddhists. Other contemporary examples include the saxophonist Joseph Jarman, who has been a practicing Buddhist since the 1960s, and the drummer Hamid Drake, who foregrounds the importance of Buddhism and Sufism to his work.[12] And these, of course, are just the most famous examples. In recent decades, Buddhism in the United States has become increasingly available and organized, with centers appearing across the country and teachers able to present the philosophy in a more nuanced and sophisticated way and to a larger audience than at the time of Coltrane and Mingus. Perhaps it is not surprising, then, that more African American jazz musicians have seriously undertaken its practice, as has the American populace at large.[13]

The connection between African American aesthetic, spiritual, and social traditions and Buddhism is an area in need of further examination. One can hypothesize a connection between the ways of understanding the self in an African American tradition of "dis-mantling" or, following Edward Brathwaite, "X-ing the self" and Buddhism. For Hancock, Buddhist approaches combined with his experiences in jazz performance lead to a way of being and acting suggestive of the characteristics Derrida has connected to "democracy-to-come."

Herbie Hancock first discovered Buddhism in 1972 and has been a diligent practitioner to the present day. In addition to his many references to Buddhism in interviews, he wrote the forward to the popular Buddhist book, *The Buddha in Your Mirror: Practical Buddhism and the Search for Self*. In numerous interviews over the decades he has recounted the importance of Buddhism to his practice of jazz improvisation and elaborated on the similarities between Buddhism and jazz (see for instance, Reiss). Although Hancock was first drawn to Buddhism in order to become a better musician, the philosophy has infiltrated his entire worldview (Reiss). I include some of his comments on both Buddhism and jazz improvisation below that I believe illuminate how the ideas above regarding nonconceptual knowing, undecidability, infinite responsibility, and the here and now are actually put into practice.

Hancock has shared many anecdotes describing how music transmits knowledge nonconceptually.[14] One of the more important accounts is his description of his introduction to Buddhism. The pianist initially discovered Buddhism through the effects it was having on Buster Williams's bass playing:

> [On a club date in Seattle in 1972] the bassist Buster Williams starts playing this introduction. And what came out of him was something I'd never heard before. And not only had I not heard it from him, I'd never heard it from anybody. It was just pure beauty and ideas and—it was magical. Magical. And people were freaking out, it was so incredible what he was playing.
>
> I let him play for a long time, maybe 10, 15 minutes. He just came up with idea after idea, so full of inspiration. And then I could feel myself waking up just before we really came in with the melody for the song. And I could tell that the whole band woke up, and there was some energy that was generat-

ing from Buster. We played the set and it was like magic. When we finished, many people ran up to the front of the stage and reached up their hands to shake ours. Some of them were crying they were so moved by the music. . . .

I knew that Buster was the catalyst for all of this, so I took him into the musicians' room, and I said, "Hey, Buster, I heard you were into some new philosophy or something and if it can make you play bass like that, I want to know what it is." . . . his eyes lit up and he said, "I've been chanting for a way to tell you about this." And I said, "What? Chanting what? What is this?" And now I know that it was the only way he could have reached me. That would be the only way I would have listened to what he had to say. If he had just come up and told me about it beforehand, I would have probably put my hand on his shoulder and said, "Hey, man, that's great. You know, whatever works for you keep doing it," which is a way of putting up a shield. But it came through the music, which was the only way to kind of reach my heart at the time, because that's what my focus was then. (Hancock, interview by Valerie Reiss)

Here Hancock describes a form of knowing, learning, and transmission that is common in Buddhist teaching—an embodied expression and manifestation of understanding that is undeniable, connected to the heart, yet difficult to describe in words. Hancock admits he would not have understood this knowledge if Williams had only spoken to him about it and Hancock hadn't had the experience of actually hearing and feeling this information. He had to experience it; he had to "know" it in a way that language could not convey. And because of Hancock's deep connection with music, it was music that could best speak to him at that time. Many students have described how the presence of great Buddhist masters can offer a soothing effect: the master's embodiment of wisdom is palpably felt in the bodies of those around them. This is not particularly mystical. Just as someone who has practiced the saxophone for many years can (seemingly magically) play the saxophone; someone who has developed knowledge from nonconceptual insight garnered over the years will embody that wisdom in their most minute actions and interactions with others. But saying that something cannot be described in words is not tantamount to saying it resides outside history. It is to say that we communicate in ways that are not only linguistic. Sometimes these nonconceptual ways offer more important, more nuanced, and more sophisticated information than what is conveyed with words. But what is communicated is often the end product of years of work and effort.

It is this type of embodied practice that can open up Derrida's concepts of undecidability, infinite responsibility, and the here and now. For example, the pianist's description of improvisation emphasizes the practice of not cohering into the decision, but continually opening to the singular moment of the here and now. Hancock states that, through his study of Buddhism:

> I've learned that any situation can be viewed from an infinite number of vantage points. . . . There is a natural tendency for us as human beings to see the situations that happen to us from one vantage point. But what Buddhism teaches us, and what life teaches us, is that a situation can be looked at in many, many different ways. And the way we look at that situation, and how we deal with it as a result of seeing it from other vantage points, can determine whether that life situation is going to have a negative or a positive effect on our future." (SGI Quarterly)

Hancock reminds us that any situation can be understood from "an infinite number of vantage points." An approach that may have worked in the past might not work when we encounter similar circumstances again. This type of openness feels riskier than sticking to a preconceived formula. Inspired by his work with Miles Davis, Hancock considers risk-taking "very important." Referring to his time in Davis's band, Hancock recounts that Davis "very much encouraged risk-taking. . . . He wasn't concerned at all about our mistakes. He was much more concerned about the courage that it takes to make mistakes" (SGI Quarterly). This is the courage to be on the edge, to remain open to the singular moment and its infinite possibilities. It is the courage not to cohere into a decision, not to invent the "subject," not to provide the predictable, comfortable formula.

Hancock stresses risk, but, importantly, "with a sense of responsibility" (SGI Quarterly). This is reminiscent of Derrida's similar words about the infinite responsibility that we hold to the here and now, to the singular other, to the to-come of democracy. This could be the practice of democracy: this vulnerable opening to the new that carries with it a "sense" of responsibility, a *feeling* of responsibility, not an idea or decision of what exactly is responsible, but a responsiveness, a willingness, an ability to respond to the singular moment in a courageous, open-ended, continuous, indeed, infinite (never-ceasing) manner. In the practice of infinite responsibility there is no need to hope, nor a need to despair. There is only the continual responsiveness to the singular other—that is, the other that is never repeated, never unified into a coherent subject, but is perpetually new. As Hancock has practiced this type of risky openness to the unknown, he has been compelled toward activities that benefit others. He cofounded the Rhythm of Life Organization, which seeks to "increase the employability of youth using technology and entertainment based software applications and to use technology to improve humanity."[15] He was also a founding board member for the Bayview Hunters Point Center for Arts and Technology, which offers free classes in media and design in the Bayview-Hunters Point community, aiming to "educate, empower, and employ" youth through both technological education and encouragement of their creative expression.[16] With a clear-seeing, clear-hearing, open attention to the present, beneficial and appropriate actions are more likely to occur than if the present is not seen or heard clearly. Undoubtedly, this can have positive benefits, social as well as aesthetic.

People, Don't Get Ready: No Hope and Democracy

The future is a concept. Hope is a concept. Democracy is a concept. That is, when we understand these ideas as an endpoint, as a goal, they are reified, coherent concepts that remain within the realm of conceptual thought. Improvising in the "here and now" offers a different relationship to the future, to hope, to democracy, and to our responsibilities to the other. If "improvisational performance is risky behavior," as Ellen Webb writes, a type of engagement that asks us to give up our "drive to strategize, and instead to stay in the open-ended situation," (241) then it is asking us to let go of expectations, opinions, decisions, and comfortable vantage points. Buddhism argues that it is expectation that leads us to the concepts of "hope" and "despair." Hoping can be an example of deferring responsibility to the here and now and looking elsewhere: perhaps the future or the past will save us.[17] The practice of jazz improvisation can be a way of stepping into the shaky and vulnerable not-knowing of the to-come. With infinite responsibility to that moment there is no need, no time, no space for hope.

The open state, or, at least, the more open state (because it is a practice), can feel precarious, because it is not stabilized into a decision. From a Buddhist perspective, human beings have such a deep attachment and need for this stabilization that it is very difficult to keep opening. It is a deep-rooted attachment to self-preservation and perhaps even deeper denial of the uncomfortable sense that there is no self to preserve. But meditation helps practitioners relax into the space of "no self" (or less self, as they practice), that is, into undecidability and openness. The practitioner begins to experience life a bit more directly, not so mediated by thoughts. She becomes familiar with a way of being that does not cohere into identity, a self against an other, a subject against an object, a past against a future. Rather, she experiences an open here and now with an infinite responsibility to listen and not cohere into a decision or judgment.

Buddhist philosophy aligns with Mackey's description (following Brathwaite) of the "X-ing of the self" and the understanding of the co-arising and continual movement of phenomena. This new "old news" understanding of self seems to suggest, much like the process of improvisation, that my actions are always connected to yours, that I work within something larger that I can't really control but I can perhaps help shape with others— that I work within a momentum of history that has a force but is not immovable; indeed, it is always moving. It suggests the wisdom of letting go of a frantic obsession with defense, that a less defensive (which becomes offensive) stance may allow for movement elsewhere. Letting go means giving up control, giving up constant vigilance in defending territory of all kinds, of coming to terms with the inevitability of the passage of time and loss. Perhaps we can learn from improvisation a sense of security that derives not from entrenched decisions and "safe" spaces, but from the ability to move with always changing circumstances, the recognition that the song never stops and therefore can't be found, and the knowledge that it is never produced by one individual alone. Jazz improvisation might be teaching us that the time has come to stop "getting ready." This is not utopian. It takes effort. We need to always practice. Our responsibility is infinite. Democracy is here, it is now. Our future is only and always now.

Notes

1. By "objectification of time" I mean, for example, the ways that "the past" is taken as an object separate from the present, an object that can then be cordoned off and observed in a museum. For excellent analyses of the way this approach to time developed since modernity, see McClintock.

2. In Buddhist philosophy, "extreme views" generally references "eternalism

and nihilism," in answer to which the Buddha advocated a middle way. "Extreme views" and the focus on the "middle path" also refer, however, to the tendency to fall into binaristic thinking and a preoccupation with borders. This is the sense in which I mean it here.

3. Regarding Amiri Baraka's comments on Albert Ayler and Sun Ra's innovations: "New Black Music is this: find the self, then kill it," Mackey writes, "the emphasis on self-expression is also an emphasis on self-transformation, an othering or, as [Edward] Brathwaite has it, an X-ing of the self, the self not as noun but as verb . . . To kill the self is to show it to be fractured, unfixed" (522).

4. See for instance, Samuel Floyd, "Ring Shout!"; Ingrid Monson, *Saying Something*; Guthrie Ramsey, *Race* Music; and Olly Wilson, "Black Music as an Art Form."

5. The most prominent current proponent of the view that jazz is tantamount to democracy is Wynton Marsalis. For Marsalis, jazz is "democracy in action" (see "An Interview with Wynton Marsalis" on the product page of his book, *Moving to Higher Ground: How Jazz Can Change Your Life* at www.amazon.com). And as Michelle Obama introduced a jazz concert as part of the "Jazz Studio" program at the White House (which that day included five members of the Marsalis family and Paquito D'Rivera) she said, "There is no better example of democracy than a jazz ensemble: individual freedom with responsibility to the group" (Ben Ratliff, "At the White House, a Blend of Jazz Greats and Hopefuls," *New York Times*, June 15, 2009). For an excellent discussion of how jazz was used to represent American democracy by the U.S. state department during the Cold War, see Von Eschen, *Satchmo Blows Up the World*.

6. Possibilities that I link elsewhere to something I call the "improvisative." See Tracy McMullen, "The Improvisative."

7. For the pragmatist philosopher Richard Rorty, democracy is connected to ideas of the future. Rorty writes, "Dewey referred to pragmatism as 'the philosophy of democracy.' What he had in mind is that both pragmatism and America are expressions of a hopeful, melioristic, experimental frame of mind. I think the most one can do by way of linking up pragmatism with America is to say that both the country and its most distinguished philosopher suggest that we can, in politics, substitute *hope* for the sort of knowledge which philosophers have usually tried to attain. America has always been a future-oriented country, a country which delights in the fact that it invented itself in the relatively recent past" (24). Rorty writes, "Asking for pragmatism's blueprint of the future is like asking Walt Whitman to sketch what lies at the end of that illimitable democratic vista. The vista, not the endpoint, matters" (28). "Pragmatists—both classical and 'neo'—do not believe that there is a way things really are. So they want to replace the appearance-reality distinction by that between descriptions of the world and of ourselves which are less useful and those which are more useful. When the question 'useful for what?' is pressed, they have nothing to say except 'useful to create a better future.' When they are asked, 'Better by what

criterion?,' they have no detailed answer, any more than the first mammals could specify in what respects they were better than dying dinosaurs" (27).

8. See previous note.

9. Derrida writes, "Music is the object of my strongest desire, and yet at the same time it remains completely forbidden. I don't have the competence. . . . I am even more afraid of speaking nonsense in this area than in any other" (Brunette and Wills, qtd. in Ramshaw). And Derrida has written further "that what sets the musician apart is the possibility of meaninglessness" (Green Gartside, qtd. in Ramshaw). I take this as a concern on Derrida's part with not being able to navigate past the limits of language, that is, past conceptual knowing.

10. An excellent introduction to structuralist thinking can be found in Silverman, *The Subject of Semiotics*.

11. Ingrid Monson (via John Work) has documented jazz musicians' association with the Ahmadiyya movement in the 1940s, a "multiracial version of the Muslim faith" (Monson 330) that had its "roots in late nineteenth century India" (333). In her essay on spirituality in post-1960s avant-garde jazz, Franya Berkman traces Eastern religious influences on African American spirituality in the nineteenth century and the twentieth, citing, for example, the work of Philip Jenkins on Theosophy and Black religion.

12. The drummer Hamid Drake has been vocal about the influence of Buddhism, Hinduism, and Sufism on his musical practice. The name of his band, Bindu, comes from a Sanskrit word meaning "subtle point" and, according to Drake, "refers to a sort of energy that was believed to reside in the body." The drummer has stressed the importance of "being able to listen in another sort of way," a way that "requires full-body and full-mind attention." Drake makes a point of saying that his philosophical borrowings are not superficial or decorative appropriations. They are "things that I actually believe in and practice. I'm not trying to be cool. It's stuff that I practice in my everyday life. A lot of it's tied to Sufism and Buddhism" (Gottschalk). The saxophonist Joseph Jarman has devoted himself to Buddhist practice for decades and has taught meditation and Aikido since the 1980s.

13. Soka Gakkai International (to which Hancock, Shorter, Williams, and Maupin belong) has been the most influential Buddhist organization in the African American community, because it has set up centers in poorer neighborhoods and has also reached out to these communities. For issues of racism in American Buddhism, as well as ways that Buddhism can help overcome racism, see Gutiérrez Baldoquín, *Dharma, Color, and Culture*, and Pintak, "Something Has to Change."

14. Another story that emphasizes the nonconceptual yet exceptionally important information conveyed through music can be found in Hancock's account of his experience with his second piano teacher at the age of nine in the forward he wrote to *The Buddha in Your Mirror*.

15. Hancock, Herbie. "Rhythm of Life Organization (ROLO)." herbiehancock .net. N.d. Web. 25 Oct. 2012.

16. "Through project-based learning and access to the latest digital technology, students are able to learn professional media applications while discovering their innate artistic abilities. By encouraging students to collaborate with each other, their families, and the world around them, we strive to build a community enriched by the experience of creative expression." "BAYCAT: Bayview Hunters Point Centre for Arts and Technology: Overview." baycat.org. N.d. Web. 25 Oct. 2012.

17. Andreas Huyssen suggests that our current "culture of memory" exemplifies our loss of faith in the future and the belief that "if the future can't save us, perhaps the past will."

WORKS CITED

Ake, David. *Jazz Cultures*. Berkeley: University of California Press, 2002. Print.

Amador, Michelle. Messages to John Brackett. 2009. E-mail.

Anderson, Iain. *This Is Our Music: Free Jazz, the Sixties, and American Culture*. Philadelphia: University of Pennsylvania Press, 2007. Print.

Ang, Ien. *On Not Speaking Chinese: Living between Asia and the West*. London: Routledge, 2001. Print.

Appadurai, Arjun. *Modernity at Large: Cultural Dimensions of Globalization*. Minneapolis: University of Minnesota Press, 1996. Print.

Atkins, E. Taylor, ed. *Jazz Planet*. Jackson: University Press of Mississippi, 2003. Print.

Austin, J. L. *How to Do Things with Words*. Ed. Marina Sbisa and J. O. Urmson. 2nd ed. Cambridge, MA: Harvard University Press, 1975. Print.

Bailey, Derek. *Improvisation: Its Nature and Practice in Music*. Cambridge, MA: Da Capo, 1992. Print.

Bangs, Lester. "Charlie Haden: *Liberation Music Orchestra*." Morthland, 35–36. Print.

———. "Free Jazz/Punk Rock." *Musician Magazine* 1979. *Notbored*. Web. 22 June 2010.

———. "The MC5—Kick Out the Jams." *Rolling Stone* 30 Apr. 1969. *Beat Patrol*. Web. 22 June 2010.

Baraka, Imamu Amiri [LeRoi Jones]. *Blues People: Negro Music in White America*. New York: Morrow, 1963. Print.

———. "The Changing Same." *Black Music*. Cambridge, MA: Da Capo, 1998. 180–211. Print.

———. *It's Nation Time*. Chicago: Third World, 1970. Print.

———. "One Night Stand." *Preface to a Twenty Volume Suicide Note*. New York: Totem/Corinth, 1961. 21–22. Print.

Barrett, Lindon. *Blackness and Value: Seeing Double*. Cambridge: Cambridge University Press, 1999. Print.

Barzel, Tamar. Conversations with Marc Ribot. Sept. 2009. E-mail.

Berkman, Franya. "Appropriating Universality: The Coltranes and 1960s Spirituality." *American Studies* 48.1 (2007): 41–62. Print.

———. "Divine Songs: The Music of Alice Coltrane." Diss. Wesleyan University, 2003. Print.

Berliner, Paul. "Give and Take: The Collective Conversation of Jazz Performance." *Creativity in Performance*. Ed. R. Keith Sawyer. Greenwich, CT: Ablex, 1997. 9–42. Print.

Born, Georgina, and David Hesmondhalgh. *Western Music and Its Others: Difference, Representation, and Appropriation in Music*. Berkeley: University of California Press, 2000. Print.

Borough of Manhattan Community College's Tribeca Performing Arts Center. "Lost Jazz Shrines." *Tribeca Performing Arts Center*. Tribeca PAC, n.d. Web. 22 June 2010.

Braxton, Anthony. *Tri-Axium Writings*. 3 vols. Hanover, NH: Frog Peak Music, 1985. Print.

Bronx Council on the Arts. "Economic Development through a Creative Economy: Executive Summary." *Bronxarts*. Bronx Council on the Arts, n.d. Web. 22 June 2010.

Brooks, David. *Bobos in Paradise: The New Upper Class and How They Got There*. New York: Simon and Schuster, 2001. Print.

Brown, Marion. *Afternoon of a Georgia Faun*. ECM, 1970. CD.

Burns, Ken, dir. *Jazz: A Film by Ken Burns*. 10 vols. PBS, 2001. DVD.

Butler, Judith. *Bodies That Matter: On the Discursive Limits of "Sex."* New York: Routledge, 1993. Print.

———. *Gender Trouble: Feminism and the Subversion of Identity*. New York: Routledge, 1990. Expt. in Price and Shildrick. 416–22. Print.

Byron, Don. Interview by Makani N. Themba. "Don Byron—On Life outside the Box." *Seeingblack*. Web. 23 Oct. 2012.

Carlson, Marvin. *Performance: A Critical Introduction*. London: Routledge, 1996. Print.

Carr, C. "Money Changes Everything: The East Village Art Mart." *Village Voice Literary Supplement* Sept. 1985. *Abcnorio*. Web. 22 June 2010.

Chicago Underground Duo. *12 Degrees of Freedom*. Thrill Jockey, 1998. CD.

Chinen, Nate. "Jazz in America, to the Beat of a Smooth One-Man Band." *New York Times* 27 Aug. 2006. Print.

Chuck D. "Strange Bedfellows: How the Clash Inspired Public Enemy." *Let Fury Have the Hour: The Punk Rock Politics of Joe Strummer*. Ed. Antonio D'Ambrosio. New York: Nation, 2004. xix–xx. Print.

City of Toronto. *Culture Plan for the Creative City*. Toronto: Toronto Culture, 2003. Print.

Cole, Bill. *John Coltrane: John Coltrane*. 1976. Cambridge, MA: Da Capo, 2001. Print.

Copeland, Stewart. "The Stewart Copeland Interview." *JamBase*. Web. 23 Oct. 2012.

Coss, Bill. "The Agonies of Exploration: Jeanne Lee and Ran Blake." *Down Beat* 13 Sep. 1962:18. Print.

Crispell, Marilyn. Personal Interview with Ellen Waterman and Julie Smith. 29 June 2003.

Cyrille, Andrew, Jeanne Lee, and Jimmy Lyons. *Nuba*. Black Saint, 1979. CD.

Dammers, Jerry. "Cosmic Engineering: Jerry Dammers; The Spatial AKA Orchestra." *Sun Ra: Interviews and Essays*. Ed. John Sinclair. London: Headpress, 2010. 129–38. Print.

de Lauretis, Teresa. *Technologies of Gender: Essays on Theory, Film, and Fiction*. Bloomington: Indiana University Press, 1987. Print.

Derrida, Jacques. "Remarks on Deconstruction and Pragmatism." *Deconstruction and Pragmatism*. Ed. Chantal Mouffe. New York: Routledge, 1996. 77–88. Print.

Descombes, Vincent. *Modern French Philosophy*. Cambridge: Cambridge University Press, 1998. Print.

DeVeaux, Scott. "Constructing the Jazz Tradition: Jazz Historiography." *Black American Literature Forum* 25.3 (1991): 525–60. Print.

Dickinson, Peter. *CageTalk: Dialogues with and about John Cage*. Rochester, NY: University of Rochester Press, 2006. Print.

Dickinson, Phil. Personal interview with Rob Wallace. 23 Sept. 2011.

Drake, Hamid. Personal Interview with Ellen Waterman and Julie Smith. 29 June 2003.

Duncombe, Stephen, and Maxwell Tremblay, eds. *White Riot: Punk Rock and the Politics of Race*. London: Verso, 2011.

Duran, Bonnie. "Race, Racism, and the Dharma." *Dharma, Color, and Culture: New Voices in Western Buddhism*. Ed. Hilda Gutiérrez Baldoquín. Berkeley: Parallax, 2004. Print.

Durant, Alan. "Improvisation in the Political Economy of Music." *Music and the Politics of Culture*. Ed. Christopher Norris. London: Lawrence and Wishart, 1989. 252–82. Print.

Early, Gerald. "The Passing of Jazz's Old Guard: Remembering Charles Mingus, Thelonious Monk, and Sonny Stitt." *Kenyon Review* 7.2 (1985): 21–36. Print.

Ellington, Duke. "'Interpretations in Jazz': A Conference with Duke Ellington." *Etude* (1947): 134, 172. Print.

———. "A Royal View of Jazz." *Jazz: A Quarterly of American Music* 2 (1959): 83–87. Print.

Ellison, Ralph. *Invisible Man*. 1952. New York: Vintage, 1995. Print.

———. *Three Days before the Shooting . . .* Ed. John F. Callahan and Adam Bradley. New York: Modern Library, 2010. Print.

Erickson, Kevin. "Reclaiming New York for Local Arts." *Wiretap: Ideas and Actions for a New Generation*. 9 Jan. 2008. *WireTapMag*. Web. 2 June 2010.

Evans, Graeme. "Measure for Measure: Evaluating the Evidence of Culture's Contribution to Regeneration." *Urban Studies* 42.5/6 (2005): 959–83. Print.

Fellezs, Kevin. *Birds of Fire: Jazz, Rock, Funk, and the Creation of Fusion*. Durham, NC: Duke University Press, 2011. Print.

Fields, Jim, and Michael Gramaglia, dirs. *End of the Century: The Story of the Ramones*. Rhino Home Video, 2003. DVD.

Fischlin, Daniel, and Ajay Heble, eds. *The Other Side of Nowhere: Jazz, Improvisation, and Communities in Dialogue*. Middletown, CT: Wesleyan University Press, 2004. Print.

Fitzgerald, F. Scott. *The Great Gatsby*. New York: Oxford University Press, 1998. Print.

Florida, Richard. *Cities and the Creative Class*. London: Routledge, 2005. Print.

———. *The Rise of the Creative Class—And How It's Transforming Work, Leisure, Community and Everyday Life*. New York: Basic, 2002. Print.

Floyd, Samuel A., Jr. "Ring Shout! Literary Studies, Historical Studies, and Black Music Inquiry." *Black Music Research Journal* 11.2 (1991): 265–87. Print.

Fontaine, Dick, dir. *Sound??* Rhapsody, 1966. Film.

Foote, Lona. "Jeanne Lee—Meet the Composer." *Ear Magazine* May 1988: 28–29. Print.

Foster, Susan Leigh. "Introducing Unnatural Acts, 1997." *Decomposition: Post-Disciplinary Performance*. Ed. Sue-Ellen Case, Philip Brett, and Susan Leigh Foster. Bloomington: Indiana University Press, 2000. 3–9. Print.

Frisell, Bill. *History, Mystery*. Nonesuch, 2008. CD.

García, Beatriz. "Cultural Policy and Urban Regeneration in Western European Cities: Lessons from Experience, Prospects for the Future." *Local Economy* 19.4 (2004): 312–26. Print.

Garnham, Nicholas. "From Cultural to Creative Industries: An Analysis of the Implications of the 'Creative Industries' Approach to Arts and Media Policy Making in the United Kingdom." *International Journal of Cultural Policy* 11.1 (2005): 15–29. Print.

Gelfand, Alexander. "Life after the Death of Jazz." *The Walrus*. July/August 2006. Web. 23 Oct. 2012.

Gilroy, Paul. *The Black Atlantic: Modernity and Double Consciousness*. Cambridge, MA: Harvard University Press, 1993. Print.

Ginder, Jenny. *Towards a New Music Venue: Report on Quantitative and Qualitative Review*. Toronto: Toronto Arts Council, Ontario Arts Council, and Canada Council for the Arts, 2008. Print.

Gioia, Ted. "Where Did Our Revolution Go? Free Jazz Turns Fifty." *Jazz*. Jazz .com. 27 Feb. 2008. Web. 22 June 2010.

Goldberg, Joe. "Cecil Taylor and the New Tradition." *Saturday Review* 9 Feb. 1963: 43. Print.

gossett, hattie. "In the Window/Monk." *African American Review* 27.4 (1993): 571. Print.

Gottschalk, Kurt. "Hamid Drake." *All about Jazz*. 10 June 2006. Web. 22 June 2010.

Griffin, Farah Jasmine. "When Malindy Sings: A Meditation on Black Women's Vocality." *Uptown Conversation: The New Jazz Studies*. Ed. Robert G.

O'Meally, Brent Hayes Edwards, and Farah Jasmine Griffin. New York: Columbia University Press, 2004. 102–25. Print.

Griffiths, Ron. "The Politics of Cultural Policy in Urban Regeneration Strategies." *Policy and Politics* 21.1 (1993): 39–46. Print.

Gutiérrez Baldoquín, Hilda. *Dharma, Color, and Culture: New Voices in Western Buddhism*. Berkeley: Parallax, 2004. Print.

Haden, Charlie. *Liberation Music Orchestra*. 1969. Impulse!, 1996. CD.

———. *Not in Our Name*. Verve, 2005. CD.

Hall, Stuart, and Paul du Gay, eds. *Questions of Cultural Identity*. London: Sage, 1996. Print.

Hancock, Herbie. Foreword. *The Buddha in Your Mirror*. Ed. Woody Hochswender, Greg Martin, and Ted Morino. Santa Monica, CA: Middle Way, 2001.

———. Interview by Valerie Reiss. "Herbie, Fully Buddhist." *Beliefnet*. Beliefnet, 2007. Web. 22 June 2010.

Harris, Jerome. "Jazz on the Global Stage." *The African Diaspora: A Musical Perspective*. Ed. Ingrid Tolia Monson. New York: Garland, 2000. 103–50. Print.

Hartley, John. *Creative Industries*. Oxford: Blackwell, 2005. Print.

Hawryluk, Maggie. "Calling All the Shots: Adrienne Albert Talks about Her Latest Strategy." *Brokers Weekly* 9 Apr. 2008: 18. Print.

Hebdige, Dick. *Cut 'n' Mix: Culture, Identity, and Caribbean Music*. New York: Routledge, 1987. Print.

———. *Hiding in the Light: On Images and Things*. London: Routledge, 1979. Print.

———. *Subculture: The Meaning of Style*. New York: Methuen, 1984. Print.

Heble, Ajay. *Landing on the Wrong Note: Jazz, Dissonance, and Critical Practice*. New York: Routledge, 2000. Print.

Heffley, Mike. *Northern Sun, Southern Moon: Europe's Reinvention of Jazz*. New Haven, CT: Yale University Press, 2005. Print.

Henderson, Stephen. "Modernity and Other Directions in Afro-American Literature: Reflections on the Past Two Decades." *Fertile Ground: Memories and Visions*. Ed. Kalamu Ya Salaam and Kysha Brown. New Orleans: Runagate, 1996. 136–43. Print.

Hesmondhalgh, David, and Andy C. Pratt. "Cultural Industries and Cultural Policy." *International Journal of Cultural Policy* 11.1 (2005): 1–13. Print.

Higgins, Dick. *Modernism since Postmodernism: Essays on Intermedia*. San Diego: San Diego State University Press, 1997. Print.

———. "A Taxonomy of Sound Poetry." *Ubuweb*. Ubuweb, 2 Oct. 2002. Web. 22 June 2010.

Hoare, Ian. "Mighty, Mighty Spade and Whitey: Black Lyrics and Soul's Interaction with White Culture." *The Soul Book*. Ed. Ian Hoare, Tony Cummings, Clive Anderson, and Simon Frith. New York: Dell, 1975. 117–68. Print.

Hughes, Langston. "The Negro Artist and the Racial Mountain." *Keeping Time:*

Readings in Jazz History. Ed. Robert Walser. New York: Oxford University Press, 1999. 55–57. Print.

Huyssen, Andreas. *Present Pasts: Urban Palimpsests and the Politics of Memory*. Stanford, CA: Stanford University Press, 2003. Print.

Infantry, Ashante. "A Jazz Niche below the Radar, but on the Map: New Parkdale Venue for the Non-mainstream Migrates to the Tranzac Club for Improv Festival." *Thestar*. Toronto Star, 15 Nov. 2007. Web. 22 June 2010.

Issue Project Room. Homepage. *Issueprojectroom*. ISSUE Project Room, 2009. Web. 22 June 2010.

Jacques, Geoffrey, moderator, with Scott DeVeaux, Krin Gabbard, Bernard Gendron, and Sherrie Tucker. "A Roundtable on Ken Burns's *Jazz*." *Journal of Popular Music Studies* 13.2 (2001): 207–25. Print.

"Jazz of a Minority." Panel Discussion. WBAI. 21 Apr. 1964. Radio.

Jenkins, Barbara. "Toronto's Cultural Renaissance." *Canadian Journal of Communication* 30.2 (2005): 169–86. Print.

Jenkins, Philip. *Mystics and Messiahs: Cults and New Religions in American History*. New York: Oxford University Press, 2000. Print.

John Coltrane Quartet. *One Down, One Up: Live at the Half Note*. Impulse!, 2005. CD.

Kelley, Robin D. G. *Freedom Dreams: The Black Radical Imagination*. Boston: Beacon, 2002. Print.

Kennedy, Gary W. "Crispell, Marilyn." *Grove Music Online*. Oxford University Press, n.d. Web. 31 May 2010.

———. "Drake, Hamid." *Grove Music Online*. Oxford University Press, n.d. Web. 31 May 2010.

Kingwell, Mark. "The $195-Million Scribble, and Other Tales of Seduction from Our Romance with Celebrity Architects." *Toronto Life* 38.6 (2004): 70–75. Print.

Kramer, Wayne. "My Night as a Tone Scientist." *Sun Ra: Interviews and Essays*. Ed. John Sinclair. London: Headpress, 2010. 125–27. Print.

Kristeva, Julia. *The Sense and Non-sense of Revolt: The Powers and Limits of Psychoanalysis*. Trans. Jeanine Herman. New York: Columbia University Press, 2000. Print.

———. *Strangers to Ourselves*. Trans. Leon S. Roudiez. New York: Columbia University Press, 1991. Print.

Lee, Jeanne. "Compositions and Arrangements." Undated, in author's possession.

———. *Conspiracy*. Earthforms, 1974. CD.

———. "In These Last Days (from The Valley of Astonishment and Bewilderment)." *Nuba*. Black Saint, 1973. CD.

———. *Jam! The Story of Jazz Music*. New York: Rosen, 1999. Print.

———. "Narrative of Career." Undated, in author's possession. Print.

———. "Overview of Artistic Achievements." Undated, in author's possession. Print.

Lee, Jeanne, and Ran Blake. *The Newest Sound Around*. 1962. BMG, 1987. CD.

Leitch, Vincent B. "The Politics of Sovereignty." *The Late Derrida*. Ed. W. J. T. Mitchell and Arnold I. Davidson. Chicago: University of Chicago Press, 2007. 229–47. Print.

Levin, Laura, and Kim Solga. "Building Utopia: Performance and the Fantasy of Urban Renewal in Contemporary Toronto." *TDR: The Drama Review* 53.3 (2009): 37–53. Print.

Lewis, David. "Jeanne Lee and David Eyges Interview." *Cadence* (1997): 4–13. Print.

Lewis, George E. "Afterword to 'Improvised Music after 1950': The Changing Same." *The Other Side of Nowhere: Jazz, Improvisation, and Communities in Dialogue*. Ed. Daniel Fischlin and Ajay Heble. Middletown, CT: Wesleyan University Press, 2004. 163–72. Print.

———. "Experimental Music in Black and White: The AACM in New York, 1970–1985." *Current Musicology* 71–73 (2001–2): 100–57. Print.

———. "Gittin' to Know Y'all: Improvised Music, Interculturalism, and the Racial Imagination." *Critical Studies in Improvisation / Études critiques en improvisation* 1.1 (2004). Web. 20 Oct. 2012.

———. "Improvised Music after 1950: Afrological and Eurological Perspectives." *The Other Side of Nowhere: Jazz, Improvisation, and Communities in Dialogue*. Ed. Daniel Fischlin and Ajay Heble, Middletown, CT: Wesleyan University Press, 2004. 131–62. Print.

———. Personal Interview with Ellen Waterman and Julie Smith. 26 June 2003.

———. *A Power Stronger than Itself: The AACM and American Experimental Music*. Chicago: University of Chicago Press, 2009. Print.

———. "Rethinking Diversity: New Music in the Global Context." Canadian New Music Network Forum. Halifax, Nova Scotia, January 7–9, 2010. Keynote address.

Lewis, George, and Miya Masaoka. *The Usual Turmoil and Other Duets*. Music and Arts Program, 1998. CD.

Licht, Alan. Comment on "Marc Ribot: Care and Feeding of a Musical Margin." *All about Jazz*. 9 June 2007. Web. 27 June 2010.

Lipsitz, George. *American Studies in a Moment of Danger*. Minneapolis: University of Minnesota Press, 2001. Print.

———. *Dangerous Crossroads: Popular Music, Postmodernism, and the Poetics of Place*. London: Verso, 1997. Print.

———. *Footsteps in the Dark: The Hidden Histories of Popular Music*. Minneapolis: University of Minnesota Press, 2007. Print.

———. "Songs of the Unsung: The Darby Hicks History of Jazz." *Uptown Conversations: The New Jazz Studies*. Ed. Robert G. O'Meally, Brent Hayes Edwards, and Farah Jasmine Griffin. New York: Columbia University Press, 2004. 9–26. Print.

Litweiler, John. "Free Jazz Today." *The Freedom Principle: Jazz after 1958*. Cambridge, MA: Da Capo, 1990. 287–99. Print.

Lock, Graham. *Blutopia: Visions of the Future and Revisions of the Past in the Work of Sun Ra, Duke Ellington, and Anthony Braxton*. Durham, NC: Duke University Press, 1999. Print.

Lowe, Allen. *That Devilin' Tune: A Jazz History [1895–1950]*. West Hills Radio Archive, 2006. CD.

Mac Low, Jackson. Liner notes. *Jackson Mac Low*. New Wilderness Audiographics, 1977. Audiocassette.

———, "The Text on the Opposite Page May Be Used in Any Way as a Score for Solo or Group Readings, Musical or Dramatic Performances, Looking, Smelling, Anything Else &/or Nothing at All." *An Anthology of Chance Operations*. Ed. La Monte Young. New York: Young and Mac Low, 1963. Print.

Mackey, Nathaniel. "Other: From Noun to Verb." *The Jazz Cadence of American Culture*. Ed. Robert G. O'Meally, 513–32. New York: Columbia University Press, 1998. Print.

———. "Paracritical Hinge." *The Other Side of Nowhere: Jazz, Improvisation, and Communities in Dialogue*. Ed. Daniel Fischlin and Ajay Heble. Middletown, CT: Wesleyan University Press, 2004. 367–86. Print.

Mandel, Howard. *Future Jazz*. Cambridge: Cambridge University Press, 2000. Print.

Marcus, Greil. *Lipstick Traces: A Secret History of the Twentieth Century*. Cambridge, MA: Harvard University Press, 1989. Print.

———. Liner notes. *Liliput*. Kill Rock Stars, 2001. CD.

Margasak, Peter, et al. *The Future of Jazz*. Chicago: A Capella, 2002. Print.

Masaoka, Miya. "Ensembles." *Miyamasaoka*. Miya Masaoka, n.d. Web. 31 May 2010.

———. Personal Interview with Ellen Waterman and Julie Smith. 26 June 2003.

Masaoka Orchestra. *What Is the Difference between Stripping and Playing the Violin?* Victo, 1998. CD.

MC5. *Kick Out the Jams!* Elektra, 1969. CD.

McClary, Susan. *Feminine Endings: Music, Gender, and Sexuality*. Minnesota: University of Minnesota Press, 1991. Print.

McClintock, Anne. *Imperial Leather: Race, Gender, and Sexuality in the Colonial Contest*. New York: Routledge, 1995. Print.

McGuigan, Jim. "Doing a Florida Thing: The Creative Class Thesis and Cultural Policy." *International Journal of Cultural Policy* 15.3 (2009): 291–300. Print.

McMullen, Tracy. "Identity for Sale: Glenn Miller, Wynton Marsalis, and Cultural Replay in Music." *Big Ears: Listening for Gender in Jazz Studies*. Ed. Nichole T. Rustin and Sherrie Tucker. Durham, NC: Duke University Press, 2008. 129–54. Print.

———. "The Improvisative." *The Oxford Handbook of Critical Improvisation Studies*. Ed. George Lewis and Benjamin Piekut. Oxford: Oxford University Press, forthcoming. Print.

McNeil, Legs, and Gillian McCain. *Please Kill Me: The Uncensored Oral History of Punk*. New York: Penguin, 1996. Print.

McPhee, Joe. *Nation Time*. 1970. Atavistic, 2009. CD.

Miles, Malcolm. "Interruptions: Testing the Rhetoric of Culturally Led Urban Development." *Urban Studies* 42.5/6 (2005): 889–911. Print.

Miller, Paul D., ed. *Sound Unbound: Sampling Digital Music and Culture*. New York: Routledge, 2003. Print.

Mingus, Charles. "Open Letter to the Avant Garde." *More than a Fake Book*. New York: Jazzworkshop, 1991. 119. Print.

Minor, William. "Koto Master Miya Masaoka." *Coda* 280 (1998): 20–22. Print.

Monson, Ingrid. "Art Blakey's African Diaspora." *The African Diaspora: A Musical Perspective*. Ed. Ingrid Monson. New York: Garland, 2003. 329–52. Print.

———. *Saying Something: Jazz Improvisation and Interaction*. Chicago: University of Chicago Press, 1996. Print.

Morthland, John, ed. *Mainlines, Blood Feasts, and Bad Taste: A Lester Bangs Reader*. New York: Anchor, 2003. Print.

Moten, Fred. *In the Break: The Aesthetics of the Black Radical Tradition*. Minneapolis: University of Minnesota Press, 2003. Print.

Moynihan, Colin. "Punk Institution Receives City Money for New Building." *New York Times* 29 June 2009. Print.

Mugge, Robert, dir. *Sun Ra: A Joyful Noise*. Mug-Shot, 1980. Film.

"Nation Time." *Alternative Press*. Nov. 2000. 118. Print.

New York State Council on the Arts. "Past NYSCA Grants." NYSCA. New York State Council on the Arts, 2004. Web. 22 June 2010.

Nicholson, Stuart. *Is Jazz Dead? (Or Has It Moved to a New Address)*. New York: Routledge, 2005. Print.

Nisenson, Eric. *Ascension: John Coltrane and His Quest*. Cambridge, MA: Da Capo, 1993. Print.

Noglik, Bert. Liner notes. *Double Holy House*. 1990. Perf. Cecil Taylor. FMP, 1999. CD.

Nuttall-Smith, Chris. "Who Can Save the ROM This Time?" *Globe and Mail* 22 Jan. 2010. Print.

Oliveros, Pauline. "Harmonic Anatomy: Women in Improvisation." *The Other Side of Nowhere: Jazz, Improvisation, and Communities in Dialogue*. Ed. Daniel Fischlin and Ajay Heble. Middletown, CT: Wesleyan University Press, 2004. 50–70. Print.

———. *Software for People: Collected Writings, 1963–80*. Barrytown, NY: Printed Editions, 1984. Print.

O'Meally, Robert, Brent Hayes Edwards, and Farah Jasmine Griffin, eds. *Uptown Conversation: The New Jazz Studies*. New York: Columbia University Press, 2004. Print.

Østergaard, Erik. "The History of Nipper." *Erikoest.* n.d. Web. 15 Sept. 2009.

Palacios, Julian. *Syd Barrett and Pink Floyd: Dark Globe.* London: Plexus, 2010.

Palmer, Robert. Liner notes. *Spirits of Havana.* Perf. Jane Burnett. MusicHaus, 2002. CD.

Parker, Andrew, and Eve Kosofsky Sedgwick. "Introduction: Performativity and Performance." *Performativity and Performance.* New York: Routledge, 1995. 1–18. Print.

Parker, Evan. Messages to the author. 2009. E-mail.

Parker, William. Liner notes. *The Inside Songs of Curtis Mayfield.* RAI Trade, 2007. CD.

———. Liner notes. *I Plan to Stay a Believer: The Inside Songs of Curtis Mayfield.* AUM Fidelity, 2010. CD.

Parsonage, Catherine. *The Evolution of Jazz in Britain, 1880–1935.* Hampshire, UK: Ashgate, 2005. Print.

Parsons, Lucy. "The Principles of Anarchism." lucyparsons.org. Web. 23 Oct. 2012.

Patterson, Matt. "The Public Legitimization of Iconic Architectural Developments: A Comparative Study of the Royal Ontario Museum and the Art Gallery of Ontario." 44th Annual Meeting of the Canadian Sociological Association. Carleton University, Ottawa. May 2009. Paper Presentation.

Peck, Jamie. "Struggling with the Creative Class." *International Journal of Urban and Regional Research* 29.4 (2005): 740–70. Print.

Peretti, Burton. "Epilogue: Jazz as American History." *Riffs and Choruses: A New Jazz Anthology.* Ed. Andrew Clark. New York: Continuum, 2001. 185–89. Print.

Peterson, Carla L. "Foreword: Eccentric Bodies." *Recovering the Black Female Body: Self-Representations by African American Women.* Ed. Michael Bennett and Vanessa D. Dickerson. New Brunswick, NJ: Rutgers University Press, 2001. ix–xvi. Print.

Piekut, Benjamin. "Testing, Testing . . . : New York Experimentalism 1964." Diss. Columbia University, 2008. Print.

Pintak, Lawrence. "'Something Has to Change': Blacks in American Buddhism." *Blackelectorate.com.* 2005. Web. 28 June 2010.

Porter, Eric. *What Is This Thing Called Jazz: African American Musicians as Artists, Critics, and Activists.* Berkeley: University of California Press, 2002. Print.

Pouncey, Edwin. "Loving the Alien." *Wire* 274 (2006): 28–29. Print.

Pravaz, Natasha. "Brazilian Music and Community Building in Toronto." Diaspora, Dispersal, Improvisation, and Imagination. The Guelph Jazz Festival Colloquium. Macdonald Stewart Art Centre, Guelph. 3 Sept. 2008. Presentation.

Price, Janet, and Margrit Shildrick, eds. *Feminist Theory and the Body: A Reader.* New York: Routledge, 1999. Print.

Radano, Ronald. *Lying Up a Nation: Race and Black Music*. Chicago: University of Chicago Press, 2003. Print.

———. *New Musical Figurations: Anthony Braxton's Cultural Critique*. Chicago: University of Chicago Press, 1994. Print.

Ramsey, Guthrie P., Jr. *Race Music: Black Cultures from Bebop to Hip-Hop*. Berkeley: University of California Press, 2003. Print.

Ramshaw, Sara. "Deconstructin(g) Jazz Improvisation: Derrida and the Law of the Singular Event." *Critical Studies in Improvisation / Études critiques en improvisation* 2.1 (2006). Web. 23 June 2010.

Ratliff, Ben. "At the White House, a Blend of Jazz Greats and Hopefuls." *New York Times* 15 June 2006. Web. 7 December 2009.

Reason Myers, Dana L. "The Myth of Absence: Representation, Reception, and the Music of Experimental Women Improvisers." Diss. University of California, San Diego, 2002. Print.

Ribot, Marc. "Crisis in Indie/New Music Clubs: The Care and Feeding of a Musical Margin." *Freejazz*. 20 Sept. 2006. Web. 5 May 2010.

———. "Marc Ribot: The Care and Feeding of a Musical Margin." *All about Jazz*. AOL Music. 5 June 2007. Web. 5 May 2010.

Riggins, Roger. "Jeanne Lee." *Coda* 1 Feb. 1979: 4–5. Print.

Roberts, Rob. "The Torontonians: William Thorsell, agent of change." *National Post*. National Post, Inc. 13 Nov. 2009. Web. 5 May 2010.

Robeson, Paul. *Paul Robeson Speaks: Writings, Speeches, Interviews, 1918–1974*. Ed. P. S. Foner. New York: Bruner/Mazel, 1978. Print.

Roe, Tom. "Generation Ecstasy: New York's Free Jazz Continuum." *Undercurrents: The Hidden Wiring of Modern Music*. London: Continuum, 2002. 249–62. Print.

Rorty, Richard. *Philosophy and Social Hope*. New York: Penguin, 1999. Print.

Rowe, Keith. "Invisible Jukebox." *Wire* Jan. 2008. 18–21. Print.

Schaffner, Nicholas. *Saucerful of Secrets: The Pink Floyd Odyssey*. New York: Dell, 1992. Print.

Schechner, Richard. *Performance Studies: An Introduction*. London: Routledge, 2002. Print.

Scott, Joan W. "The Evidence of Experience." *Critical Inquiry* 17 (1991): 773–97. Print.

Searle, Chris. *Forward Groove: Jazz and the Real World from Louis Armstrong to Gilad Atzmon*. London: Northway, 2008. Print.

SGI Quarterly. "The Art of Life: Interview with Herbie Hancock." *SGI Quarterly: A Buddhist Forum for Peace, Culture, and Education* (2001). Print.

Shange, Ntozake. "Did I Hear the Congregation Say Amen?" *Village Voice* 29 Apr. 1981: 77. Print.

Shantz, Adam. "Organized Sound from Chicago's Underground." *New York Times* 18 Mar. 2001. Web. 22 June 2010.

Shepp, Archie. Liner notes. *Mama Too Tight*. Impulse!, 1998. CD.

Shukaitis, Stephen. "Space Is the (Non)Place: Martians, Marxists, and the

Outer Space of the Radical Imagination." *Sociological Review* 57.1 (2009): 98–113. Web. 15 Jan. 2010.

Silverman, Kaja. *The Subject of Semiotics*. Oxford: Oxford University Press, 1983.

Sinclair, John, ed. *Sun Ra: Interviews and Essays*. London: Headpress, 2010.

Sisario, Ben. "An Avant-Garde Arts Group Bites Off a Lot to Chew." *New York Times* 8 July 2009. Print.

———. "Avant Garde Music Loses a Lower Manhattan Home." *New York Times* 31 March 2007. Web. 11 Nov. 2011.

Small, Christopher *Musicking: The Meanings of Performing and Listening*. Middletown, CT: Wesleyan University Press, 1998. Print.

Smith, Julie. "Playing Like a Girl: The Queer Laughter of the Feminist Improvising Group." *The Other Side of Nowhere: Jazz, Improvisation, and Communities in Dialogue*. Ed. Daniel Fischlin and Ajay Heble. Middletown, CT: Wesleyan University Press, 2004. 224–43. Print.

Snead, James. "Repetition as a Figure of Black Cultures." *Out There: Marginalization and Contemporary Cultures*. Ed. Russell Ferguson, Martha Gever, Trinh T. Minh-ha, Cornel West. New Museum of Contemporary Art and MIT Press, 1990. 213–30. Print.

Sorbara, Joe. "Leftover Daylight Series." *Oval Window Music*. N.p., 2003–9. Web. 22 June 2010.

Spooner, James, dir. *Afro-Punk*. Image Entertainment, 2003. Film.

Stanbridge, Alan. "Detour or Dead-End? Contemporary Cultural Theory and the Search for New Cultural Policy Models." *International Journal of Cultural Policy* 8.2 (2002): 121–34. Print.

———. "Display Options: Discourses of Art and Context in the Contemporary Museum." *International Journal of Cultural Policy* 11.2 (2005): 157–70. Print.

———. "From the Margins to the Mainstream: Jazz, Social Relations, and Discourses of Value." *Critical Studies in Improvisation / Études critiques en improvisation* 4.1 (2008). Web. 23 June 2010.

———. "Live Reviews: Aim Toronto Interface Series with Evan Parker." *Signal to Noise (The Quarterly Journal of Improvised, Experimental and Unusual Music)* 53 (2009): 42–43. Print.

———. "The Tradition of all the Dead Generations: Music and Cultural Policy." *International Journal of Cultural Policy* 13.3 (2007): 255–71. Print.

Stanyek, Jason. "Transmissions of an Interculture: Pan-African Jazz and Intercultural Improvisation." *The Other Side of Nowhere: Jazz, Improvisation, and Communities in Dialogue*. Ed. Daniel Fischlin and Ajay Heble. Middletown, CT: Wesleyan University Press, 2004. 87–130. Print.

Stewart, Jesse. "Freedom Music: Jazz and Human Rights." *Rebel Musics: Human Rights, Resistant Sounds, and the Politics of Music Making*. Ed. Daniel Fischlin and Ajay Heble. Montreal: Black Rose, 2003. 88–107. Print.

Strom, Stephanie. "Grants Nurture Arts Spaces and Housing." *New York Times* 4 Apr. 2010. Print.

Stuffco, Jered. "ROM Condo Project Takes Heat from Critics." *Globe and Mail* 2 Nov. 2005. Print.

Sun Ra. *Heliocentric Worlds, Vol. II.* 1965. Get Back, 1999. CD.

———. Interview by John Sinclair. "It Knocks on Everybody's Door: Detroit Interview with Sun Ra." Sinclair, 22–30.

Szwed, John F., et al. *The Future of Jazz.* Ed. Yuval Taylor. Chicago: A Capella, 2002. Print.

———. *Jazz 101: A Complete Guide to Learning and Loving Jazz.* New York: Hyperion, 2000. Print.

———. *Space Is the Place: The Lives and Times of Sun Ra.* Cambridge, MA: Da Capo, 1998. Print.

Tarthang Tulku. *Milking the Painted Cow: The Creative Power of Mind and the Shape of Reality in Light of the Buddhist Tradition.* Berkeley: Dharma, 2005. Print.

Taylor, Arthur. *Notes and Tones: Musician-to-Musician Interviews.* New York: Perigree, 1977.

Taylor, Cecil. *Double Holy House.* 1990. FMP, 1999. CD.

———. Interview with Chris Funkhouser. "Being Matter Ignited: An Interview with Cecil Taylor." *Hambone* 12 (1999): 17–39. Print.

———, perf. Jazzfestival Hamburg Performance. NDR TV Recording. 12 Nov. 1995. Television.

Teachout, Terry. "Can Jazz Be Saved?" *Wall Street Journal* 9 Aug. 2009. Web. 18 May 2010.

Terlizzi, Roberto, Francesco Martinelli, and Stefano Archangeli. "Jeanne Lee and Gunter Hampel." *Coda* 1 Feb. 1979: 6–9. Print.

Thomas, Lorenzo. *Don't Deny My Name: Words and Music and the Black Intellectual Tradition.* Ed. Aldon Lynn Nielsen. Ann Arbor: University of Michigan Press, 2008. Print.

Thompson, Stacy. *Punk Productions: Unfinished Business.* Albany: SUNY Press, 2004.

Thomson, Scott. "The Pedagogical Imperative of Musical Improvisation." *Critical Studies in Improvisation / Études critiques en improvisation* 3.2 (2007). Web. 23 June 2010.

Thomson, Scott, Ken Aldcroft, Rob Clutton, Nick Fraser, Rob Piilonen, and Joe Sorbara. "Roundtable Discussion: The Association of Improvising Musicians Toronto." *Critical Studies in Improvisation / Études critiques en improvisation* 2.1 (2006). Web. 23 June 2010.

Threadgold, Terry. "Performativity, Voice, Corporeality, Habitus, Becoming, Assemblage: Some Reflections on Theory and Performing Metaphors." *Musics and Feminisms.* Ed. Sally Macarthur and Cate Poynton. Sydney: Australian Music Centre, 1999. 63–77. Print.

"Transliteration." *Oxford Reference Online.* Oxford: Oxford University Press, n.d. Web. 31 May 2010.

Tucker, Sherrie. "Big Ears: Listening for Gender in Jazz Studies." *Current Musicology* 71–73 (2001–2): 375–408. Print.

Von Eschen, Penny M. *Satchmo Blows Up the World: Jazz Ambassadors Play the Cold War.* Cambridge, MA: Harvard University Press, 2004. Print.

Walser, Robert, ed. *Keeping Time: Readings in Jazz History.* New York: Oxford University Press, 1999. Print.

Watson, Ben. *Derek Bailey and the Story of Free Improvisation.* London: Verso, 2004.

Watt, Mike. "Revising History: Mike Watt on John Coltrane, Miles Davis, Sun Ra, More " *The Bad Penny.* Web. 23 Oct. 2012.

Webb, Ellen. "For the Taste of an Apple: Why I Practice Zen." *Taken by Surprise: A Dance Improvisation Reader.* Ed. Ann Cooper Albright and David Gere. Middletown, CT: Wesleyan University Press, 2003. 239–43. Print.

Weinreich, Regina. "Play It Momma." *Village Voice* 3 July 1978: 64–65. Print.

Whyte, Murray. "Why Richard Florida's Honeymoon Is Over." *Thestar.* Toronto Star. 27 June 2009. Web. 17 Apr. 2010.

Williams, Martin. "With Blake and Lee in Europe." *Down Beat* 7 May 1964: 14–17. Print.

Wilmer, Valerie. *As Serious as Your Life: The Story of the New Jazz.* London: Serpent's Tail, 1977. Print.

Wilson, Olly. "Black Music as an Art Form." *Black Music Research Journal* 3 (1983): 1–22. Print.

Zorn, John. *Spy vs. Spy—The Music of Ornette Coleman.* Elektra, 1989. CD.

CONTRIBUTORS

THE ASSOCIATION FOR THE ADVANCEMENT
OF CREATIVE MUSICIANS

Internationally renowned for unparalleled contributions to modern music, the Association for the Advancement of Creative Musicians (AACM) has been an inspirational leader within the cultural community since 1965. A nonprofit organization chartered by the State of Illinois, the AACM is a collective of musicians and composers dedicated to nurturing, performing, and recording serious, original music. The AACM may best be known for its leading-edge public concerts featuring some of the most accomplished, versatile and innovative musicians performing original, creative music. The organization takes particular pride in developing new generations of talent through the free music training program conducted by members for city youth, the AACM School of Music. Another equally important aspect of the AACM's mission is the high moral standard members seek to provide in their capacities as performers, artists, teachers, and role models.

TAMAR BARZEL

The ethnomusicologist Tamar Barzel is an assistant professor of music at Wellesley College. She is currently completing a book manuscript, *Downtown and Disorderly: Radical Jewish Culture and Its Discontents on Manhattan's Downtown Music Scene.*

JOHN BRACKETT

John Brackett is a lecturer in music at the University of North Carolina, Chapel Hill. His book, *John Zorn: Tradition and Transgression*, was published in 2008.

DOUGLAS EWART

Douglas Ewart has served as chairman of the AACM and as an instructor in the AACM School of Music. He performs original music and is known for his work as a lecturer, teacher, and workshop director throughout the United States, Europe, and Japan.

AJAY HEBLE

Ajay Heble is professor of English in the School of English and Theatre Studies, University of Guelph. He is the author or editor of several books, including *Landing on the Wrong Note: Jazz, Dissonance, and Critical Practice, The Other Side of Nowhere: Jazz, Improvisation, and Communities in Dialogue,* and *Rebel Musics: Human Rights, Resistant Sounds, and the Politics of Music Making.* Heble is also the artistic director of The Guelph Jazz Festival.

VIJAY IYER

The composer-pianist Vijay Iyer has released fourteen albums, including *Historicity,* which was named the number one jazz album of 2009 by the *New York Times.* His writings appear in *Music Perception, Journal of Consciousness Studies, Current Musicology, JazzTimes, Wire, The Guardian,* and the anthologies *Uptown Conversation, Sound Unbound,* and *Arcana IV.*

THOMAS KING

Thomas King is a writer and photographer who has photographed the Guelph Jazz Festival for the last ten years. His second novel, *Green Grass, Running Water* was short-listed for a Governor General's Award and his non-fiction essays, *The Truth About Stories,* won the Ontario Trillium Award. King currently teaches in the English department at the University of Guelph in Guelph, Ontario.

TRACY MCMULLEN

Tracy McMullen is a jazz saxophonist and Assistant Professor in the Department of Music at Bowdoin College. She is currently working on a book entitled *Replay: Repetition and Identity Compulsion from ABBA to Žižek.*

PAUL D. MILLER (DJ SPOOKY)

Paul D. Miller (also known as DJ Spooky) is a composer, multimedia artist, and writer. His written work has appeared in *The Village Voice, The Source, Artforum* and *Rapgun,* among other publications.

NICOLE MITCHELL

Nicole Mitchell has been celebrated for bringing an exciting new approach to flute improvisation. She is copresident of the AACM and founder of the critically acclaimed Black Earth Ensemble and Black Earth Strings.

ROSCOE MITCHELL

A founding member of the world-renowned Art Ensemble of Chicago, the composer and multi-instrumentalist Roscoe Mitchell was a major contributor to the creation of the body of musical literature that ushered in the post-Coltrane period. He is currently the Darius Milhaud Chair of Composition at Mills College.

FAMOUDOU DON MOYE

Famoudou Don Moye is best known for his work with the most highly acclaimed avant-garde combo of the 1970s and 1980s, the Art Ensemble of Chicago.

ALDON LYNN NIELSEN

Aldon Lynn Nielsen is the George and Barbara Kelly Professor of American Literature in the Pennsylvania State University's Department of English. His works of scholarship include *Writing between the Lines, C.L.R. James: A Critical Introduction, Black Chant*, and *Integral Music: Languages of African American Innovation*.

ERIC PORTER

Eric Porter is professor of American studies at UC, Santa Cruz. He is the author of *What Is This Thing Called Jazz: African American Musicians as Artists, Critics, and Activists* (2002) and *The Problem of the Future World: W. E. B. Du Bois and the Race Concept at Midcentury* (2010).

MARC RIBOT

Guitarist Marc Ribot has released 19 albums under his own name over a thirty-year career. He has collaborated with many musicians, including producer T Bone Burnett (on the grammy-award-winning *Raising Sand*).

MATANA ROBERTS

Matana Roberts is a saxophonist, composer, and improviser. She is a faculty member for the School for Improvised Music, in New York City, and is an associate member of the AACM.

JARIBU SHAHID

Jaribu Shahid is a bassist with a career-long involvement with the Roscoe Mitchell Sound Ensemble and, currently, the Roscoe Mitchell Note Factory. Shahid has recorded with Sun Ra, James Carter, David Murray, Geri Allen, and others.

JULIE DAWN SMITH

Dr. Smith is a research associate in the Department of English at the University of British Columbia and was most recently the executive director of Coastal Jazz and Blues. She has served on the boards of the New Orchestra Workshop Society, the Chicago Music Alliance, and the UBC Arts Co-op Advisory Committee.

WADADA LEO SMITH

Wadada Leo Smith is a jazz trumpeter, multi-instrumentalist, composer and improviser active in music for over thirty years. He has taught at the University of New Haven and Bard College, and has been the Dizzy Gillespie Chair at the California Institute of the Arts since 1993.

ALAN STANBRIDGE

Alan Stanbridge is an associate professor in visual and performing arts at the University of Toronto. He is working on a book entitled *Rhythm Changes: The Discourses of Jazz*.

JOHN SZWED

John Szwed, professor of music and jazz studies at Columbia University, is an anthropologist and jazz scholar. Among other books, he has published *Space Is the Place: The Lives and Times of Sun Ra* (1997), and *Jazz 101* (2000). *Doctor Jazz*, a book included with the CD set *Jelly Roll Morton: The Complete Library of Congress Recordings*, by Alan Lomax, was awarded a Grammy in 2005.

GREG TATE

Greg Tate is a founding member of the Black Rock Coalition and a former staff writer at *The Village Voice*. Tate's books include *Flyboy in the Buttermilk* and *Everything but the Burden: What White People Are Taking from Black Culture*. He is currently completing a book on James Brown.

SCOTT THOMSON

Scott Thomson is a trombonist and composer based in Toronto. He was a founding board member of the Association of Improvising Musicians Toronto and was the artistic director of Somewhere There, a performance space in Toronto.

ROB WALLACE

Writer, musician, and teacher, Rob Wallace has performed and recorded with many artists. He is the author of *Improvisation and the Making of American Literary Modernism*.

ELLEN WATERMAN

Ellen Waterman is professor and director of music at Memorial University, in St. John's, Newfoundland. She is both a music scholar and a flutist, specializing in creative improvisation and contemporary music. She is founding coeditor of the online journal *Critical Studies in Improvisation / Études critiques en improvisation.*

COREY WILKES

Corey Wilkes burst onto the Chicago jazz club scene in 2002 and filled the vacant trumpet seat in the Art Ensemble of Chicago. He is an artist in residence and board member with the Jazz Institute of Chicago and a member of the AACM.

INDEX

191; as traditional, 52–58; and
Washington, D.C., 22
Free Jazz, 114
Frisell, Bill, 27n2, 151n6
Frith, Fred, 20
Fugs, 127
Fujii, Satoko, 213
funk, 2, 120, 125, 161, 218–20, 240–41
fusion, 4, 50, 104, 111, 118, 121, 127,
219

Gaddy, Christopher, 254
Garner, Errol, 39
Garrison, Jimmy, 39
Gaye, Marvin, 218
Gebers, Jost, 11
gender, 119, 133n3, 147; boundaries,
10; diversity in, 117; and free jazz,
137n23; in George Lewis's "Dream
Team," 59–87; and Jeanne Lee,
22–23, 88–110; and performativity,
83. *See also* women
Gennaro, Mike, 181n2
George Coleman-Frank Foster Big
Band, 218
Gerson, Alan, 144, 150, 152n11
Ghostface Killa, 222
Gillespie, Dizzy, 15–17, 44
Ginsberg, Allen, 33, 36
Gioia, Ted, 12–14
Giuffre, Jimmy, 51–52
Gjerstad, Frode, 134n10
Gnarls Barkley, 38
Golia, Vinny, 20
Gonsalves, Paul, 48
Goodman, Benny, 9
Gordon, Dexter, 218
gossett, hattie, 155–56
Grand Master Flash, 237
Graves, Milford, 20, 54, 124–25,
136n18
Great Black Music, 10, 85n8, 118, 225.
See also Art Ensemble of Chicago
Great Gatsby, The, 8, 27n7
Guelph Jazz Festival and Colloquium
(Guelph, Ontario), 17, 21, 23–25,

62, 67, 73–74, 85n3, 175, 179–80,
191, 193, 225, 244
Haden, Charlie, 4, 20, 51–52, 116–18,
136n19, 210
Haley, Geordie, 181n4
Hamer, Fannie Lou, 107
Hammond, John, 151n3
Hampel, Gunter, 92
Hancock, Herbie, 26, 219; as Bud-
dhist, 271–75, 278nn13–15
Happenings, 91, 97
Harper, Billy, 223
Harris, Jerome, 151n5, 153
Hasson, Bill, 36
Hazelton, David, 41, 91
Hebdige, Dick, 11, 119, 127, 134n12,
135n16
Heble, Ajay, 60, 62, 82, 85, 90, 228
Hemingway, Gerry, 20
Hemphill, Julius, 57, 218, 220
Henderson, Joe, 222
Higgins, Billy, 57
Higgins, Dick, 91, 109n1, 109n6
hip-hop, 219, 237–39; and black iden-
tity, 257; commerciality of, 255,
261; and improvisation, 257; and
jazz, 137n26, 222–24; and poetry,
38, 40; and punk, 129, 137n26
His Master's Voice, 37–38
history: living, 5–6, 19, 25; and mys-
tery, 5, 17, 20–26, 27n2, 112
History, Mystery, 27n2
Hodges, Johnny, 57
Holiday, Billie, 88, 101
Hopkins, Fred, 86n10
Hughes, Langston, 8, 27n6, 43, 114
Humphries, Lex, 125
Hwang, Jason, 150n1

Iaffaldano, Michelangelo, 181n2
Ibarra, Susie: trio, 66
Impressions, The, 265
Improvisation, 1; as activism, 227–28;
as artistic practice, 25, 88–89; and
the audience, 242; and boundaries,
16–18; collective, 53, 55; and com-

memory (*continued*)
improvisation, 78–81; material,
230, 236–37, 239
Messiaen, Olivier, 231
Mingus, Charles, 33, 115, 218; and
Buddhism, 271; Duke Ellington's
influence on, 44–45, 47, 56
Minutemen (band), 119, 136n19
Mitchell, Nicole, 212
Mitchell, Roscoe, 20, 86n10, 207, 227
Molvaer, Nils Petter, 16
Moncur, Grachan, III, 92
Monk, Thelonious, 101, 132n2, 153
Monson, Ingrid, 6, 63, 85n6, 266,
277n4, 278n11
Moore, Angelo, 133n7
Moore, Michael, 177
Moore, Rebecca, 144, 150n1, 166
Moore, Thurston, 130, 135n17
Morgan, Lee, 36
Mori, Ikue, 171
Morris, Butch, 151n5
Morton, Jelly Roll, 45, 116
Moshe, Ras, 151n5
Mostly Mozart Festival, 149
Moten, Fred, 40
Motian, Paul, 116
Motown, 31, 218
Moye, Famoudou Don, 26, 55, 207,
209, 244–64
Mozart, Wolfgang Amadeus, 149, 185
Murray, Albert, 106
Murray, David, 218, 222
Music Gallery, 176, 181n5, 190
mystery: history and, 5, 17, 20–26,
27n2, 112

Nanton, Tricky Sam, 48
Nathanson, Roy, 151n5
nation: as improvisation, 32, 43
National Endowment for the Arts,
92, 146
"Nation Time," 31–32, 36, 43
Nation Time, 31–32
Neal, Gaston, 32–33
Neal, Larry, 33

Neidlinger, Buell, 57
Neues Kabarett, 142, 145
Neuhaus, Max, 103
Newborn, Phineas, Jr., 218
Newman, Paul, 181n2
New School for Afro-American
Thought, 32–34. *See also* Neal,
Gaston
New Thing, 4, 5, 10, 12, 33, 35, 45
Newton, James, 257
New York State Arts Council, 154,
164n3
Nichols, Herbie, 36
Nichols, Janine, 150n1
Nielsen, Aldon Lynn, 21–22, 137n25
Nipper, 37–39, 43
Noglik, Bert, 41–42
nostalgia: innovation and, 2–6, 18, 23
No Wave, 132n3, 153–54, 219

October Revolution in Jazz, 35
Ohio Players, 218
Olatunji, Babatunde, 34
Oliveros, Pauline, 4, 16–17, 20, 86n15,
109n8
Ontario Arts Council, 182n11
Original Dixieland Jazz Band (ODJB),
113, 115
Osibisa, 219
Oxley, Tony, 135n15

Page, Jimmy, 218
Parachute Center, 260
Parker, Charlie (Bird), 43, 56, 60, 79,
100, 123, 136n18, 136n20, 221, 227,
242; and Buddhism, 271
Parker, Evan, 15, 177, 182n9, 196n19
Parker, Maceo, 31
Parker, Patricia Nicholson, 142, 145,
148, 150n1, 151n5
Parker, William, 14, 150n1, 177, 200;
on Curtis Mayfield, 1–2, 26
Parsons, Lucy, 113–14, 133n5
pedagogy, 6, 19–21
Perera, Nilan, 181n3, 183n12
performativity: in George Lewis's